THOMAS MERTON

the world in my bloodstream

for Michael & Maureen

Enjoy!

Angus

THOMAS MERTON

the world in my bloodstream

Papers

presented at
THE FOURTH
GENERAL CONFERENCE
of the THOMAS MERTON SOCIETY
of GREAT BRITAIN AND IRELAND
at OAKHAM SCHOOL,
APRIL 2002

Edited by
ANGUS STUART

P³P

Published in Great Britain 2004
THREE PEAKS PRESS
9 Croesonen Road
Abergavenny,
Monmouthshire NP7 6AE
mail@p3p.org   http://p3p.org

The illustration on the front cover is reproduced courtesy of
the Thomas Merton Center, Bellarmine University, Louisville, Kentucky,
and with the permission of the Trustees of the Merton Legacy Trust.
Merton's poem 'With the World in my Blood Stream' is the copyright
of the Trustees, and is printed with the permission of
New Directions Publishing Corporation.

Designed & set in Joanna at Three Peaks Press

Printed in Wales at Gwasg Dinefwr, Llandybie

A CIP record for this publication
is available from the British Library

ISBN   1-902093-08-9

Contents

"...I am glad to be able to tell someone at Oakham that I really bear the school a deep affection, with sentiments of gratitude that will not die... I never regret having gone to Oakham. On the contrary, I am very glad that I was sent there rather than to some larger school, for Oakham had something of simplicity and sincerity about it that one might look for in vain elsewhere."

THOMAS MERTON to C.J. DIXON,
November 9th, 1954

INTRODUCTION

As I have edited the papers presented at the Fourth General Meeting of the Thomas Merton Society, I have been struck both by their variety and by the ways in which they connect together and complement one another. I suppose I should not be surprised by this in that they were all in one way or another seeking to respond to the theme of the conference: *The World in My Blood Stream: Thomas Merton's Universal Embrace*. The first part of this derives from the title of one of Merton's *Eighteen Poems*, 'With the World in my Blood Stream,' inspired by his encounter and friendship with the young student nurse in the summer of 1966. The subtitle derives from that sense of universality and inclusiveness that is increasingly apparent in his writings as he grew and developed as a monk, and as a person, in his years at Gethsemani.

This theme of the conference springs from the simple question, how do we relate to the 'world'? In particular, how do we relate to the modern (or post-modern) world, the world of technology, of commerce and consumerism, the material world, contemporary culture. How are we to live in this shrinking world of instant communication and globalization? The world of multinational companies and power politics where might is right, or *makes* right, the world where overwhelming force is a legitimate instrument of peace. I write this in the immediate aftermath of the Iraq War; at the time of the conference we were a little over six months after 'September 11th' and still very much in its shadow. This was the specific context in which the conference took place and to which many of the presenters were responding, either implicitly or explicitly, and perhaps also explains some of the coherence found in taking the papers as a whole. The question of how we are to live in the world seemed to have taken on an added poignancy and an increased urgency in the light of recent events.

It is also a question (if not *the* question) Merton wrestled with throughout his monastic life and even before—his entry into the monastery in the first place can be construed as his response to such a question. His writings in books, articles and essays, and in his letters, journals and poems manifest the twists and turns and the development of his own answer to the question of how to live in the world. His writings give us much material on which to reflect, but more than this we are able to see how his thinking developed and changed over time—how he grew as a person through his life. Beyond the writings we are able to appreciate something of the man whose life, like that of his hero Gandhi, was his message.

Merton's struggles resonate with our own because they are essentially the same – how to live in this world – and they are not new: it's the question Christians have wrestled with since Constantine adopted Christianity and made it the official religion of the Roman Empire in the fourth century—and probably before. Indeed, how to live (in the world, for there is no other) is the question for those who would be 'holy' men and women of whatever tradition and in any age.

The question implies some sort of distinction between us and the world – a distinction clearly felt by the early Christians who regarded themselves as strangers and aliens, sojourners and pilgrims, not of this world – a sense of not belonging. It's the tension experienced by all those who seek to follow Christ whilst living in the 'world.' Similar tension is found also in other traditions—perhaps put most simply it is the tension between living for peace and justice in a world dominated by power and commerce. Or again perhaps it is the tension, more strongly antipathy, between truth and illusion. It is this distinction that drove the early saints into the desert and into the monasteries—and drove Thomas Merton into the monastery of Gethsemani. Yet through his years there he came to experience a new relationship with the world and discovered (or rediscovered) his place in the world – and no longer the aphoristic 'in the world but not of the world' but in the world and in a real sense very much part of it – with the world in his blood stream.

The question of how to live in the world gives rise to two further questions concerning our own identity and our vision of the world: 'Who am I?' and 'How do we see the world?' The two questions are related: how we understand our own identity (how we see ourselves) will affect how we understand the world and relate to it. Merton's universal embrace derives from his own sense of identity in the hidden ground of love. For Merton time and again we find that the answer to the question 'Who am I?' and the answer to the question 'Who is the world?' is the same: when we get beyond the illusions of superficiality, the identity of both is 'Christ.' This is not a narrowly defined 'Christ' in the sense of the historical figure of 'Jesus Christ' but rather relates to the 'ground of being'—the Divine identity hidden in the depths of our being. It is the mystical oneness with the creator and source of life that permeates and unites all creation. Our true identity that is identified with universal identity.

These two dimensions, the inward and the outward, permeate the papers gathered here—sometimes implicitly, sometimes explicitly. In his presidential address, Donald Allchin finds the heart of Merton's universal vision in his learning to recognise God's presence in the depths of his own inmost spirit—enabling him in turn to read God's presence in all things. He comments (as he did in his 2000 address) on how Merton seems to be coming closer to us as we get further away from him in time, echoing Ed Rice's contention that Merton was born at least a century ahead of his time.

Robert Inchausti is implicitly responding to the question of how we are to live in the world in his paper 'Beyond Political Illusion: the Role of the Individual in Troubled Times.' In this paper he contrasts Merton's contemplative vision with two very different contemporary ethics: the 'neo-paganism' of Robert Kaplan's 'Warrior Ethics' and the 'Christian Realism' of Reinhold Niebuhr. Merton, he suggests, allows us to re-think our relationship to secular categories (to the world). In this he draws on the Dante imagery of The Seven Storey Mountain which sees the modern world as purgatory—paralleling Allchin's concluding quote about keeping your mind in hell and not despairing.

Inchausti's paper raises questions about how we are to respond to the world and the times in which we live and the role each individual person can play. Our other two keynote papers address different aspects of Merton's universal embrace. Bonnie Thurston explores Merton's relationship with Islam through a consideration of his seven explicitly 'Islamic poems.' In this she parallels Merton's interest in Zen with the 'nonlogical logic of mysticism' found in Sufism and its emphasis on direct experience and 'essence without form.' She makes the point that the reason for Merton's embrace of Islam is Christian— it is Merton's Christian view of God's universal embrace that inspires his reaching out to others. Donald Grayston makes a similar point in tracing Merton's transculturalism to Christ, 'the true pioneer of transcultural reality.' Interfaith dialogue is very much in accord with the heart of Christianity—it is intrinsically, though not exclusively, a Christian activity. For Christians the theological rationale for being transcultural (crossing the frontiers) is Christ.

Like Bonnie Thurston, Grayston also draws on Merton's contact and interaction with Islam as well as Zen Buddhism. In an unwitting carry-over from the Third General Meeting (*A Mind Awake in the Dark*), he uses Merton's *Day of a Stranger* as a vehicle for his discussion of Merton's universal embrace. He specifically identifies the two dimensions of this embrace outlined above—inner and outer. In the inner dimension he identifies an 'inner ground' that is both more universal than the empirical ego and yet entirely his own and he then relates this to ideas of being reborn. Though not limited to Christianity such ideas found a natural resonance in the post-Easter context of the conference of dying and rising with Christ. In the outer dimension, Grayston picks up the resurrection theme again in what William H. Thompson calls 'the creative underpinnings of a deeper view of Christology.' It is this 'deeper view of Christology' – what we mean by 'Christ' – that enables us to uncover our own true identity and reach out to the world.

The exploration of the themes pertaining to Thomas Merton's universal embrace continue through the variety of the concurrent session papers presented in the morning and afternoon of that warm Saturday in April. Michael Sobocinski gives a very specific illustration of the connection between finding connectedness with others and finding one's own inner identity in the context of his work in the Denver Children's Home. Here we find the transformative power of love, both for the giver and the receiver, as children are helped in the process of healing and becoming fully human through an active empathy in which the carer identifies with the suffering of the child. Merton's distinction between the isolated 'false self' and the connected 'true self' is evident and again the identification of 'Christ' in both oneself and the other.

Two papers follow exploring Merton's relationship with 'the beats.' This falls under that part of Merton's universal embrace that extends towards contemporary culture. David Belcastro characterises Merton's friendship with the beats as a new dimension of his monastic vocation in which he identifies with their position on the margins of, or outside, contemporary society. They like him experience tension with the 'world,' like him they do not 'belong.' Belcastro explores Merton's take on the beats as 'inside-out Christians' or 'monks in reverse'—'inside-out Christians' refers to their 'fully integrated vision' and their approach from the 'human dimension' of the body and 'the holiness of direct desire'; 'monks in reverse' points up the gap between, for example, Christianity and the churches, and the incongruities and inconsistencies of modern life (the world) in the hope of opening up a larger vision of life. The idea of being outside the institutional Church and yet being able to participate in the Gospel clearly has resonance for many today who feel they do not belong—neither in the world ('square society', etc.) nor in the Church (and here Merton had his own ambivalences and ambiguities!) Merton's relationship with the beats also perhaps helped to get the world pumping in his blood stream by reintegrating back into his life things he'd left at the monastery door.

The second paper dealing with Merton and the beats considers Merton's embrace of Buddhism and the traditions of the east and how this relates to a parallel interest and involvement by beat writers, and in particular Jack Kerouac. The paper emphases the notion of parallel lives by beginning and ending with autobiographical snap-shots taken within the same time-frame for both Merton and Kerouac. The key aspects of eastern thinking that attracted Kerouac and the beats are identified as the ideas of direct unmediated experience of reality and notions of compassion and awareness of human suffering. Both of these strike a chord with Merton and are epitomized in his 'Fourth and Walnut Epiphany' referred to also in a number of other papers. Clearly these resonate too with the twin themes of inward search for true identity and outward relation to reality and the world at the heart of the conference theme.

The next two papers, by Dick Berendes and Earl Madary and by Tom Del Prete, pick up these twin concerns by drawing on the ideas of personalism originating with Emmanuel Mounier and introduced to the Catholic Worker Movement by co-founder Peter Maurin. Berendes and Madary use personalism as a unifying paradigm for their discussion of Thomas Merton and Dorothy Day and the relationship between contemplation and action. A 'person' is contrasted with an 'individual' in the sense that a person is seen as in relation whereas an 'individual,' on this definition, is isolated. Personalism is therefore both a way of being and a way of seeing others—it is about identity and relating; it is about self-discovery and other discovery. Each person is of infinite value, each person is an epiphany of God—again the twin themes of recognising 'Christ' in ourselves and in others. Berendes and Madary then take these ideas and develop them in a discussion of the relationship between prayer, conscience, obedience (not least to one's true self) and action before reflecting more specifically on how they relate to Gandhi and non-violence and our responses post September 11th.

Tom Del Prete explores in more detail the inner realization of Christ in us – the 'deeper Christology' referred to above – as the true basis for relatedness. Picking up Merton's exhortation to his brothers that it is better to become 'related' than virtuous, Del Prete contrasts relatedness with virtue in Merton's writing and in particular draws on his reading of Chuang Tzu, Gandhi (again) and the Russian Orthodox idea of *sobornost* which emphasises the Holy Spirit and personal encounter with God. He then explores how relatedness works out in community life and, at a wider scale, contrasts an 'atomistic society' as a collective based on self-interest with a 'personalistic society' as a 'mutuality of personhood and love.' Wider still, cultural and transcultural perspectives are introduced linking in to those of Donald Grayston's paper. For Tom Del Prete the phrase 'with the world in my blood stream' is itself a metaphorical statement of relatedness.

Merton's interest in world faiths is examined by Judith Hardcastle's paper where she explores his interaction with correspondents in Hinduism, Buddhism, Islam and Judaism. She draws out the creative tension between Merton's rootedness in Christianity and his dialogue with people of other faiths. Again his dialogue appears to be motivated by, rather than despite, his Christianity. And again it is apparent that Merton was way ahead of his time and, in the area of multi-faith, is perhaps still some way ahead of ours too. The key to Merton's embrace outward of those of other faiths (whilst acknowledging the differences) seems to be his ability to journey inward beyond doctrines to the 'intuitions and truths' to be found in the 'inner and ultimate spiritual "ground" that underlies all articulated differences' (*Mystics and Zen Masters*, p.204). Again there is that sense of discovering Christ in that 'part of humanity that is most remote from our own' (*Collected Poems*, p.388).

A number of papers draw on Merton's *Conjectures of a Guilty Bystander* but Paul Pearson focuses in more detail on this book as a whole, using it as a means to examine the issues Merton was facing in the 1960s and how he responded to them. In particular he considers Merton's development in the intervening years since the *Sign of Jonas* was published in the early 1950s. 'Redeeming the Rhinoceros' relates to the underlying question of the Christian's relationship with the modern world that we continue to struggle with. 'The Night Spirit and the Dawn Air' refers to the importance of place and nature for Merton as he seeks to live in the world, and the role of solitude and stability in rediscovering the 'divine child' within and so experiencing God's mercy, which in turn leads outward in the embrace of compassion. Again the encounter with 'Christ' both inward and outward is very much in evidence—'guard the image of man for it is the image of God.'

The final paper here, by Fernando Beltrán Llavador and Sonia Petisco Martínez, draws together many of the themes of the conference. The first part of the paper contrasts Thomas Merton's universal embrace with trends towards economic globalization. Like Robert Inchausti at the beginning of the conference, they help us to 'rethink our relationship to secular categories dominating contemporary thought' (Inchausti)—specifically here *globalization* and its manifestation in the ethics of ends justifying means and in increasingly compulsive consumption by parties that are essentially unconnected. In contrast Merton's universal embrace derives from finding his true identity in Christ (*as* Christ) which is bound up both with the identity of each and every person in Christ (*as* Christ) and the Trinitarian relationship of Christ in the Godhead. Like Berendes and Madary, and like Del Prete, they make use of the idea of a 'person' as being constituted by love and openness (connectedness, relatedness) to both radical Other and neighbouring others—the Biblical relationship to both God and neighbour. This understanding of 'person' is rooted in the Trinity whereby each member is living only for the others—God is understood as the dynamic of three relationships. To be fully human is to be in the image of God (echoing Pearson) and therefore to reflect this dynamic of relationship whereby self-interest cannot but include the interest of others—the kind of mutuality encountered in the Denver Children's Home with Michael Sobocinski. Paradoxically this very Christian understanding provides both the *rationale* for inter-faith encounter and transculturalism (as we see also in the papers by Thurston, Grayston and Hardcastle), and the meeting point with any on or beyond the margins of our cultural frontiers (Belcastro). Thus this Trinitarian understanding is both the impetus that brings us to the table of dialogue and is itself what we bring to the table.

In the second part of their paper, Llavador and Martínez develop this dynamic of identity and relatedness, appropriately enough, in a detailed discussion of Merton's poem 'With the World in my Blood Stream.' In the poem Merton finds his identity not only in Christ (as we heard in our President's address) but also in 'the star's plasm' that runs in his veins—'the star's plasm,' the stuff of the universe, stardust, the material of which are all made. With the world (literally) in his blood stream Merton finds his relatedness not only with his inmost self (Christ), not only with humanity in a general sense (universal embrace), but with another person, a woman, flesh and blood, also Christ incarnated in the world . . . that flows in his blood stream with all the attendant risk, danger, elation, foolhardiness, scandal and betrayal that beset those who would truly embrace the universe.

A fitting point at which to draw this introduction to a close and invite you to experience for yourself the varied and enriching contributions that follow—save to point out that the theme of the conference was inspired by a poem and we therefore begin and end with poetry. We begin with Merton's poem 'With the World in my Blood Stream' and conclude with a (judicious) selection of poems read by participants on that Saturday night, both uproarious and mellow. Enjoy!

ANGUS STUART

With the World in my Blood Stream

I LIE ON MY HOSPITAL BED
Water runs inside the walls
And the musical machinery
All around overhead
Plays upon my metal system
My invented back bone
Lends to the universal tone
A flat impersonal song
All the planes in my mind
Sing to my worried blood
To my jet streams
I swim in the world's genius
The spring's plasm
I wonder who the hell I am.

The world's machinery
Expands in the walls
Of the hot musical building
Made in maybe twenty-four
And my lost childhood remains
One of the city's living cells
Thanks to this city
I am still living
But whose life lies here
And whose invented music sings?

All the freights in the night
Swing my dark technical bed
All around overhead
And wake the questions in my blood
My jet streams fly far above
But my low gash is no good
Here below earth and bone
Bleeding in a numbered bed
Though all my veins run
With Christ and with the stars' plasm.

Ancestors and Indians
Zen Masters and Saints
Parade in the incredible hotel
And dark-eyed Negro mercy bends

And uncertain fibres of the will
Toward recovery and home.
What recovery and what Home?
I have no more sweet home
I doubt the bed here and the road there
And WKLO I most abhor
My head is rotten with the town's song.

Here below stars and light
And the Chicago plane
Slides up the rainy straits of night
While in my maze I walk and sweat
Wandering in the low bone system
Or searching the impossible ceiling
For the question and the meaning
Till the machine rolls in again
I grow hungry for invented air
And for the technical community of men
For my lost Zen breathing
For the unmarried fancy
And the wild gift I made in those days
For all the compromising answers
All the gambles and blue rhythms
Of individual despair.

So the world's logic runs
Up and down the doubting walls
While the frights and the planes
Swing my sleep out the window
All around overhead
In doubt and technical heat
In oxygen and jet streams
In the world's enormous space
And in man's enormous want
Until the want itself is gone
Nameless bloodless and alone
The Cross comes and Eckhart's scandal
The Holy Supper and the precise wrong
And the accurate little spark
In emptiness in the jet stream
Only the spark can understand
All that burns flies upward
Where the rainy jets have gone
A sign of needs and possible homes

An invented back bone
A dull song of oxygen
A lost spark in Eckhart's Castle.
World's plasm and world's cell
I bleed myself awake and well.

Only the spark is now true
Dancing in the empty room
All around overhead
While the frail body of Christ
Sweats in a technical bed
I am Christ's lost cell
His childhood and desert age
His descent into hell.

Love without need and without name
Bleeds in the empty problem
And the spark without identity
Circles the empty ceiling.

THOMAS MERTON

PRESIDENTIAL ADDRESS

The Hesychastic Heart
of Thomas Merton's Universal Embrace

A.M. 'Donald' Allchin

I AM SURE that I am not alone in feeling that the events of last September 11th in New York have had the effect of bringing Thomas Merton much nearer to us. I think already, long before that day, people were becoming aware of ways in which Merton seemed to be drawing nearer to us as we got further away from him in time. I began to think that a way to understand that apparent paradox was to recognise that Merton was so far ahead of his own time, it was only as we moved further away from him that we were gradually catching up with him.

September 11th changed things. Change became sudden not gradual, unpredictable not predictable, improbable rather than probable. I have been surprised, sometimes almost thrown, by the strength of my own reactions to these events, and in particular to the strength and disarray of my feelings towards the United States of America, a country which I have known for almost forty years, where I have frequently stayed and taught, where I have many friends and acquaintances, people to whom I am greatly indebted. I thought I knew the USA fairly well, for better and for worse, and that I knew my own reactions to that vast country, the favourable and the less favourable ones.

Forgive me if I speak personally. I have been remembering in the last months two lines from *King Lear*, which were very much with me at the end of the 1960s.

> The weight of this sad time we must obey,
> speak what we feel, not what we ought to say.

The events of September 11th have affected me in two ways. First in a strong sense of identification, not only with the country as a whole, but with the city and people of New York in particular, a place where I stayed quite a number of times in the sixties and seventies. I was in

Italy on the 11th of September, at Bose, in a predominantly Italian environment. Suddenly I was aware that I was not only a European. I was also an Anglo-Saxon, and I felt almost a New Yorker. I found the same thing when I got to New York some three weeks later, to stay with friends in a parish on 29th Street in Manhattan, not so far from the World Trade Center. I had an unexpectedly deep sense of satisfaction, of at-homeness, as the taxi drove into those familiar streets and I saw they were still there. But I must say that once I was there in Manhattan I became aware, in a way I could never have foreseen, of the weight, the burden, the sense of loss which people seemed to be carrying, particularly in that part of New York.

But if on the one hand I have found a sense of identification with America and with American friends, which was stronger than I had expected, I have also known within myself a revulsion from some of the attitudes and actions of the American government, which has astonished me by its violence; I hadn't expected myself to react so powerfully.

I think for instance of the treatment of the prisoners at Guantanamo Bay in Cuba. A treatment which seems to me to have been grotesque in its inhumanity, its stupidity and indeed its wickedness. In relation to those men, and to others whom the administration seems anxious to dispose of, I have felt that the difference that opens up between a country which retains the death penalty and one which has decided to reject it, is perhaps deeper and more decisive than I imagined it would be.

If you look in The Merton Annual, Volume 11, you will find the text of a keynote address given at the International Society's meeting in Mobile, Alabama, in 1997 by James Douglass, director of a House for Homeless People in Birmingham, Alabama.[1] In it he speaks of the American prison system with its huge population, he speaks of those on Death Row,

> surrounded by the thickest walls on earth, guarded twenty-four hours a day, monitored constantly by electronic devices and video cameras...

He speaks of the particular way in which that system weighs on the black community,

> at the judicial scape-goating of the poor and the massive expansion of our prison system into a new Harlem. On our Death Row we

have lost compassion. At the time of the unspeakable there is Death
Row at the center of our history.

Perhaps it is not so surprising that the authorities at Guantanamo Bay
are obviously perfectly at ease with the system they have devised.
They evidently took it for granted that the rest of the world (even,
apparently, the rest of the Muslim world) would have been as pleased
as they were with the photographs they released of prisoners in
process of being processed.

If my own reaction against a certain kind of aggressive and
unreflecting American reaction to September 11th is stronger than I
had expected, perhaps it has something to do with the two people
who first welcomed me to the United States in the summer of 1963,
when I was visiting that country for the first time, and who gave me,
needless to say, a very different picture of what America is called to be.

The first was Dale Moody, New Testament Professor at the Southern
Baptist Seminary in Louisville, with whom I stayed first of all. He was
in many ways a rather typical American; perhaps untypical in his deep
sense of rootedness in Kentucky, the state in which he had not only
been born and grown up, but in which he lived and worked and to
which he was devoted. Dale Moody was a man felt by many of his
colleagues to be dangerously liberal in matters of theology. He was a
man loved by his students for his combination of scholarly accuracy
with Baptist warmth and enthusiasm, a combination which got his
lecture room the nickname 'Hallelujah Hall!' It was he who took me to
visit Lincoln's birthplace, to visit Shakertown at Pleasant Hill, it was he
who took me to Gethsemani and introduced me to Merton.

Merton was of course a man of a more complex kind than Dale
Moody. Brought up in England and France, his father a New
Zealander, his mother an American, it was in the end with his mother's
country that he stayed and cast down his anchor. He became an
American and identified himself with the country of his adoption, in
many ways wholeheartedly if never uncritically. He too was a man
who lived both with his heart and his head, and who joined clarity
with devotion. I suppose, almost without being aware of it, I gained
my deepest impressions of the United States not only through
our conversations, but above all from the book of his which is
still particularly dear to me, *Conjectures of a Guilty Bystander*, the book
in which he lives through, thinks through and prays through those
tumultuous years of the 1960s.

I have never ceased to be amazed at the strange fact that we should have been spending the day together in April 1968 at the moment when Martin Luther King was shot in Memphis. We finished the day in a little restaurant in Bardstown, Colonel Hawke's Diner, under the watchful eye of the restaurant's proprietor and manager Colonel Hawke, a remarkable and memorable African-American, a friend of Tom and a friend of the community at Gethsemani.

It would be tempting to try to imagine what Merton's reaction would be today to some of the stranger and more troubling aspects of our contemporary tumults. But I intend to try to look a little beneath the surface of things to the deeper motivations of his life. Recognising for instance how closely some of his deepest concerns in that last decade of his life correspond to some of the deepest needs of our own time.

There is for instance the need to work towards a non-violent way of resistance to war and violence, the need to develop a positive peace movement, a way of working towards both truth and reconciliation. There is also the urgent need to press forward on the way of inter-faith dialogue, towards a greater mutual understanding, respect and love between people of very different religious and cultural traditions. There is above all the urgent need to rediscover a wholeness and liberty in our way of living and thinking and praying the Christian tradition, a new awareness, a new sense of the all-embracing divine humanity of Christ, which leaves no-one outside the scope of divine love. It is the subtitle of our conference this year, *Thomas Merton's Universal Embrace*. How far is it our continuing fears, prejudices, divisions, within the family of Christ, which block us from this truly universal vision, this truly universal embrace?

I have long believed that something of the very heart of Merton's theological and spiritual vision is to be found in the unpublished lectures on *Ascetical and Mystical Theology*, which he gave to the community at Gethsemani in 1960, and in those lectures above all about the remarkable chapter on *Natural Contemplation*, on *physike theoria*, in the work of Maximus the Confessor. Of Maximus, Merton says

> He has the broadest and most balanced view of the Christian cosmos of all the Greek fathers and therefore of all the fathers.

He indeed can tell us what it means to have the world in our bloodstream.

Last October, on my visit to the States, I went from New York to Louisville, to take part in a day symposium on *Merton and Hesychasm, Merton and the Prayer of the Heart*, and the morning after the meeting I had the chance to spend two or three precious hours at the Merton Study Center, and with Paul Pearson's expert and perceptive guidance I was able to discover many things in a brief space of time. Above all I had the chance to examine one of the volumes of Mignes' *Patrologia Graeca*, from the monastic library, which contains the works of Maximus the Confessor, and there I could trace in Merton's discreet careful notes and marks in the margin of that volume, how thoroughly he had read his way through that great and complex thinker. Of course he shouldn't have been making those notations, I think he perhaps reckoned that no-one else in the monastery would read the volume at all!

There I saw something of the work which lay behind the words he spoke to the community in those lectures on the spiritual tradition of the Church through the centuries, or, as he says in those lectures, 'the mystical tradition of the Church, a collective memory and experience of Christ living and present within her,' and of the vital place of natural contemplation within that memory and experience. *Theoria Physike*, 'the reception of God's revelation of himself in creatures, in history, in scripture,' learning to read God's presence in all things, finding the world despite all its apparent darkness as still God's good creation.

> We must not believe that sin caused this unique masterpiece, which is the visible world in which God manifests himself by a silent revelation. (Maximus).

> The vision of *theoria physike* is essentially *sophianic*, through the vision we are able to unite the hidden wisdom of God in things with the hidden light of wisdom in ourselves. The meeting and marriage of these two brings about a resplendent clarity within man himself, and this clarity is the presence of the divine wisdom fully recognised and active within us. (Merton).

It is that 'resplendent clarity' which we see shining out in the photograph of Merton and the Dalai Lama at the end of the third of their momentous meetings.

This contemplation of God in and through the things he has made, and in and through the vicissitudes of history, personal and public, works at many levels. It involves a discovery of God's presence in the spirit of scripture and not in the letter. It liberates us from a deadly literalism of scriptural understanding, the root of fundamentalism, it involves discovering God's presence in the *logoi* of created things, not in their materiality, that is to say in the things in themselves, in their own true being, not simply as things to be manipulated and exploited by us; it means 'recognising God's presence in our own inmost spirit and true self, rather than in the ego'; the discovery of the true person within, the hidden person of the heart; 'recognising God's action in the inner meaning of history and not in its externals; in the inner sense of the divine judgement and mercy, not in the superstitious and pseudo-apocalyptic interpretation of events.' How that speaks to some of the dangerous nonsense of our time, which treats the vision of St John on Patmos, for instance, as if it contained the predictions of an astrologer!

The wisdom which comes from the encounter with God in history and in our own lives is liberating and integrating, enabling us through turmoil to find balance and clarity and equilibrium.

The will of God is no longer a blind force plunging through our lives like a cosmic steamroller and demanding to be accepted willy-nilly. On the contrary we are able to understand the hidden purposes of the creative wisdom and the divine mercy of God, and we can co-operate with him as sons and daughters with a loving father.

There is much more in Merton's monastic interpretation of the patristic ideal of natural contemplation, receiving and apprehending the revelation of God in and through the things that God makes and the things that he does. There is his whole consideration of what that means for the work of the artist, the poet, the musician in our times.

He must be in communication with things in their deepest centre, in their most real value, he must be attuned to their voice, he must sense something of their logic, their vocation.

There is also his brilliant use of the architecture and craftsmanship of the nineteenth century Shakers to illustrate the nature of the true sacred art and meaning of this seventh century theologian. 'Shaker handicrafts are a real epiphany of the *logoi*;' in them we see the inner logic, the calling, the vocation of stone and wood and bricks and mortar. The Shaker building always fits right into its location, manifests the *logos* of the place where it is built, grasps and expresses the hidden *logos* of the valley or hillside which forms its site.

But rather than dwell on such material, fascinating though it is, I want to come back again to the very heart of our topic, to Merton's description of the inner, mystical tradition of the Church, its 'collective memory and experience of Christ living and present within her.'

The symposium in which I was taking parting, in Louisville, was on the theme of Merton and Hesychasm, Merton and the Prayer of the Heart but it was unfortunate that none of the four speakers, of whom I was one, seem to have been aware of the tape of Merton speaking directly on the subject of prayer of the heart, i.e. the Jesus Prayer, to the brothers of the community at Gethsemani and showing how that extremely simple way of prayer is a true way of keeping alive, in one's own inmost being, as well as in the life of the whole Church, this memory and experience of Christ living and present within and amongst us.

Only on Tuesday last did I get from David Scott this tape of Merton speaking on this subject to the community of Gethsemani. It is a wonderful tape, a talk full of humour and joy, given with immense vigour and immense freedom. It begins with Merton telling us of a meeting he has had recently with a person who had struck him as someone truly holy, someone in whose presence he seemed to feel the touch of God's presence, and in her saw the truth of what Irenaus means when he says that the vision of God is a human person truly alive. Merton then speaks about the Jesus Prayer and its use, its practice, its meaning and its power. Ultimately its power is in the name which stands at its centre, the name in which human and divine meet in their fullness and integrity.

Throughout the talk one is aware of Merton's enormous desire to communicate to his brethren in the community something of his own sense of discovery of this way of prayer, so simple that it can unite itself with all the times and circumstances of our life, can bring us at the end to discover that through the action of the Holy Spirit the memory and presence of Christ in indeed living within us.

If we ask how it was that Merton came to know that prayer, we can confidently say that he came to know it by praying it. If we want to see how carefully he had pondered on the depth of its meaning, how ready he was to learn from the Orthodox world in which it had its origin, we can turn to his journal entry for September 11th 1960 when he observes the anniversary of the death of Staretz Silouan, the monk of the Russian Monastery on Mount Athos who had died on September 11th 1938.[2] It was Staretz Silouan, unknown in his lifetime, and still very little known in 1960, who is now becoming well known as St

Silouan the Athonite, having been canonised by the Ecumenical Patriarchate of Constantinople.

If you want an introduction to the prayer and vision of St Silouan you cannot do better that to turn to the little book of Brother Ramon and Bishop Simon Barrington-Ward, *Praying the Jesus Prayer Together*.[3] There you will see something of the unifying power of that prayer, drawing together Evangelical, Catholic and Orthodox, and not only that, you will see the way in which that prayer speaks far beyond the boundaries of Christendom, especially to Muslims and Hindus. There too you will find, as you will in Merton's Journal for 1960, reflections on the words of the Lord spoken to the Staretz at the turning point of his life, 'Keep your mind in hell and do not despair.' I had long thought of those words as a message of hope from heaven addressed particularly to men and women of the twentieth century. Hearing them now I can see that they are no less urgently addressed to the people of our own century, our third millennium.

'Keep your mind in hell and do not despair.' What else could we possibly say to our brothers and sisters, Muslim, Jewish and Christian, in the Holy Land, to those who shelter at this moment in the Church of the Nativity in Bethlehem, to those who go into the Church of the Resurrection in Jerusalem. 'Keep your mind in hell and do not despair.'

Notes and References

1. James W. Douglass, 'Compassion and the Unspeakable' in *The Merton Annual Vol.* 11, Sheffield Academic Press, 1998, pp.67-87
2. Thomas Merton, *Turning Toward the World – The Journals of Thomas Merton Vol. 4* (ed. Victor A. Kramer), USA, HarperSanFrancisco, 1996, pp.44-46
3. Brother Ramon and Simon Barrington-Ward, *Praying the Jesus Prayer Together*, Oxford, The Bible Reading Fellowship, 2001

THOMAS MERTON

the world in my bloodstream

KEYNOTE ADDRESSES

ROBERT INCHAUSTI

BONNIE THURSTON

DONALD GRAYSTON

Beyond Political Illusion: The Role of the Individual in Troubled Times

ROBERT INCHAUSTI

For THOMAS MERTON, 'the world' was not some static, scholastic concept but an ever-changing, mutating, living reality, alive in his bloodstream. And when he described it, particularly in his poetry and later essays, it was always as a co-participant, struggling to understand himself in and through the particulars of existence. In *Conjectures of a Guilty Bystander* he wrote:

> We are living in the greatest revolution in history—a huge spontaneous upheaval of the entire human race: not the revolution planned and carried out by any particular party, race, or nation, but a deep elemental boiling over of all the inner contradictions that have ever been in man, a revelation of the chaotic forces inside everybody. This is not something we have chosen, nor is it something we are free to avoid.

> This revolution is a profound spiritual crisis of the whole world, manifested largely in desperation, cynicism, violence, conflict, self-contradiction, ambivalence, fear and hope, doubt and belief, creation and destructiveness, progress and regression, obsessive attachments to images, idols, slogans, programs that only dull the general anguish for a moment until it bursts out everywhere in a still more acute and terrifying form. We do not know if we are building a fabulously wonderful world or destroying all that we have ever had, all that we have achieved!

> All the inner force of man is boiling and bursting out, the good together with the evil, the good poisoned by evil and fighting it, the evil pretending to be good and revealing itself in the most dreadful crimes, justified and rationalized by the purest and most innocent intentions.[1]

So how does one find one's bearings amid such tumult and confusion? What is the place of the individual in troubled times?

I hope to make clear Merton's radically original answer to these questions by comparing his contemplative vision to two very different interpretations of contemporary ethics. Firstly, the Neo-Machiavellianism represented by Robert Kaplan, whose book *Warrior Politics: Why Leadership Demands a Pagan Ethos* became very popular in the United States shortly after the events of 9/11. And secondly, the Christian-Realism of Reinhold Niebuhr, whose ideas provided the ethical underpinning to both American Cold War Policy and Martin Luther King's Birmingham Campaign.

I'll begin with Kaplan because, although he represents the absolute antithesis to Merton's prophetic Christianity, there are some very interesting parallels. For one thing, Kaplan argues that our world is not 'modern' or 'postmodern,' but *ancient*, 'a world that, despite its technologies, the best Chinese, Greek, and Roman philosophers would have understood, and known how to navigate.'[2] Works such as Sun Tzu's *Art of War*, Augustine's *City of God*, and Hobbes' *Leviathan* have acquired odd new relevance – as have all our classics – as prescient anticipations, albeit unconsciously and in pre-modern terms, of the movement toward a global civilization as it struggles through uneven economic developments and the clash of civilizations.

Kaplan's central thesis, however, is better illustrated by the following quote:

> a policy is defined not by its excellence but by its outcome: if it isn't effective, it can't be virtuous... Machiavelli believes in pagan virtue—ruthless and pragmatic but not amoral. 'All armed prophets succeed,' he writes, 'whereas unarmed ones fail.'[3]

I can think of no more succinct summation of the values of our modern politicized world than this little paragraph. No wonder Kaplan's book was praised by former secretary of state Henry Kissinger, former secretary of defense William Cohen, Newt Gingrich, and the CEO of Lockheed Martin! And yet every prophetic religious figure – from Samuel to Thomas Merton – has been struggling against just such sentiments.

What is at stake here is not exactly whether the ends justify the means, but more whether we can ever really know the ends we should seek. Machiavelli, Kissinger, and Kaplan say that we can, and so they advocate a pagan leadership ethos that is both pitiless and calculating; whereas Merton, like the prophets before him, argues for a more existential vision. Since we can't know what the good truly is, we must temper our ambitions with moral caution and a sense of historical irony.

For Merton, causality in human affairs is largely an illusion; the future can't be understood through the categories of the present, and human calculations of self-interest are simply not objective enough given the unseen hand of providence operating behind the scenes. The pagan virtues of Pilate are short-sighted and inaccurate; however clever they might have seemed to tacticians and men of the hour.

But let us not miss Kaplan's point: by bringing the realities of coercion and violence into our discussion of social policy, he makes it clear that *authentic ethical achievements can't be merely an extension of our idealism.* If we are serious about furthering the good, the true, and the beautiful, we must factor in those forces working against them. That is to say, acquiring an ethical vision of life cannot be divorced from exercising our civic responsibilities, and to that we need to add understanding of what is really going on in the world around us. Public service, in this sense, may be the very means through which a more accurate understanding of the world is acquired.

What strikes a Merton reader most about Kaplan's argument is how surprisingly bookish he is in his acceptance of the price *others must pay* so that we might forge a political consensus. His focus upon so-called 'realities' belies a very truncated view of both real historical possibilities and actual human suffering. What is needed if we want to really grasp the current state of the world is a repudiation of our prerogative 'to be safe' and a turn to the ascetic heroism of the selfless statesman, the struggling artist, the altruistic soldier, the dedicated philosopher, noble scientist, and servant saint; perhaps, a marriage of working class endurance with aristocratic *noblesse oblige*: the stoic courage of the New York firefighter coupled with the intellectual reach of a Franklin Delano Roosevelt and wit of Mark Twain.

What Kaplan fails to realize in his call for a pagan leadership ethos is that Orthodoxy has already been there and back. Traditional Christian theology is largely what is left of Classical Thought after history has been seen through as a power play. It doesn't try to redeem our times, improve them, redirect, or even change them; it just describes reality, and by so doing liberates us from the tyranny of pagan philosophers and petty tyrants so that we can experience real hope. Hope not that the world is getting better or that our dreams will come true – it's not, and they won't – but hope that life itself is a great good and that love and courage matter. Indeed, love, courage, fortitude, and the struggle for justice are not tools for progress at all, but ends in themselves—who we are.

Perhaps the post-war theologian who offered the most sophisticated take on the role religion plays in contemporary power politics was Reinhold Niebuhr. Like Merton, he began his academic career as a Marxist, but World War II made it clear to him that 'moral' individuals could inhabit 'immoral' societies, and that the clash between a private ethics and the public good required serious theological reflection.

Politics could not give us all that we seek, but there was no way to know what we could seek without confronting intractable political realities and actual human limitations. Christian realists were needed to temper the utopian excesses of both Left and Right wing political extremes without giving up on the possibility of progress or succumbing to cynicism, acquiescence, or despair. The West may not have all the solutions to every problem, but if it was honest enough to admit that no easy solutions existed, then this tragic awareness offered more hope for slow, sustained progress than the easy, revolutionary 'proposals' offered by the ideologues of the Soviet Bloc.

For Niebuhr, the Biblical ideal of the Kingdom of God stood in radical judgment not only of current social reality but also to every conceivable alternative to it. Cultural and social achievements, however impressive, could provide no final good. History was driven by an insatiable human desire for more. We are best able to direct our energies toward reform only when we understand what is really going on, and in most cases what is going on is not merely a clash of competing ideals but also a clash of competing interests.

A 'realistic' Christian ethic has to take into account all the factors in a situation, especially those born of unconscious self-seeking and entrenched privilege. Any perspective that ignores these forces may allow its advocates to feel good about their selfless idealism but at the expense of true and effective moral action. These are Hegel's 'beautiful souls' who opt out of history for the moral comfort of an illusory absolute, as opposed to engaged Christian realists who own up to their limitations as flawed human beings who nevertheless must act in a morally compromised world.

Given Niebuhr's perspective, the fanaticism of Pontius Pilate is the fanaticism of all good men, who do not know that they are not as good as they esteem themselves. Pilate represents the moral mediocrity of all political leaders who simply cannot distinguish between a criminal and the Saviour because they judge everything by the same reductive laws of minimal order.[4] Or as John Millbank has so eloquently put it,

> In Pilate, precisely, we see what human rule and reason is: the slaying through indifference and impatience of the God-man or the human future.[5]

As a result, all political decisions tend to devolve into questions of the lesser of two evils which inevitably devolves further into concessions to expediency. Prophetic leadership can challenge this narrowing of possibilities, but it is seldom if ever successful. The best one can hope, Niebuhr argues, is for a hovering irony that keeps the powerful perpetually self-effacing and subject to criticism.

But, educating the American public into the paradoxes and ironies of history was a risky thing given the assault upon ethical thinking that had already taken place due to the propaganda barrages of World War II. 'Christian realism' pitched to this frightened and cynical post-war population could only served to heighten Cold War paranoia and justify a tendency to shoot first and ask questions later—a point of view summarized in that chilling slogan that emerged from the Vietnam war: 'Kill them all, and let God sort them out.'

This is why Thomas Merton's *The Seven Storey Mountain* (1948) resonated powerfully with those looking for a non-materialistic, alternative to the ideologies of the new super states. To meet the dangerous new power alignments of the post-war world, a new America had emerged: corporate, consolidated, internationally connected, and militarily ready, run by professional managers, social scientists, and experts. The most pressing question of the era was not how the country's unique democratic character was going to be preserved, that was already gone, but rather whose interests this new class of technocrats were going to serve.

Merton offered a refreshingly frank answer to this question. The new class would serve exactly the same worldly interests as the old ones: progress, money, power, and development. The Allies' victory may have saved the world from entering into a new dark age, but if they failed to recognize the empty cultural forms that had preceded it and that threatened to follow in its wake, there was a very real danger that their victory could become hollow.

The Seven Storey Mountain, by examining the place of mysticism in the life of the mind, or rather by examining its 'absence,' raised the troubling question of the role of individual conscience in the new technological society. Merton, more or less, agreed with Mahatma Gandhi, that history was 'the record of every interruption of the even working of the force of love'—everything that stood between the individual and God. It was an account – and this was confirmed by the GIs now returning home from the war – of the accumulated sins of the fathers visited upon the sons, shadows playing upon the inside of a cave; a nightmare from which all of us were trying to awake.

Yet for Merton human experiences – existential reality, events – were no mere fictions. If life's time-bound particulars sometimes obscured their transcendental source, and if the chronicles of human strife often hid the mystery of existence behind a veil of self-justifications, that did not mean that Reality itself could not be known. Only that it was usually misnamed. And it was in this process of mis-naming that the significance of experience itself got fatally distorted, causing individuals to oscillate between personal preoccupation with their own subjective experiences and a pseudoscientific materialism posited as a presupposition for conventional sanity.

As the allusion to Dante in the title implies, *The Seven Storey Mountain* represented the modern world as a purgatory—a spiritual Diaspora where the most profound human values and experiences were rapidly being exiled, left for dead, or buried at sea. The Allies, in an instinctual rejoinder to the militarism of the totalitarian states, had themselves embraced the values of production, might, and control, and, in the process had lost track of their single greatest moral strength: the ascetic ideal. If Western civilization was going to survive, Merton suggested, it would have to go inward to get back in touch with its own spiritual core:

> The way to find the real world is not merely to measure and observe what is outside us, but to discover our own inner ground. For that is where the world is, first of all: in my deepest self. This "ground," this "world" where I am mysteriously present at once to my own self and to the freedoms of all other men, is not a visible, objective and determined structure with fixed laws and demands. It is a living and self-creating mystery of which I am myself a part, to which I am myself my own unique door.[6]

Protestant America in its conversation with Enlightenment skepticism had accepted the epistemological preoccupations of the new sciences as central, and so became concerned with evidences for the faith, but never came to grips with the wisdom tradition still lurking within the medieval imagination. This rootless, invented, American Protestant self longed for a spiritual home, but given its preoccupation with Cartesian certainties had no means for arriving there. The Catholic contemplative tradition, however, updated by a healthy dose of theistic existentialism, could bring the Western religious imagination back in touch with its experience and go beyond William James' focus on the philosophical reasonableness and moral helpfulness of faith, to what Kierkegaard called 'the absolutely, paradoxically, teleological placed' radicalism of the apostle.

Seen in the light of Merton's contemplative spirituality, Christianity takes on new meaning as a mediating position between classical metaphysics and contemporary theory. It supplies a post-mythological perspective that leads to a view of human development as a movement away from mimetic desire[7] to a universal, transcendent ethic of solidarity with the outcast, the alienated, the excluded, and the poor.

Thomas Merton described this as a movement away from the values of the *false self*, that part of us created by culture and identified with success, achievement, and others' good opinions, to the values of the *real self*, that part of us known only to God which is glimpsed by us from time to time in moments of prayer, service, and contemplation. This self is revealed when we experience personal loss or some form of psychological disintegration that reconstitutes our identity within some more inclusive comprehension of life.

This distinction between the social self and the mystical self holds far reaching political implications: shifting the entire focus of culture criticism away from sociological categories to existential analysis, recollection, and the revelations of prayer. Merton remarks:

> One of the most widespread errors of our time is a superficial "personalism" which identifies the "person" with the external self, the empirical ego, and devotes itself solemnly to the cultivation of this ego. But this is the cult of a pure illusion, the illusion of what is popularly imagined to be "personality" or worse still "dynamic" and "successful" personality. When this error is taken over into religion it leads to the worst kind of nonsense—a cult of psychologism and self-expression which vitiates our whole cultural and spiritual self. Our reality, our true self, is hidden in what appears to us to be nothingness and void. What we are not seems to be real, what we are seems to be unreal. We can rise above this

unreality, and recover our hidden identity. And that is why the way to reality is the way of humility which brings us to reject the illusory self and accept the "empty" self that is "nothing" in our own eyes and in the eyes of men, but is our true reality in the eyes of God: for this reality is "in God" and "with Him" and belongs entirely to Him.[8]

Many secular scholars have a difficult time accepting this distinction, and so as a result the Christian tradition they study – much like the Islamic World they imagine – is either static, lethal or dead. So they administer inoculations against its supposed poisons or conduct autopsies, never suspecting that the body of thought they are working on is not only still alive but highly conscious. Merton, by accepting the spiritual premises inherent to Christian spirituality, allows us to rethink our relationship to the secular categories dominating contemporary thought, giving us distance from them, and liberating us from their ethical blindness.

The events of 9/11 confronted Americans with a problem not faced since the last war: what do we do with an implacable, relentless, and suicidal enemy sworn to our destruction? The pacifist approach would have us make this enemy into our friend through dialogue, self-sacrifice, and negotiation. Air-drop supplies into Afghanistan rather than bombs, and use this opportunity to reflect upon our own sins and excess as well as theirs. The militant would simply eliminate our enemies wholesale by killing them. This approach – equally unrealistic – has at least the bureaucratic advantage of advancing a measurable goal!

Niebuhrian realism, however, offers another approach: we must simply own up to the fact that life itself is a tragic affair, that there will always be those who oppose our interests and plans, even those who will our destruction. We cannot make them our friends whatever we do because we cannot in good conscience change ourselves to reflect their values, nor can we physically eliminate them from the face of the earth, and so we must temper our ambitions both in peace and in war with a longer view of things that recognizes both our moral and our practical limitations as human beings.

George W. Bush's mixed strategy of sending both bombs and humanitarian supplies to Afghanistan doesn't qualify as Niebuhrian irony, however, because Bush never owned up to the contradictory nature of his policies. For him, the bread and the bombs were simply two sides of the same coin, the carrot and the stick of 'infinite justice.' Niebuhr, however, would caution against such a naive view. Bombs don't just eliminate enemies, they also create them, and humanitarian aid doesn't only generate good will; it also creates resentment and dependencies. Political dialogue must be preceded by real cultural and theological exchanges if peace is ever to be achieved, but these are seldom to be found either among today's Machiavellian policy makers or those enforcing their tough-minded policies on the front lines.

Jean Baudrillard described the American war in Afghanistan as 'the continuation of non-politics by other means,' and his point is well taken.[9] If no conversation was taking place between the West and the Islamic countries before the war began, the war itself certainly won't cure that; it will simply continue the *silence* more vociferously. The terrorist attacks didn't clarify the ambiguities of our relationship to the Islamic World any more than they obscured them. We are exactly where we were before 9/11: in the middle of an economic transition to globalization without any real vision why we are doing it or what kind of ancient animosities we are setting off in the process.

Christian realists accept this state of affairs as the tragic context within which all of us must work out our shared human destiny— accepting our moral culpability, our partial virtue, and our limited vision as givens, tempering our confidence in ourselves and in our nation through our faith in a universal God greater than both. But Christian contemplatives like Merton, suspect that even this measured, reasonable approach might be a misreading of our true situation, and that only through recollection and prayer can our illusions be lessened and the windows of perception cleansed.

Here is where Thomas Merton comes in as a key twentieth century social thinker. Tempted by Marxism in his youth, he ultimately chose to carry 'the ignorant perfection of ordinary people' to its logical conclusion by turning away from the false values of modernity to a deep reflection upon the sources of his own dignity, joy, and desire for human justice in the religious traditions of the West.

His witness, of course, was largely misunderstood within the bifurcated, politicized social contexts of Cold War America and the protests of the sixties. Appropriated first by the Catholic sectarians and then later by the counter-culture, his true significance as a post-liberal critic of secular optimism and the 'perfect crime' of simulated modern existence went largely unnoticed.[10] And yet as time goes by, his insights, his refusals, his troubled relationship to both the church and to his times, become more and more telling as a prophetic commentary on contemporary existence.

Merton was more than a diagnostician; he was a soldier of the spirit; like Gandhi, he conducted 'experiments in truth.' They were interior experiments, and so his 'discoveries' were not as easily transferable to the political environment as say the deft political discernments of Niebuhr or the radical certainties of the Berrigans. And yet in the long run, Merton's tragic, religious plebeian view that history is not the primary theatre of the self-making but that conscience is, may be in fact the more important and telling observation.

Elie Wiesel tells a parable that eloquently describes the current state of spiritual affairs: Man once prayed to God to let him be God for a few moments so that he might know what it was like. God refused saying that if he changed places with Man, Man might not change back. But Man promised he would, so God allowed the switch. But once he became God, Man refused to switch back. We live in a world in which Man has become God, and God has become man, and only just recently have both parties begun to feel uncomfortable with the arrangement.

Merton's return to the sources of Western asceticism in the contemplative traditions of Benedict and Cassian was not a switch back to pre-modern Orthodoxy but to a right relation with God that transformed all our current knowledge in the light of as yet unknown categories of spiritual understanding—not in a retro-embrace of paganism, nor a modern pragmatism that evades the possibility of radical change.

Niebuhr was the single most influential religious intellectual in post-war America because he embraced the paradoxes of modern Christianity as powerfully as Merton, insisting that there could be no salvation in human history and yet no grace apart from it. But ultimately the kind of activist public intellectual he became was the very antithesis of Merton's monastic 'marginal man.'

Merton spent over a third of his day in prayer and silence, while Niebuhr attended conferences, met with public officials, published rejoinders to public policy statements, and generally made himself a force in the corridors of power. He spent forty weekends a year traveling around the country giving sermons and making sure his 'realist' Christian morality entered into the public debates of his day. Merton, on the other hand, retired from the world, lived the life of a peasant, kept close to nature and solitude, eventually even becoming a hermit. He played down the public acclaim and the business of an 'important man' in order to celebrate the duties of a monk—to teach, to serve, to work, to pray, and to stay close to the poor. For Merton, the first duty of the Christian apostle in both good and bad times was to *practice* what he preached, not to become a *spokesman* for a 'Christian world view.' Merton understood that creative living was an act of generosity, of giving, or extravagance, and that the message of any work of art, love, or witness is always the same: this will disconnect you from your fused personality.

As a result, Merton's vows of poverty, chastity, and obedience put him in a much more radical relationship to his times than Niebuhr, who may have been a more consistent social theorist but did not live an alternative way of life. And yet Merton, like Niebuhr, understood the dangers of too one-sided a rejection of the world. He too advocated a tragic awareness of man's limitations. He too took the 'long view.' But Merton's public work was more 'private,' if I can put it that way. He addressed specific individuals through personal correspondence and conversation. And he wrote books for ordinary men and women seeking wholeness in a fragmented age. He did not write – as Niebuhr did – 'with one eye firmly fixed on social and political forces.' He wrote directly to other disoriented modern souls, with one ear tuned to the eternal silence.

Merton understood that we cannot perceive a truly inclusive reality until we have discarded the solidity, the boundedness, the unfreedom, the negativity inherited from our cultural and political ethos. The contemplative life allowed him to acknowledge the exquisite co-existence of opposites and inverted dimensions beyond consensus reality, so that he could align himself with raw, creative energy—the Holy Spirit, the Muse, the non-material stuff that is the source, meaning, and value of the material world.

Niebuhr moved beyond tragedy to point out the 'ironies' of American history, whereas Merton threw his life into the mystic, contemplative abyss in order to reveal our hypocrisies and complicities. Merton wasn't as interested in distinguishing between the lesser of two political evils as he was in *describing the impact our politicized world was having upon our ability to attain purity of heart.* He described the situation this way:

> This is no longer a time of systematic ethical speculation, for such speculation implies time to reason, and the power to bring social and individual action under the concerted control of reasoned principles upon which most men agree.
>
> There is no time to reason out, calmly and objectively, the moral implications of technical developments which are perhaps already superseded by the time one knows enough to reason about them.
>
> Action is not governed by moral reason but by political expediency and the demands of technology—translated into the simple abstract formulas of propaganda. These formulas have nothing to do with reasoned moral action, even though they may appeal to apparent moral values—they simply condition the mass of men to react in a desired way to certain stimuli.
>
> Men do not agree in moral reasoning. They concur in the emotional use of slogans and political formulas. There is no persuasion but that of power, of quantity, of pressure, of fear, of desire. Such is our present condition—and it is critical![11]

How do we escape this?

Perhaps, this is the role of the individual in trouble times: to manage his or her own escape. And Merton's suggestions as to how this may be done are very clear: we must refuse to be duped by the claims and desire of our false selves, refuse to insult our own souls by making intellectual and moral compromises with the prevailing half truths, and insist upon the greater reality of our unknowable, transcendent identities whose true existence is known only to God.

We can say 'Yes' to Niebuhrian Christian Realism only to the degree we go beyond politics to embrace the Contemplative Surrealism of Jesus Christ whose resurrection disclosed the hitherto unseen potentialities lurking within the spiritual darkness of our own lost lives.

Notes and References

1. Thomas Merton, *Conjectures of a Guilty Bystander*. Garden City, New York, Doubleday, 1966, pp.54-55. Image edition 1989, pp.66-67
2. Robert Kaplan, *Warrior Politics*. New York, Random House, 2001, p.vii
3. Ibid. pp.viii-ix
4. Reinhold Niebuhr, *The Irony of American History*. New York, Scribners, 1962, p.160

5. John Millbank, 'Knowledge: The theological critique of philosophy in Hamann and Jacobi' in *Radical Orthodoxy: A New Theology* (ed. John Millbank, Graham Ward and Catherine Pickstock). London, Routledge, 1999, p.30

6. Thomas Merton, *Contemplation in a World of Action*. Garden City, New York, Doubleday, 1971, p.234

7. 'Mimetic desire' is a term used by René Girard to describe the plasticity of human longing. We are born with certain survival needs, but we are conditioned into desires by seeing what others want and copying them. What we really want is to appropriate the things others want in order to gain status, prestige, and identity. Contemplation, meditation, and prayer are antidotes to mimetic desire—the hypnotic trance cast upon all of us by culture after the fall.

8. Thomas Merton, *New Seeds of Contemplation*. New York, New Directions, 1962, pp.281-282, republished in England as *Seeds of Contemplation*. Wheathampstead, Anthony Clarke Books, 1972, pp.218-219

9. *Harpers Magazine*, February 2002, p.18

10. See Jean Baudrillard's telling analysis of our virtual age, *The Perfect Crime*, translated by Chris Turner. London and New York, Verso, 1996

11. Thomas Merton, *Conjectures of a Guilty Bystander*. Garden City, New York, Doubleday, 1966, pp.53-54. Image edition 1989, pp.65-66

Some Reflections on Islamic Poems by Thomas Merton

BONNIE THURSTON

Who could have imagined in February 2001, when Angus Stuart did me the honor of asking me to give this address, that our universal embrace of Islam would need to be so particularly tender. I come from a country which is currently demonizing Islam and which seems to be trying to drag yours along in this wickedness. How particularly important it is, therefore, that we understand something of the beauty of Islam and those who embrace it. Therefore, let us begin our session with a moment of silent prayer for those who know God by the beautiful name of Allah.

IN WHAT FOLLOWS I will give a brief chronological (by publication date) listing of Merton's seven explicitly Islamic poems and say a word about each. This will introduce us to the breadth of Merton's interest in Islam in line with the theme of our conference, *Thomas Merton's Universal Embrace.* First, though, a general word about Merton's interest in Islam and a few suggestions of sources for further study.

Introduction

It seems to me that mutual comprehension between Christians and Moslems is something of very vital importance today, and unfortunately it is rare and uncertain, or else subjected to the vagaries of politics.[1]

This might be a remark by an academic summoned by this morning's television news program for an interview. But in fact it is a comment of Thomas Merton in a letter on December 26, 1962 to the Pakistani Muslim, Abdul Aziz, with whom he had a long and fruitful correspondence. Thomas Merton's profound study and understanding of Buddhism, particularly its Mahayana 'incarnations,' Zen and Tibetan, is well known. But he was equally interested in and conversant with Islam, particularly its mystical manifestation, Sufism. And until very recently this went largely unremarked among Merton scholars.

Of course Merton was not the first Roman Catholic, or even the first Cistercian, to be seriously interested in the Islamic tradition. Charles de Foucauld (d.1916), who became a Cistercian and then left the order to live among the poor in Algeria (where he was subsequently martyred), was, in fact, converted to authentic Christianity when he encountered the deep piety of Islam during his military service in North Africa. Merton knew and venerated Foucauld (as, indeed, I do). Another Frenchman, Louis Massignon (d.1962), deeply influenced by Foucauld, was, himself, the pre-eminent Catholic Islamic scholar of his day, producing a classic study of the technical vocabulary of mysticism in Islam as well as introducing the martyr mystic Ibn Mansur al-Hallaj (d.922) to the West. It is from al-Hallaj via Massignon that Merton gleaned the phrase le point vierge which figures so prominently in the 'Fourth and Walnut' revelation.[2]

In view of these Franco-Islamic connections (which would make an interesting study for someone whose French is better than mine), it is even odder that, until the perfectly splendid volume Merton and Sufism: The Untold Story edited by Bob Baker and Gray Henry[3] in 1999, there was no book-length study of Merton and Islam. (And in so far as this is a collection of articles, we are still without one.) One had to dig in the bibliographies provided by The Merton Seasonal to find studies on Merton and Islam. Before the turn of the century, to my knowledge there were only six scholars who had written or spoken seriously about the subject: Sr. Madeline Abdelnour and Burton Thurston (both now, alas, deceased), Terry Graham, Sidney Griffith, Erlinda Paguio and me. The volume Merton and Sufism collects work by Griffith, Paguio, and the Thurstons and adds essays by its editors. Additionally, it anthologizes excerpts from Merton's lectures on Sufism, prints all his Sufi poems and his reviews of books on Islam for various Cistercian publications.

In addition to the material in the Baker-Henry volume, primary source material for a study of Merton and Islam is found in his journals, especially Conjectures of a Guilty Bystander (CGB)[4] and in the journals of the 1960s. In Learning to Love (LL)[5] it is clear that the October, 1966 visit of Sidi Abdesalam, an Algerian Sufi, was of great, personal importance to Merton. Merton called it a 'momentous visit' (LL, p.152) perhaps because the Sufi told him that he was 'very close to mystical union and the slightest thing now can so to speak push me over the edge' (LL, p.153). A secondary account of the visit is to be found in the article in *Merton and Sufism* by Nicole Abadie, who was present for the encounter.[6]

Shannon's collection of letters, *The Hidden Ground of Love* (HGL), includes letters to Reza Arasteh (an Iranian psychologist), Abdul Aziz (a Pakistani Sufi to whom Merton opened the secret doors of his prayer life) and Martin Lings (an English Orientalist). In my view the Aziz letters are particularly important for students of Merton. The American, Herbert Mason, with whom Merton corresponded, introduced him to Louis Massignon. The Massignon-Merton letters are found in Shannon's collection, *Witness to Freedom* (WF).[7]

Perhaps the most interesting and frustrating body of primary material are the tapes of the Sufi talks Merton gave to the novices at Gethsemani from 1966-68. Much of this material is available commercially from Credence Cassettes,[8] but don't expect cogent, outlineable academic lectures. Merton's style is breezy and meandering. Frankly, it drives me crazy. Students will find it more helpful to consult Merton's reading notebooks, especially number 18, which are available at the Thomas Merton Studies Center at Bellarmine University in Louisville, Kentucky.

Merton, himself, summarized his work on Islam in a letter of October 31, 1967 to the Egyptian, Aly Abdel Ghani.

> I am very familiar with the traditions of Sufism, and have of course read much of the Holy Qur'an. I have read Avicenna, or some of his writing, and very much like others such as Ibn-Arabi, Ibn-Abbad (of Morocco), the Persian Rumi, etc. I wish I knew Arabic, as I could read more in the original. (WF, p.335)

Reviewing Merton's studies in Islam what strikes one is, first, that his reading is primarily in the Sufi traditions, and, second, that the list of authors he read is a sort of 'who's who' of Islamic scholars of the mid-20th century: A. Reza Arasteh, Arthur Arberry (translator of the Qur'an), Titus Burckhardt, Henry Corbin, Martin Lings, Louis Massignon, Seyyed Hossein Nasr, Paul Nwiya, Cyprien Rice, Frithjof Schuon; the list goes on.

That Merton was deeply interested in and influenced by Islam is evident. Let us consider briefly why he might have been attracted by Islam, and, in particular, Sufism. Merton's studies focused on central Islamic concepts like the unity of God (*TAWHID*) and the revelation of God's word (*TANZIL*). But his real fascination was with its spiritual realities, the way in which Islam set people 'free to travel in a realm of white-hot faith as bare and grand as the desert itself, faith in the One, God, the compassionate and the merciful. What are compassion and mercy but the gifts of freedom to freedom?' (CGB, p.90) Merton deeply appreciated the Sufi analysis of the human condition and of progress in the spiritual life.[9] He was much taken by the *TARIQ* (the Sufi path), the *JIHAD AL-AKHBAR* (the greater Jihad, or struggle with/ against the self), the concept of *FANA* (annihilation, extinction or passing away of the self/ego), and the prayer practice of *DHIKR*[10] (remembrance, recollection, recitation of the Holy, Beautiful Names of God). As did study of Zen Buddhism, Merton's study of Sufism gave him another set of concepts, another language if you will, in which to speak of Christian spiritual experiences, of the deepest life of prayer.

Merton once quipped to his novices that 'One Sufi did everything to be as shocking to the Ulema as possible. They have a tendency to break all of the laws from A to Z down as a way of hiding their inner life. That is what I have been doing the last 25 years to hide my Sufi experience.'[11] The tone of Merton's voice indicates his approval of what he called this Sufi 'beatnik style.' But the stylistic affinity was not only personal, but literary. The way the Sufis spoke and taught about religious experience appealed to Merton.

In commenting on Ibn al'Arabi and Al'Hujwiri in *Conjectures of a Guilty Bystander* Merton speaks of the 'nonlogical logic of mysticism and of direct experience, expressed in statements which do not agree and which nevertheless finally explode into a meaning that can be seized if one has some experience of what is being said' (CGB, p.210). Merton found non-logical, metaphorical expression of the truths of religious experience attractive. One hears this 'stylistic affinity' in a remark he made in another of the talks to the novices. Sufis, he notes, 'don't have formulas or public answers. . . [t]hey have stories and sayings and hints and proverbs and things like that and you make out the best you can.' In *Conjectures of a Guilty Bystander* Merton said 'Sufism is essence without form' (CGB, p.211). (Parenthetically, I think this was part of Merton's attraction to Zen, as well. Zen seeks direct, essential religious experience without the encumbrance of doctrinal formulation.) As a writer, Merton was more poet than systematic theologian (much to the delight of some of us and the devilment of others!) Sufis use of story and poem to express religious truth was natural for him—and brings us naturally to a consideration of his Islamic poems which are often reworkings of extant Sufi or Islamic narratives.

Thomas Merton's Islamic Poems

While there are a number of poems which evince Merton's profound understanding of Islam, there are seven explicitly Islamic poems in *The Collected Poems* (CP).[12] Three of these are longer, multi-section compositions. Let me comment very briefly and roughly in chronological order on each.

On a visit to the Cincinnati Museum of Art on October 27, 1960 Merton saw the 'beautifully designed cloth that was once spread over the tomb of a holy man, Imam Riza' (to Abdul Aziz in HGL, p.45). Merton remarked to both Louis Massignon (Oct. 29, 1960, WF, pp.279-80) and Abdul Aziz (Nov. 17, 1960 in HGL, p.45) on the impact of this experience. ('This encounter had a deep effect on me. . .' WF, p.280) He felt that by means of it he had 'come into contact with a great spirit.' (HGL, p.45) Merton noted to Massignon, 'It had on it a wonderful Sufi poem, translated for those who were interested.' (WF, p.280) The poem 'Tomb Cover of Imam Riza' is his version of the poem embroidered on the cloth. As Erlinda Paguio notes, Merton's poem 'is derived from the English translation made by the Islamic scholar, Arthur J. Arberry, and from the subsequent reformulation made by the art expert, Phyllis Ackerman.'[13] The poem emphasizes the importance of the Imam in Shiia Islam. Shiites believe that the Imam to be descended from The Prophet (via Ali) and not only the spiritual leader of the community but also the proper interpreter of Islamic tradition. Imam Riza was a Persian, and his tomb became a place of pilgrimage. The poem calls it 'the threshold of holiness in the dust of the road/where mighty kings have laid their heads and crowns' (CP, p.985).

The last collection of lyrics which Merton, himself, prepared for publication was *Emblems of a Season of Fury*, published in 1963. It contains two Islamic poems, 'The Moslems' Angel of Death' and 'Song for the Death of Averroes.' In a passing note in his journal on January 8, 1961 Merton says, 'Reading . . . Schuon on Moslem angels.'[14] On January 14, 1961 he writes to Herbert Mason about the poem 'The Moslems' Angel of Death' (WF, p.269) which he subsequently sent both to Louis Massignon and Ernesto Cardenal. Islam has a lively sense of the spiritual world and especially of angels and jinn. The Angel of Death is 'Izra'il, one of four archangels, whose description sounds to me a bit like something from the Biblical books of Ezekiel or Daniel. In addition to four faces (one for each compass point), 'Izra'il has 4,000 wings and his body consists of all eyes and tongues. Perhaps for this reason Merton's poem compares him to a 'jeweled peacock' that 'stirs all over/With fireflies' (CP, p.307). The peacock's long tail feathers are, of course, tipped with 'eyes.' In Islamic mythology 'Izra'il was able to snatch from earth a handful of its main constituents so that God could make human beings from them. God then made him the angel of death, so he figures in humankind's beginning and ending. The light imagery in Merton's poem no doubt comes from Merton's knowledge that in 'Izra'il's roll of human beings, the names of the blessed are surrounded by a bright circle.[15] The poems says 'He takes his pleasure in/Lights.' 'He turns the city lights in his fingers like money' (CP, p.307). 'He is a miser. His fingers find the money./He puts the golden lights in his pocket' (CP, p.308). The subtitle of the poem, 'Algeria 1961,' is perplexing. Is it a reference to the many lives being taken by 'Izra'il in the Algerian civil war? And, if so, are the final two lines of the poem ('Azrael! Azrael!/See the end of trouble!' CP, p.308) a note of consolation or bitterly ironic? The dominant metaphor of the poem is the figure of 'Izra'il counting out human lives like a miser counts out his money. I find it none too cheerful.

'Song for the Death of Averroes' is a collection of three poems 'after the Spanish version of Asin Palacios' (CP, p.325). Miguel Asin Palacios (1871-1944) was a Spanish scholar of Islam who translated Arabic works into Spanish and in 1933 wrote a long article on Ibn 'Abbad (whom we shall meet shortly), 'Un Precursor Hispano-Musulman de San Juan de la Cruz.'[16] Written in the first person singular, these poems describe Ibn Al Arabi's interactions with Averroes. Both were 'Moors,' Spanish Muslims. Averroes (Ibn Rushid, d. 1198) was a great philosopher, a commentator on Aristotle and a rationalist who sought to reconcile religion and philosophy. Ibn Arabi (d. 1240) was a Sufi, a mystic and, interestingly, the disciple of two women Sufi Masters. He wrote a complete system of mystic knowledge which has been extensively studied by later Muslim theologians. We know from his letter to Abdul Aziz on September 24, 1961 that Merton was reading Henry Corbin's book on Ibn Arabi (HGL, p.50) to whom he refers at least twice in Conjectures of a Guilty Bystander.

The tension in the poems in 'Song for the Death of Averroes' is that between two ways of knowing, the rational way of Averroes and the mystical way of Ibn Arabi. Epistemology is a frequent subject in Islamic theology and philosophy. The great Persian Sufi teacher of the 13th century, Jelaluddin Rumi, wrote a poem, 'Two Kinds of Intelligence,' selections of which bear repeating here:

> There are two kinds of intelligence: One acquired,
> as a child in school memorizes facts and concepts
> from books and from what the teacher says,
> collecting information from the traditional sciences
> as well as from the new sciences. . . .
>
> There is another kind of tablet, one
> already completed and preserved inside you.
> A spring overflowing its springbox. A freshness
> in the center of the chest. This other intelligence
> does not turn yellow or stagnate. It's fluid
> and it doesn't move from outside to inside
> through the conduits of plumbing-learning.
>
> This second knowing is a fountainhead
> from within you, moving out.[17]

In Merton's poem, these two ways of knowing are personified in Averroes and Ibn Arabi. Arabi, the speaker of the poem, believes he understands the way of Averroes ('he saw that I had understood him right away' CP, p.325), but Averroes cannot understand Arabi's way ('For though I had understood him, he had not understood me' CP, p.326). Averroes is described as 'an eminent philosopher, dedicated entirely/to a life of thought, study and rational investigation' (CP, p.327); Ibn Arabi is 'one of those endowed with mystical/gifts, one able to unlock His door' (CP, p.327). In *Conjectures of a Guilty Bystander* Merton remarks on the 'the story of Averroes' contact with and interest in the young Sufi mystic, Ibn al' Arabi, and his *angustia* at not being able to grasp what Arabi had seen clearly through a divine gift. It is a poignant story and I made a poem of it' (CGB, p.208). A very fine poem in my view.

'Readings from Ibn Abbad' occurs in the volume, *Raids on the Unspeakable* (RU) which is a collection of prose pieces and calligraphy prepared for publication in 1964-65. In one way or another the pieces in the book deal with the arts and religious experience. Merton opens the set of ten 'readings' from Ibn 'Abbad with a prose introduction. He was very familiar with 'Abbad and had reviewed the classic by Paul Nwyia, *Ibn 'Abbad de Ronda* (Beruit, 1961) for *Collectanea Cisterciensia*. Nwyia believed 'Abbad to be the most important mystical writer of the 14th century.[18] Born in Ronda in 1333, he emigrated to Morocco where Sufi life flourished. Inclined to solitude and meditation, he devoted himself to asceticism and mysticism and wrote letters of spiritual direction and a manual of devotion. (By the way, the letters are now readily available in English in the Paulist Press series 'Classics of Western Spirituality' in the volume *Ibn 'Abbad of Ronda, Letters on the Sufi Path* translated and introduced by John Renard.[19]) Writing in *The Sufi Orders in Islam*, Spencer Trimingham remarked that the mystic 'Abbad 'stands out simply because of the spiritual aridity of the age.'[20] Be that as it may, it is not hard to understand Merton's attraction for the Shadhili Sufi, especially in view of his apparent influence on John of the Cross (about whom Merton also wrote). Merton had mentioned the Ibn 'Abbad-John of the Cross connection with Reza Arasteh in a letter of December 18, 1965 (HGL, p.41). Writing to Abdul Aziz on November 7, 1965 Merton says

> I am sure that...I spoke of Ibn Abbad, by whom I was very much impressed, and later I even did some adapted versions of his thought, in semi-poetic fashion, based of course on the French version. These will be published next year in a book... (HGL, p.61).

There are ten 'adaptations' in *Raids*, a description of the Sufi by a friend, a description of his burial place (which became a pilgrimage destination), a 'prayer and sermon,' and seven of his teachings, two framed as letters, and three 'to a novice.' Not surprisingly, the biographical matter, though poetically presented, is accurate. I am quite struck when I read this material by how the paradoxical presentations of 'Abbad's teaching sound like Zen material. Three short sections of the poem give a sense of what I mean (RU, pp.146-147, 149):

4: *Desolation* [recall John of the Cross' Dark Night of the Soul]

For the servant of God
Consolation is the place of danger
Where he may be deluded
(Accepting only what he sees,
experiences or knows)
But desolation is his home:
For in desolation he is seized by God
And entirely taken over into God.
In darkness, in emptiness,

In loss, in death of self.
Then the self is only ashes. Not even ashes!

5: *To Belong to Allah*

To belong to Allah
Is to see in your own existence
And in all that pertains to it
Something that is neither yours
Nor from yourself,
Something you have on loan;
To see your being in His Being,
Your substance in His Substance,
Your strength in His Strength:
Thus you will recognize in yourself
His title to possession of you
As Lord,
And your own title as servant:
Which is Nothingness.

8: *To a Novice* [remember Merton was Master of Scholastics]

Be a son of this instant:
It is a messenger of Allah
And the best of messengers
Is one who announces your indigence,
Your nothingness.
Be a son of this instant,
Thanking Allah
For a mouthful of ashes.

(This last poem sets up echoes in my mind of the poem 'A Messenger from the Horizon' in *Emblems of a Season of Fury*). In his introductory notes Merton says the purpose of the pieces 'is to share something of an encounter with a rich and fervent religious personality of Islam, in whom the zeal of the Sufis is revealed. . .'[21] In this he certainly succeeds.

At the time of his departure for Asia in 1968 Merton was preparing two volumes of verse for publication, the long and difficult poem *The Geography of Lograire* and a collection of lyrics entitled *Sensation Time at the Home*. *Lograire* is divided into four sections, one for each point of the compass. The section 'East' begins with a six part poem entitled 'East with Ibn Battuta' (CP, pp.537-544). In the notes he prepared to go with the manuscript, Merton records that Ibn Battuta (1304-1369) was a Muslim from Morocco who wrote an account of his travels between 1325 and 1354. Merton's poems are entitled 'Cairo,' 'Syria,' 'The Nusayris' (a heretical sect of Islam), 'Mecca,' 'Isfahan,' 'Delhi,' and 'Calicut,' obviously tracing Ibn Battuta's journeys eastward. They record a wonderful and charming travelogue in the voice of a fourteenth century Muslim. As was 'Song for the Death of Averroes' and 'Readings from Ibn Abbad,' the poems are re-workings of translations of the Arabic originals.

Sensation Time at the Home 'and other new poems' form Appendix I of Merton's *Collected Poems*. The origin of the poem 'Lubnan' was also Merton's reading of Ibn Arabi in which he apparently encountered Idris, whom we know in Biblical tradition as Enoch. 'Lubnan' is Lebanon, the location of Baalbeck to which Idris comes down. Idris is mentioned twice in the Holy Qur'an. In Surah 19.56-57 he is called 'a saint, a Prophet; And we raised him to high station.' In Surah 21:85 he is called 'steadfast,'[22] one of the 'patient ones.' Like the Biblical Enoch (with whom some Islamic scholars connect him), Idris is a pious man who lives a long life and is taken by God to himself. In Islamic lore he is the first to use pens, to sew and wear clothing and so was a patron saint of tailors.[23]

As Erlinda Paguio points out in her excellent commentary on the poem, in Ibn 'Arabi's work, *Bezels of Wisdom*, Idris and Ilyas (Elias) are two names assigned to the same person. Idris had a vision in which he saw Lubnan (Mt Lebanon) splitting open and disgorging a fiery horse. Ilyas mounted it (rather like The Prophet, himself, mounted a heavenly steed for his visit to the divine realms) and became pure intellect.[24] Merton's poem describes this vision and the ride on 'a horse harnessed in flame/A car of fire' (CP, p.614). It reminds the reader that

> Far away the red saint rides the shouting fire of that horse
> Idris—Ilyas one interpreter
> May be back tomorrow morning
> When the vision
> Will be total. (CP, p.614)

In view of the fact that the imagery of the poem is apocalyptic, and that it was written in a time when Merton was much taken up with the threat of nuclear war, I am not sure whether it represents promise or threat.

The poem 'The Night of Destiny' from the same collection also describes visionary experience. The 'Night of Destiny' is the 27th day of Ramadan when, Muslims believe, The Prophet received his first revelation. The very early Meccan Surah of the Qur'an, Surah 96 known as 'The Clot,' refers to this night when the first verses of the Qur'an were revealed in Muhammad's vision on Mt Hira. The passage begins as follows:

> In the name of Allah, the Beneficent, the Merciful.
> Read: In the name of thy Lord who created.
> Created man from a clot.
> Read: And thy Lord is the Most Bounteous,
> Who taught by the pen,
> Taught man that which he knew not.
> Nay, but verily man is rebellious.
> That he thinketh himself independent!
> Lo! unto thy Lord is the return. (Surah 96:1-8)

Merton provides a gloss on the poem 'The Night of Destiny' explaining, not quite accurately, that it 'celebrates the end of the Moslem fast, Ramadan, and commemorates the giving of the Koran to Mohammed. Hence it has something of the Spirit of Christmas, a feast when the heavens open and the "Word" is heard on earth' (CP, p.634).

Merton's poem is about this coming of the 'Word.' It begins with the T.S. Eliotesque line, 'In my ending is my meaning' (CP, p.634). In the poem the speaker seems to be reading at night by a lamp, a 'Weak friend/In the knowing night.' But he is, in fact, illuminated by the 'tongue of flame/Under the heart.' The poem asks, very beautifully, Who illuminates: 'Who holds the homeless light secure/In the deep heart's room?' The enigmatic, but very precise answer is 'Midnight!/ Kissed with flame!' Life, interior life, may be dark ('love is black'), but there are moments, however fleeting, of illumination, of being kissed by Love (a very Sufi notion and turn of phrase). In fact, all of the images of darkness in the poem are positive: Night is 'knowing;' love is 'black' and 'darkness,' but it is love; in the night the lamp provides 'the small circle of seeing;' midnight is 'kissed with flame;' and in the night all the lost are found. The speaker of the poem exclaims 'My love is darkness!' (CP, p.635) and the poem closes

> Only in the void
> Are all ways one:

Only in the night
Are all the lost
Found.

In my ending is my meaning.

This, I think, is a good line with which to end this catalogue of Merton's Islamic poems.

Conclusion

In *Conjectures of a Guilty Bystander* Merton noted

> I am more and more convinced that my job is to clarify something of the tradition that lives in me, and in which I live: the tradition of wisdom and spirit that is found not only in Western Christendom but in Orthodoxy, and...in Asia and in Islam (CGB, p.194).

In these seven Islamic poems Merton is working at this 'job.' His interest in Islam, like his interest in Buddhism, tended to be focused on its mystical traditions and on its ways of articulating mystical or visionary experience. This is self-evident in the poems. But the world and culture of Islam was also very much in Merton's bloodstream. The transfusion came by means of his European roots, his 'French connection,' if you will, and his knowledge of Romance languages. But the result was very much Islamic and not European, which is to say Merton embraced Islam, not some European Orientalist's version of it.

The reason for this embrace, it seems to me, was profoundly Christian. Writing to Abdul Aziz on June 2, 1963 Merton said,

> We must strive more and more to be universal in our interests and in our zeal for the glory of the one God, and may His Name be magnified forever in us. (HGL, p.55)

The Christian's 'universal embrace' reflects the nature of the God of Christians who, as Jesus taught us, stands in the road waiting to embrace the ones who come.

While it would be very nice to end these remarks on Merton's Islamic poetry on this attractive, and I believe accurate, note, our present troubled times suggest, to me at any rate, that Merton's remarks to Abdul Aziz on November 7, 1965 are a more appropriate and timely conclusion:

> Well, my friend, we live in troubled and sad times, and we must pray the infinite and merciful Lord to bear patiently with the sins of this world, which are very great. We must humble our hearts in

silence and poverty of spirit and listen to His commands which come from the depths of His love, and work that men's hearts may be converted to the ways of love and justice, not of blood, murder, lust and greed. I am afraid that the big powerful countries are a very bad example to the rest of the world in this respect. (HGL, pp.61-62)

Notes and References

1. Thomas Merton, The Hidden Ground of Love, Letters (ed. William H. Shannon). New York, Farrar, Straus, Giroux, 1985, p.53 (HGL)

2. For more on the Merton-Massignon connection see the article by Sidney H. Griffith, 'Merton, Massignon, and the Challenge of Islam,' in the Baker-Henry volume listed below.

3. Bob Baker and Gray Henry (eds.), Merton and Sufism, the Untold Story: A Complete Compendium. Louisville, Ky, Fons Vitae, 1999

4. Thomas Merton, Conjectures of a Guilty Bystander. New York, Doubleday/Image, 1968. See pp. 90, 147, 151, 181, 194, 205, 208. (CGB)

5. Thomas Merton, Learning to Love: The Journals of Thomas Merton Vol. 6 (ed. Christine M. Bochen). San Francisco, HarperSanFrancisco, 1997 (LL)

6. Baker and Henry (eds.), op.cit. pp.183-192

7. Thomas Merton, Witness to Freedom (ed. William Shannon). New York, Farrar, Straus, Giroux, 1994 (WF)

8. Credence Cassettes, P.O. Box 22582, Kansas City, MO 64141, U.S.A.

9. For an exposition of this see Burton Thurston, 'Merton's Reflections on Sufism' in Baker and Henry (eds.), op.cit. pp.33-39.

10. For more on this see my article 'Thomas Merton and Islam: The Example of Dhikr,' American Benedictine Review 45/2 (1994) which is reprinted in the Baker-Henry volume.

11. My source for the Sufi lectures is a transcription by Burton B. Thurston of some copies of the tapes.

12. Thomas Merton, The Collected Poems of Thomas Merton. New York, New Directions, 1977 (CP)

13. Erlinda Paguio, 'Islamic Themes in Merton's Poetry' in Baker and Henry (eds.), op.cit. p.90.

14. Thomas Merton, Turning Toward the World: The Journals of Thomas Merton Vol. 4 (ed. Victor Kramer). San Francisco, HarperSanFrancisco, 1997, p.86 (TTW)

15. For a brief description of 'Izra'il see the entry of that title in H.A.R. Gibbs and J.H.H. Krammer, Shorter Encyclopedia of Islam. Leiden, E.J. Brill, 1953 p.190

16. M. Asin Palacios, 'Un Precursor hispano-musulman de San Juan de la Cruz,' al-Andalus, i (1933) pp.7-79

17. Rumi Jeleluddin, Jalalu'l-Din Rumi, John Moyne (Translator), Maulana Jalal al Din Rumi, This Longing: Poetry, Teaching, Stories and Letters of Rumi. Putney, Vt, Threshold Books, 1988, p.36

18. Paul Nwyia, 'Ibn 'Abbad,' The Encyclopedia of Islam, B. Lewis, et al. (eds). Leiden, E.J. Brill, 1971, III p.670

19. John Renard, Ibn 'Abbad of Ronda, Letters on the Sufi Path. New York, Paulist Press, 1986

20. Spencer Trimingham, The Sufi Orders in Islam. Oxford, Oxford University Press, 1971, p.84

21. Thomas Merton, Raids on the Unspeakable. New York, New Directions, 1966, p.141

22. This and subsequent Qur'anic citations are from Muhammad M. Pickthall, The Glorious Qur'an: Text and Explanatory Translation. Mecca, Muslim World League, 1977

23. Gibbs and Krammer, op. cit., pp.158-159

24. Paguio, op. cit. p.95

Finding 'the Great Compassion, *Mahakaruna*': Thomas Merton as Transcultural Pioneer

DONALD GRAYSTON

L ET THOMAS MERTON SPEAK FIRST:

The hills are blue and hot. There is a brown, dusty field in the bottom of the valley. I hear a machine, a bird, a clock. The clouds are high and enormous. Through them the inevitable jet plane passes: this time probably full of passengers from Miami to Chicago. What passengers? This I have no need to decide. They are out of my world, up there, busy sitting in their small, isolated, arbitrary lounge that does not even seem to be moving—the lounge that somehow unaccountably picked them up off the earth in Florida to suspend them for a while with timeless cocktails and then let them down in Illinois. The suspension of modern life in contemplation that *gets you somewhere!*

There are also other worlds above me. Other jets will pass over, with other contemplations and other modalities of intentness.

I have seen the SAC plane, with the bomb in it, fly low over me and I have looked up out of the woods directly at the closed bay of the metal bird with a scientific egg in its breast! A womb easily and mechanically opened! I do not consider this technological mother to be the friend of anything I believe in. However, like everyone else, I live in the shadow of the apocalyptic cherub. I am surveyed by it, impersonally. Its number recognizes my number. Are these numbers preparing at some moment to coincide in the benevolent mind of a computer? This does not concern me, for I live in the woods as a reminder that I am free not to be a number.

There is, in fact, a choice.[1]

So begins Merton's magnificent *Day of a Stranger*. It was written in May 1965 in response to a question from a Venezuelan editor, Ludovico Silva,[2] about how Merton spent a typical day.

It was first published in the *Hudson Review* and then as a small book on its own, with an introduction by Robert E. Daggy, in 1981.[3] It is now most readily available in Lawrence Cunningham's excellent anthology, *Thomas Merton: Spiritual Master*. A mere eight pages in length, it has sometimes permitted me to devote two classes and part of a third in presenting it to undergraduate students taking my Merton course. And why?

Because it is vintage Merton (Cunningham calls it 'quintessential Merton,' DS, p.214), and includes, in one way or another, all his major themes and concerns. He wrote it while he was in the process of moving into the hermitage which was to be his dwelling for the last three years of his life (he moved in full-time in August 1965); and it seems to me that it is written out of a deep sense of ripeness, satisfaction and gratitude that the solitary life towards which he had for so long moved was now his. To read it is to be invited to stand with him within the circle of an astonishing communion of saints, a multireligious and multicultural assembly representing many ages, many traditions and many viewpoints, all of whom appealed in some way to his transcultural sensibility, what this conference is calling his 'universal embrace.' Cunningham speaks of it thus:

> One reads in it a fusion of his liturgical, artistic, and contemplative interests as well as his ever present sense of the destructive capacity of the modern world symbolized here by the lofty presence of the Strategic Air Command (SAC) bombers which flew over the monastery carrying their load of atomic weapons (DS, p.214).

And, comparing it to the 'Fire Watch' episode from *The Sign of* Jonas, written fifteen years earlier, Cunningham says that although it

> still reverberates with monastic and liturgical rhythms...[its] tone is more ironic, more playful, and more engaged with the world outside the cloister. [It is written with] a sense of wry detachment which may well reflect both the author's maturity and the leavening effect of his encounter with Zen (DS, p.214).

Yes, there it is: Zen. Having tried and failed to make himself into a Thomist (although he continued to admire St Thomas), he

> found himself attracted to the meta-synthetic and intuitive perspectives of Zen, to its delicacy and grace, and to the opportunities it gave him to encounter Asian contemplatives and traditions.[4]

Day of a Stranger is in fact permeated by the humour, the directness and the integrative character of Zen, or, more personally, it comes out of 'a mind awake in the dark' (DS, p.218), the mind – and heart – of a Christian monk, writer and artist who has been profoundly influenced by Zen. It is written by a man who is freer, less overtly pious and more playful than the monk who wrote the 'Fire Watch,' as witness this dialogue between Merton and an imaginary interlocutor (DS, pp.218-19):

- Why live in the woods?
- Well, you have to live somewhere.
- Do you get lonely?
- Yes, sometimes.
- Are you mad at people?
- No.
- Are you mad at the monastery?
- No.
- What do you think about the future of monasticism?
- Nothing. I don't think about it.
- Is it true that your bad back is due to Yoga?
- No.
- Is it true that you are practising Zen in secret?
- Pardon me, I don't speak English.

Part irritating journalist, part Trappist censor, part self-deprecating alter ego, Merton's interlocutor offers him a stage on which to play the role of trickster-monk, the monk who never thinks about monasticism, because he has been born again into the realm to which the true monastic calling has pointed him. Having crossed the river, he has no further need of the raft.

So what I propose to do in this paper, as I reflect on Thomas Merton's *universal embrace*, is to use *Day of a Stranger* as the basic framework for my reflections. Within this framework, I will distinguish two dimensions of this embrace: inner and outer. In regard to the inner dimension of what ultimately was, let me affirm, a single embrace of the one and only universe available to any of us, I will revisit his review article on Reza Arasteh's book, *Final Integration in the Adult Personality,*[5] and in exploring the outer dimension, I will revisit William M. Thompson's paper for the first ITMS Conference which took place in Vancouver in 1978, on Merton's transcultural consciousness,[6] concluding with a brief look at how spiritual formation in our own day connects with this universal embrace of Merton's.

Merton's review of the Arasteh book was called 'Final Integration: Toward a "Monastic Therapy."' Published by Brill in 1965, Merton read the book in January 1968. Merton particularly liked the book because it integrated reference to Sufi mystical attainment with other goals of psychotherapy, rather than calling for mere adjustment or acquiescence in the Freudian mode, which, in his view, was all that 'ordinary psychotherapy'[7] could offer. By including the word 'monastic' in his subtitle, he was indicating that he saw Arasteh's understanding of therapy as supportive of what he thought should be the result of monastic *conversatio* or *conversio morum*: self-renewal, liberation, transformation, rebirth, 'the final and complete maturing of the human psyche on a transcultural level.'[8] Surely speaking out of his experience as novice master, he asserted that people were

> called to the monastic life so that they [might] grow and be transformed, "reborn" to a new and more complete identity, and to a more profoundly fruitful existence in peace, in wisdom, in creativity, in love.[9]

But in his experience, the institutions of the monasticism of which he was a part were often less than conducive to this kind of growth. Some novices discovered that the way the monastic life was structured made 'a genuine response to the summons impossible,'[10] and so they would leave to seek other contexts where it might be possible. Others, 'the mildly neurotic,' would 'stay and make some sort of compromise adjustment, nestling fearfully in the protection of the monastery with the obscure sense that further painful growth will not be demanded!'[11]

What, then, is that final integration to which psychoanalyst, Sufi and Christian monk could all commit themselves? Here Merton answers that question with a description of the finally integrated 'man' (I note here, as have many others, that Merton wrote before the rise of concern for inclusive language, and that it is probably best simply to acknowledge this and quote his original words).

> Final integration is a state of transcultural maturity far beyond mere social adjustment, which always implies partiality and compromise. The man who is "fully born" has an entirely "inner experience of life." He apprehends his life fully and wholly from an inner ground that is at once more universal than the empirical ego and yet entirely his own. He is in a certain sense "cosmic" and "universal man." He has attained a deeper, fuller identity than that of his limited ego-self which is only a fragment of his being. He is in a certain sense identified with everybody; or in the familiar language of the New Testament...he is "all things to all men." He is able to experience their joys and sufferings as his own, without however becoming dominated by them. He has attained to a deep inner freedom—the Freedom of the Spirit we read of in the New Testament.[12]

I wonder to what extent Merton was aware as he wrote that passage that he was describing himself, or at least expressing a sense of his own spiritual *telos*. It is often said that all of Merton's work is in some way autobiographical, much of it consciously so, much of it unconsciously so. Whether conscious or unconscious, however, this passage speaks very directly to us of its writer, as we have come to know him through the aspirations and struggles which he has shared with us in his journals. As an example of what I mean, let me match this last passage with a passage from *Day of a Stranger* (DS, p.217):

> What I wear is pants. What I do is live. How I pray is breathe. Who said Zen? Wash out your mouth if you said Zen. If you see a meditation going by, shoot it. Who said "Love"? Love is in the movies. The spiritual life is something that people worry about when they are so busy with something else they think they ought to be spiritual. Spiritual life is guilt. Up here in the woods is seen the New Testament: that is to say, the wind comes through the trees and you breathe it.

With that last sentence, he is pointing us towards another and much older reference to rebirth, John 3, where Jesus says to Nicodemus: 'I tell you that you must be born over again. The wind blows where it wills; you hear the sound of it, but you do not know where it comes from, or where it is going. So with everyone who is born from spirit' (John 3:8, *New English Bible*). Perhaps this emphasis in Merton is why so many evangelicals have given major credit to him for nudging them towards faith, towards their becoming born-again Christians.[13] He spoke whereof he knew, from his own experience and that of his novices.

Even so, he asserted that the experience of rebirth was not limited to Christians. Applying to others the thought of the passage we have applied to Merton himself, he recognized the reality of rebirth for Sufis, Taoist masters and Zen Buddhists.[14] It was a transcultural and transreligious experience, what Sufis, for example, would call *Fana* and *Baqa*.

The consecrated term in Sufism is *Fana*, annihilation or disintegration, a loss of self, a real spiritual death. But mere annihilation and death are not enough: they must be followed by reintegration and new life on a totally different level. This reintegration is what the Sufis call *Baqa*. The process of disintegration and reintegration is one that involves a terrible interior solitude and an "existential moratorium," a crisis and an anguish which cannot be analyzed or intellectualized.[15]

In sum, it is an experience of disintegration, existential moratorium and reintegration on a higher and universal level – and here I think of Merton's description in *The Sign of Jonas*[16] of his breakdown or dark night – and it is the attainment to which all the great spiritual traditions summon their seekers. It is, in the Easter week in which I wrote the first draft of this paper, Egypt, the desert and the Promised Land; it is Romans 6 as well as John 3, the dying with Christ and the rising with him. And, according to Merton, the risen ones in every tradition can recognize each other, because the finally integrated human being, while retaining all that is best in his or her own culture, can pass beyond these 'limiting forms,'[17] can become a transcultural person, 'able to bring perspective, liberty and spontaneity into the lives of others.'[18] The transcultural person is, in one word, a peacemaker, if by 'peace' here we understand what the Hebrew word *shalom* means: physical, relational and interior wellbeing, wholeness. And in this spirit, says Merton, such a person embraces all of life, offers a universal embrace to pilgrims from other traditions as well as his own. 'What Merton has in mind,' says William Thompson in his discussion of Merton's thoughts on Arasteh,

> is the emergence of a person of such inner calm and personal and cultural detachment that he/she is capable of recognizing and perspectivizing the genuine values present in every person and every culture he/she encounters.[19]

In his conclusion to *Silent Lamp*, William H. Shannon also discusses Merton's review of Arasteh, and affirms the personal and monastic significance that the concept of final integration had for Merton, calling it 'the goal of the inner journey.'[20] He then asks whether Merton did achieve final integration and concludes that it would be presumptuous for him (and, if for him, then certainly for us) to attempt to answer the question. But he does assert that 'final integration was the direction in which Merton was always moving in the real journey of life that is interior and [in] . . . "an ever greater surrender to the creative action of love and grace in our hearts."'[21] Given the eschatological as well as transcultural character of final integration, it may even be posited that there is, paradoxically, no final achievement of final integration, but rather an entry into and continuing journey in *epektesis* (Gregory of Nyssa's term), the 'continued pursuit of an ever more vital experience of the light and truth of God, which, because of God's infinity, can only be itself an infinite pursuit.'[22]

I turn now to the other dimension of Merton's *universal embrace*, the outer-directed love, the great compassion, the *mahakaruna*[23] with which he reached out to the world of politics and culture, of violence and nonviolence, of intra-faith and interfaith encounter. In *Day of a Stranger*, the most striking reference to this dimension is that of the SAC bomber, the apocalyptic metal cherub, with which he both begins and ends the piece. Between these two references we note his ecological concern through his reference to the birds, 'precise pairs' (DS, p.216) of which, perhaps 15 or 20 of them, surround his cabin. We note also the 'mental ecology' of writers with whom he was in dialogue, either internally or through actual correspondence: Vallejo, Rilke, Edwin Muir, Chuang Tzu, Suzuki, Philoxenus, Sartre, John of Salisbury, Flannery O'Connor, Teresa of Avila, Raïssa Maritain. Marshall McLuhan also makes an unacknowledged appearance in his references to the 'cool' character of the hermit life, 'a life of low definition' (DS, p.216). His monastic commitment is evoked by his description of how he gets up at 2.15 a.m. to say the office.

> A light appears, and in the light an ikon. There is now in the large darkness a small room of radiance with psalms in it. The psalms grow up silently by themselves without effort like plants in this light which is favorable to them. The plants hold themselves up on stems which have a single consistency, that of mercy, or rather great mercy. *Magna misericordia* (DS, p. 218).

A page later he nods whimsically in the direction of sexuality, ruminating on the fact that 'monks, as is well known, are unmarried, and hermits more unmarried than the rest of them' (DS, p.219). He was yet to meet Chadral Rinpoche,[24] a longtime hermit, indeed in his own tradition's view, a hermit still, who had married shortly before meeting Merton.[25] What kind of conversation would have taken place between them if Chadral had thought to mention his wife to Merton? I picture Merton marrying Chadral's elder daughter (unmarried when I was there in 2000; the younger daughter is married to a monk), and settling down in transcultural domesticity in the Himalayas. With more justification than this speculation warrants, however, I would assert that the erotic character of this section of *Day of a Stranger* is unmistakable, with its references to the 'sweet dark warmth of the whole world,' and 'the secret that is heard only in silence… [which is] the root of all the secrets that are whispered by all the lovers in their beds all over the world' (DS, p.219). When Merton met Margie the following year, his heart, as clearly evidenced by this section of *Day of a Stranger*, was already open to womankind, to erotic encounter, to love.

Later in *Day of a Stranger* he describes his visit to the monastery for mass and the noon meal, where he encounters the political world in a message of the Pope being read in the refectory which denounces the bombing of civilians, killing of hostages and torturing of prisoners by the US forces in Vietnam. Then he returns to the hermitage, where he works, reads, prays and listens to a 'devout Cistercian tractor' growling in the valley (DS, p.222). Thus in eight pages he has embraced all our major concerns, modern and contemporary: the arms race, the environment, the ecology of transcultural intellectual exchange, the role of the media, sexuality and politics, all in the context of his monastic vision and his poetic and whimsical sensibility, his life as monk and writer.

All of these emphases find their place in transcultural consciousness, as William M. Thompson characterizes it, crediting Merton in fact with inspiring the very term 'transculturalization.'[26] Thompson's starting point is the fact that the planet has become 'a single whole dominated by the technology of communications,'[27] in Karl Jaspers' words. Few have done more than Merton, he says, to forge a new 'unifying myth'[28] (a term from Raimundo Panikkar), or, if not a completely functional or fully accepted unifying myth, then a transcultural *consciousness* out of which the challenges of globalization can be tackled. He quotes Merton's well-known statement from *Conjectures of a Guilty Bystander*:

> If I can unite in myself the thought and the devotion of Eastern and Western Christendom,[29] the Greek and the Latin fathers, the Russians with the Spanish mystics, I can prepare in myself the reunion of divided Christians... We must contain all divided worlds in ourselves and transcend them in Christ.[30]

Strangely, in view of his transcultural concern, he does not cite the statement with which the previous quotation is so often twinned:

> If I affirm myself as a Catholic merely by denying all that is Muslim, Jewish, Protestant, Hindu, Buddhist, etc., in the end I will find that there is not much left for me to affirm as a Catholic: and certainly no breath of the Spirit with which to affirm it.[31]

This is particularly germane, in as much as Thompson points to what he calls Merton's 'Christ-fidelity' as the matrix of his transcultural consciousness, and, as such, the potential source of transcultural break-through for Christians whose understanding of Christian faith and life has been influenced by Merton. Merton has provided us, says Thompson, with

> the creative underpinnings of a deeper view of Christology itself, and thus, if you will, with a new Christ-Vision capable of fostering in the Christian West our transcultural consciousness.[32]

This is centred, asserts Thompson, in the risen humanity of Jesus, who 'forever remains a present object of monastic prayer.'[33] Thus Merton, says Thompson, is asking us to view the resurrection as the event in which Jesus himself reached, in the term we have been exploring, final integration. Beyond an understanding of the resurrection as vindication of the just and innocent Jesus, we can therefore also think of it as an event 'which marked a decisive development in Jesus' very own being.'[34] It is fascinating, in this regard, to recall that the resurrection was a central topic of discussion in Merton's encounter with Chadral.[35] This, then, from an interview in Tricycle magazine with Merton's companion on his visit to Chadral, Harold Talbott:

> **Talbott:** We caught up with Chatral[36] Rinpoche down the road from Ghoom. Chatral Rinpoche started by saying, "Ah, a Jesus lama; you know I have never been able for the life of me to get a handle on Christianity so I'm real glad you came this morning."
>
> **Tricycle:** Did he know who Merton was?
>
> **Talbott:** No. But he explained his perplexity about Christianity. He said, "The center of your religion is a man who comes back to life after death and in Tibetan Buddhism when you have one of these people, a rolog, or a walking corpse, we call our lama to put him down. So I want to know what kind of a religion is Christianity which has at its center a dead man coming back to life." So Merton explained the Resurrection in tantric terms about the overcoming of fear and the utter and complete power of liberation which is the center of Christianity. And this satisfied Chatral Rinpoche.
>
> **Tricycle:** Freedom from fear?
>
> **Talbott:** Freedom from constraints and restraints. A man has died and he has come back in a glorious body and he has freed us from fear of death and fear of life. That's freedom.
>
> **Tricycle:** Because it's eternal?

Talbott: No. If the universe is a place where a man can live again in a glorified body and teach the truth, then the world is a free place. And Chatral Rinpoche says "At last I understand Christianity. Thank you very much."[37]

Jesus then, at least for Christians, is the true pioneer of transcultural reality, its paradigm and its vehicle, 'the most complete way in which God could possibly reveal himself to [humankind] in human terms,'[38] Merton's model and our model of a capacity for universal embrace.

So far I can go with Thompson. However, his conclusion, it seems to me, is open to critique on the grounds of spiritualization; in that, in stressing the eschatological character of final and transcultural integration, he rejects a 'this worldly realization of it.'[39] As so often happens, he is restricting eschatology to its futuristic dimension, and neglecting its realized or present dimension. In so doing, I would assert that he has not given due weight to what Merton shows us about the universal embrace of the finally-integrated person in *Day of a Stranger*, nor, indeed, to the mystical truth of what is meant by the eternal now. Merton lived as a contemplative at a particular historical moment, a moment he embraced fully. So 'your kingdom come,' yes; but 'yours *is* the kingdom' as well. The concerns of economics and politics and sexuality and social justice present themselves to the finally-integrated person with no less justification than the claims of mystical union itself.

I conclude with some thoughts about spiritual formation. If in Christian understanding Jesus is the finally-integrated human being, and if Merton is a pioneer in our own time on the path of final integration, does this not challenge the low level at which we typically set the bar for spiritual formation? The global priorities of war and peace, justice and human rights, and the encounter in transforming depth of the great religious traditions cannot be adequately addressed by the spiritually unformed. Somehow we have to integrate these understandings with catechesis and formation at the level of the local congregation. We have no interest in creating little clones of Thomas Merton, of course. What we want to do is to nurture as many as possible, to do in their own time and place what Merton did in his: engage in the great affair, open himself to the great realization, find and live out a compassion great enough to embrace the universe. We need to nurture holy women and men in our own time, with the capacity, in John S. Dunne's terms, 'to pass over and come back'—to pass over from our own cultures into those of others, with equanimity and respect, and to come back bearing the gifts of that experience.

Merton saw himself in some sense as a stranger, a marginal man, a guilty bystander; he was also a pilgrim, as his final journey attests. He lived out the reality to which the Letter to the Hebrews points in its description of great figures of faith:

> They were not yet in possession of the things promised, but had seen them far ahead and embraced them, confessing themselves to be strangers and pilgrims (Hebrews 11.13, *New English Bible*).

Merton's day as a stranger is over. However, as we assimilate his insights into our own understanding, we find that our own day challenges us to embrace the universe in a way which will eventually make us no longer strangers, speaking of ethereal perceptions to our own secular and uncomprehending communities, but ourselves pioneers, both in our own place and transculturally, of a new norm of spiritual formation the very opposite of parochial or exclusive, indeed of a universal embrace. To this challenge that well-known 'stranger,' Thomas Merton, summons us now.

Notes and References

1. 'Day of a Stranger' (hereafter, DS), in *Thomas Merton: Spiritual Master* (ed. Lawrence S. Cunningham). New York, Paulist, 1992, p.215

2. Christine Bochen provides this name in 'Radiant Darkness: The Dawning into Reality' in *Thomas Merton: A Mind Awake in the Dark* (ed. Paul M. Pearson, Danny Sullivan and Ian Thomson). Abergavenny, Three Peaks Press, 2002, p.28. This book contains papers presented at the Third General Conference of the Thomas Merton Society of Great Britain and Ireland at Oakham School in April 2000. I confess here that I chose to make substantial use of *Day of a Stranger* in my address to the Fourth General Conference not having realized that it had been the source of the theme for the Third.

3. *Hudson Review* 20 (Summer 1967) pp.211-18; *Day of a Stranger* (ed. and introd. Robert E. Daggy). Salt Lake City, Gibbs M. Smith, 1981

4. Donald Grayston, *Thomas Merton: The Development of a Spiritual Theologian*. New York and Toronto, Mellen, 1985, p.169

5. Thomas Merton, 'Final Integration—Toward A "Monastic Therapy"' in *Contemplation in a World of Action* (ed. Naomi Burton, introd. Jean Leclercq). Garden City, New York, Doubleday, 1973, pp.219-231

6. William M. Thompson, 'Merton's Contribution to a Transcultural Consciousness' in Donald Grayston and Michael W. Higgins (eds), *Thomas Merton: Pilgrim in Process*. Toronto, Griffin, 1983, p.147-169

7. Thomas Merton , 'Final Integration,' *op.cit.* p.219

8. *ibid.* p.222

9. ibid. p.221-222

10. ibid. p.224

11. ibid. p.224

12. ibid. p.225

13. Cf. Richard F. Lovelace: 'I . . . was initially converted to Christianity from atheism through reading Thomas Merton's *Seven Storey Mountain* and . . . my effort [in this book] . . . strives in the same direction he was travelling in his later years' - *Dynamics of Spiritual Life: An Evangelical Theology of Renewal*. Downers Grove, Illinois, Inter-Varsity Press, 1979, p.17

14. Thomas Merton, 'Final Integration,' *op.cit.* p.225

15. ibid. p.227-28

16. Thomas Merton, *The Sign of Jonas*. Garden City, NY, Doubleday, 1953, p.226

17. Thomas Merton, 'Final Integration,' *op.cit.* p.226

18. ibid. p.226

19. William M.Thompson, *op.cit.* p.154

20. William H. Shannon, *Silent Lamp: The Thomas Merton Story*. New York, Crossroad, 1992, p.288

21. ibid. p.288; the quoted words are from *The Road to Joy: Letters to New and Old Friends* (ed. Robert E. Daggy). San Diego, Harcourt Brace Jovanovich, 1989, p.118

22. Donald Grayston, 'Autobiography and Theology: The Once and Future Merton,' in Grayston and Higgins, *Thomas Merton: Pilgrim in Process*, *op.cit.* p.82

23. My title comes from *The Asian Journal of Thomas Merton* (ed. Naomi Burton Stone, Patrick Hart and James Laughlin; consulting ed. Amiya Chakravarty). New York, New Directions, 1973, p.4

24. Cf. *Asian Journal*, ibid. pp.142-44

25. As I discovered when I visited Chadral in December 2000.

26. Cf. William M.Thompson, *op.cit.* p.166, n.1.

27. ibid. p.147

28. ibid. pp.148-49

29. Not 'Christendoms,' as in Thompson, ibid. p.149

30. Thomas Merton, *Conjectures of a Guilty Bystander*. Garden City, NY, Doubleday, 1966, p.21

31. ibid. p.144

32. William M.Thompson, *op.cit.* p.159

33. ibid. p.161

34. ibid. p.161

35. Thomas Merton, *Asian Journal*, *op.cit.* p.143

36. His name is spelled this way in the *Asian Journal*. He now prefers to use the spelling Chadral.

37. Helen Tworkov, 'The Jesus Lama: Thomas Merton in the Himalayas - An Interview with Harold Talbott' in *Tricycle: The Buddhist Review* (Summer 1992) pp.21-22

38. William M.Thompson, *op.cit.* p.162

39. ibid. p.165

THOMAS MERTON
the world in my bloodstream

PAPERS & WORKSHOPS

The Role of Love in the Discovery of the True Self and Healing in Psychotherapy

Michael R. Sobocinski

THE THOUGHTS that I wish to share today represent an attempt to engage in a personal dialogue with the Divine nature of Love as it manifests itself in psychotherapy with physically, emotionally, and spiritually damaged children. Most of these children have experienced a level of violence and neglect in their young lives that few of us can truly imagine. While the experiential foundation for this paper derives from a highly specialized mental health practice, the insights and wisdom that these children offer are universal, speaking to us regardless of our particular life circumstances.

For the past eight years I have been blessed to work as a staff psychologist alongside a gifted and compassionate group of professionals at the Denver Children's Home, a residential treatment center whose mission over the last 125 years has been to serve the indigent children and families of the Denver metropolitan area. In coming to know the children who pass through our care, I have been challenged to respond to the spiritual questions and concerns that inevitably arise during the course of their treatment. These realities are frequently only thinly disguised within their desperate and self-destructive attempts to make sense of and cope with overwhelming life experiences, and to establish meaningful connections with others while protecting themselves from further harm. It has been here, in the midst of such extreme violence and chaos, that the transformative power of Love in healing from trauma has somewhat unexpectedly announced itself.

What I have gradually learned is that the presence of Divine Love shapes in mysterious and wonderful ways the relationship between therapist and client, becoming a third silent presence in the room if we are but willing to open ourselves carefully and reverently to its call. Once we become still and responsive to the voice of Love, our efforts at reaching across the gulf separating children whose lives have been disfigured by abuse and neglect from those of us who would walk alongside them in their healing are altered in subtle and mysterious ways.

The therapeutic process, as is true of all authentic human encounters, is ultimately a call to love one's neighbour in her brokenness. Through seeking to love in this manner, we discover that it is impossible to approach another's suffering in genuine care and compassion without first having learned to love ourselves in our own brokenness and shame, our own feeling of being damaged and 'dirty.' If genuine healing is to occur, we must confront in solitude our sadness and grief, mourn our lost possibilities, and, finally, let go of the false hope that we can through our own efforts transform these aspects of our human existence. This process ultimately allows us to transcend the false self, that shadowy and illusory ego construction which doggedly follows us throughout life. The person who embraces another's pain and suffering, whilst not simply identifying them with his own experience, in Merton's words, 'finds himself simply in the ground of life.' He continues:

> He is "in Love." He lives, then, as a seed planted in the ground. As Christ said, the seed planted in the ground must die. To be as a seed in the ground of one's life is to dissolve in the ground in order to become fruitful. One disappears into Love, in order to "be Love."[1]

What Merton is referring to in this passage is that process by which each of us works out our true identity in communion with others through the unity of Love. As the illusory differences of the false self which distract us from union with our sisters and brothers gradually fall away, we gain an appreciation for what Merton was referring to when he wrote in 'The Inner Experience' that one's 'inner self is, in fact, inseparable from Christ and hence in a mysterious and unique way inseparable from all the other "I"s who live in Christ, so that they all form one "mystical person" which is "Christ."'[2]

As is apparent by now, my talk also addresses the process of becoming fully human, which means becoming the person God wills as a physical, cognitive, emotional, social, and spiritual being. The psychologist James Garbarino, writing in his book *Lost Boys*, reminds us:

The process of kindling the divine flame begins with connection. Child development is fundamentally social: a human infant can neither survive physically nor develop normally on its own. This is why there is no such thing as "a baby"; there is only "a baby in relation to someone else."[3]

I would contend that Garbarino's words are as true for each of us as they are for the infant gazing into her mother's eyes in a dance of two souls united through Love.

We are slowly realizing that the very notion of mind itself makes sense only within the context of sustaining and transforming relationships with other persons, and that the long-cherished ideal of the autonomous, independently existing self is a fiction. Garbarino's words therefore represent a major paradigm shift in our understanding of the self, one which moves us away from the predominant view of self as an entity to be discovered, or as a psychic 'prize' that is somehow wrested away from the world through a titanic, though solitary, struggle.

Throughout his writings Merton develops a sophisticated theory of self, one that is conversational, communal, and dialectical in nature. His thought poses a serious challenge not only to the field of psychology, but also to Christianity as it has developed over the centuries in the West. Both Merton and Garbarino, in highlighting the interpenetration of the true self in the larger human community, provide a necessary corrective to the excessively self-focused, self-preoccupied view that has long dominated our intellectual tradition. While a detailed exploration into the nature of the true self is beyond the scope of the present talk, I would argue that the uniquely Christian gospel of Love contains within it a fully developed and vital psychology of the self which avoids the major limitations of both psychoanalysis and Buddhism, which until now have played the most critical roles in this productive cross-cultural encounter. The Christian voice has been largely and strangely missing from the ensuing dialogue, and Merton's thought brings to the conversation a truly revolutionary element, one which we ignore at our peril.

Merton dares us to re-capture the original message behind the Gospel's call to love our neighbour as we love ourselves. He emphasizes that our true self can only be discovered in and through others, as individually we are incomplete. In a particularly revealing note recorded in one of his reading notebooks from 1955, Merton foreshadows this understanding of the communal, dialectical self as it has evolved:

> This gift (the psychic gift of the self to another) makes us in fact *receptive* to others, and this enables us *to be ourselves in the true self integrated with God and other men*—and thus our own self is achieved by contact with others.[4]

In I Corinthians, St Paul writes of the human members who make up the living body of the Church, comparing them to the various parts of the body in a beautifully vivid metaphor celebrating the diverse gifts and identities that God has collectively given us. He emphasizes that the body is not identified with any one of its parts, and the fact that these are different from one another in no way detracts from their importance to the overall functioning of the organism. What is perhaps most revealing in this passage is the *constitutive nature* of the relationship between members of the body. It is only by means of the relationship existing between the eye and the ear, for example, that either of them is capable of realizing its essential nature. Furthermore, the relationships amongst the members of the body are *dialectical* in nature, as it is only through this interrelatedness that we can properly speak of the individual members of the body as being arms or hands or eyes in the first place. Not only are such relationships essential in bringing forth and defining the individual members of the body, but they are *transformative* as well. The loss or diminution of a function in one sense, such as sight, leads oftentimes to a heightened degree of sensitivity in another, such as hearing. Weakness and strength, wholeness and fragmentation cannot be considered in isolation from one another, but are utterly dependent upon a shifting relational context for their very being.

What St Paul is suggesting in this oft-quoted passage does not sound to me like the notion of the self as cultivated by traditional academic psychology, but rather more closely resembles an understanding arising out of the Eastern tradition. The implications of this teaching for our daily interactions seem profound, if unsettling, and have posed particular emotional and spiritual challenges in my work with the children we treat. If their burning sense of rejection and isolation are an essential aspect of my developing self, and cannot exist apart from this process of becoming, how do I respond in a manner that understands and respects their experience, yet which nonetheless seeks to transcend it in a truly loving manner? My strength must then somehow be theirs, and their journey of healing mine, just as my invested presence in the psychotherapy process is in fact an investment in my own transformation and healing, for only thus can each of us develop as God intends. I must be open to my clients loving me as I seek to love them from within a dialectic which transforms each according to St Paul's words, 'I live, now not I, but Christ lives in me' (Galatians 2:20).

To realize our true self, we must remain in communion with other persons. Apart from this sustaining connectedness, we grow increasingly preoccupied and even obsessed with, though unable to truly love, ourselves—a dynamic that many feel lies at the root of the narcissistic disorders so common in our age. We grow to believe that love of both self and other flows out from our own efforts, and learn very quickly to experience shame and a deep, burning inadequacy over our perceived shortcomings and faults.

It is as though we view life through the lens of a microscope, which provides an exquisitely detailed image of a limited aspect of the ever-changing panorama unfolding around us. As we dare shift our gaze away from the eyepiece and attend to the interpenetration of self and other that constitutes the core of our true self, we discover that our collective efforts at working out our unique identity in the communal Body of Christ are necessary for each of us to have any hope of attaining our own salvation:

> Every other man is a piece of myself, for I am a part and a member of mankind…What I do is also done for them and with them and by them. What they do is done in me and by me and for me. But each one of us remains responsible for his own share in the life of the whole body. Charity cannot be what it is supposed to be as long as I do not see that my life represents my own allotment in the life of a whole supernatural organism to which I belong.[5]

Ordinarily, one does not find the healing process within psychotherapy described as an attempt to love the person of our client, but rather we find references to the role of 'reparative experiences,' 'working through' and 'mutative interpretations.' What has become obvious to me through the stories of the children I have known in treatment is that these explanations fail to embrace the richness of the overall movement that transpires within therapy. While these concepts address important technical aspects that characterize a healing relationship, they fail to take into consideration that which is most central: the power of Love as it is lived out in the here-and-now of a genuine encounter between two souls.

The concept of *empathy* as developed by the founder of the humanistic movement in psychology, Carl Rogers, provides us with the most productive entrée into the present thesis. When this most familiar concept is approached anew, we find that empathy is most properly understood as *love lived in the world*, as a way of being that transcends the boundaries of our individual concerns. Rather than being synonymous with a vague if reassuring feeling of compassion, or a sympathetic identification with another's suffering, empathy challenges us to *act* so as to facilitate the realization of the other's innermost potential for becoming. That which remains at the level of a cognitive and affective understanding of the subjective experience of another, no matter how accurate, misses the mark and cannot truly be considered empathy.

The transcendent power of empathy is perhaps most evident when we consider a parent's interactions with an infant, who is not only utterly dependent upon others for an accurate understanding of her internal needs and affective states for her physical survival, but is equally reliant upon their continuing responsiveness. Good-enough parenting requires, for example, not only an accurate discrimination from amongst the various possible nuances in an infant's cries, but also that this understanding lead to action which helps realize the meaning inherent in the infant's experience. Our understanding of another's experiential world must translate into an active participation in that person's journey of becoming, whether this entails changing a wet diaper, helping a young child pronounce a printed word, or sitting with a suicidal teen who cannot make sense of the sexual abuse she has known at the hands of her father.

Rogers wrote long and eloquently on the nature and role of empathy in human growth and development, summarizing much of his thinking on the subject in an essay written toward the end of his life in which he states:

> It [empathy] means entering the private perceptual world of the other and becoming thoroughly at home in it. It involves being sensitive, moment by moment, to the changing felt meanings which flow in this other person, to the fear or rage or tenderness or confusion or whatever that he or she is experiencing. It means temporarily living in the other's life, moving about in it delicately

without making judgments; it means sensing meanings of which he or she is scarcely aware. . . It includes communicating your sensings of the person's world as you look with fresh and unfrightened eyes at elements of which he or she is fearful. It means frequently checking with the person as to the accuracy of your sensings, and being guided by the responses you receive... By pointing to the possible meanings in the flow of another person's experiencing, you help the other to focus on this useful type of referent, to experience the meanings more fully, and to move forward in the experiencing. [6]

Several elements of this view of empathy are central to our considerations here. First, empathy involves an immersion within the felt subjective world of the other, seeking to understand the experience of that person from within their perspective, without taking on that view as one's own. Empathy further requires that one accurately communicate this understanding to the other person. Empathy therefore serves to dissolve to some degree the alienation that defines the human condition. Second, empathy entails our joining the other person along their trek of self-discovery, by helping bring together and integrate meanings that are not currently available to them at a level of conscious awareness. Third, empathy involves a complete acceptance of the totality of the other person's subjective experience, including that which they find most frightful, anxiety-provoking, or repulsive in themselves. In seeing beyond those aspects of the other's experiential world that serve to distract and distance them from the essential core of their true self, we in effect accept the person in a manner that they may be unable to do for themselves. Fourth, our empathic immersion and subsequent responsiveness are guided by the degree of 'fit' between our understanding and the organic process of becoming residing within the other. The 'rightness' of our efforts is assessed by their correspondence with this organic process. Finally, empathy transforms the person who participates in the other's journey of becoming as surely as it does the recipient of our empathic strivings. Essentially, if we consider each of these aspects of empathy as they interact with one another, what we arrive at is an operational definition of love of both self and other.

The essence of genuine human freedom lies in discerning that our true self is to be found far beyond the countless external distractions that surround us. We grow up in Western culture taught, as Merton notes in *New Seeds of Contemplation*, that people 'can only find themselves by asserting their own desires and appetites in a struggle with the rest of the world. . . [and] can only conceive one way of becoming real: cutting themselves off from other people and building a barrier of contrast and distinction between themselves and other men.'[7] Our senses are constantly impinged upon by messages that imply that we will complete ourselves, find happiness and true satisfaction, and achieve 'fulfillment' by embracing the world of material beings. We remain frenzied, driven to ever-greater activity and a deeper immersion in the addictive world of these distractions. Again, as Merton describes the false self in *New Seeds of Contemplation*:

> I have what you have not. I am what you are not. I have taken what you have failed to take and I have seized what you could never get. Therefore you suffer and I am happy, you are despised and I am praised, you die and I live; you are nothing and I am something, and I am all the more something because you are nothing. And thus I spend my life admiring the distance between you and me; at times this even helps me to forget the other men who have what I have not and who have taken what I was too slow to take and who have seized what was beyond my reach, who are praised as I cannot be praised and who live on my death.[8]

The self thus understood is a 'zero-sum game,' where there are clear winners and losers, and where my satisfaction comes at your expense. Given this backdrop, the commonly observed allure of these external distractions becomes more readily understood, for to step out of this exhausting frenzy of doing and acquiring is to risk an existential encounter with one's inner world. This may be terribly threatening to someone who has not known the loving presence of another person willing to accompany them in their journey of becoming, with its inherent anxieties and uncertainties. Many of the self-destructive, illegal, and problematic behaviors displayed by the children we treat, such as drug and alcohol abuse, promiscuous sexuality, gang activity, violence, depression and anxiety, extreme difficulty falling asleep at night, the need for constant activity—all may be understood as attempts at escaping from the false self, and the nagging sense of unworthiness that is its hallmark.

To slow down and become familiar with their internal experience is to confront the terrible fear that they are in fact abnormal and 'crazy,' and that others can clearly discern the deep sense of shame that they mistakenly believe represents their true self. The feverish activity of their lives reflects the urgency with which they avoid the gnawing fear that they are fundamentally lacking, inadequate, unworthy, and unlovable. For on some unconscious level they understand all-too-well that to be unworthy of love is to be isolated and alone, with no hope for union with others. And such is the nature of the hell that these children seek to avoid, that they tragically continue to sacrifice the possibility of others coming to know them in their pain and brokenness, which is the one thing that would allow them to see through the deceptions of the false self.

While the presenting issues, the life histories and the diagnoses accompanying these children vary significantly, a common theme is their core experience of self. This refers to whether or not each of them has, again in Garbarino's words, been 'connected rather than abandoned, accepted rather than rejected, and nurtured rather than neglected and abused.'[9] In each instance one is drawn to the manner in which these youths have grown up lacking the experience of care-taking adults who have responded consistently to the Spark of the Divine residing within them. Those who were responsible for their care have often literally as well as metaphorically not seen them. They have become invisible to those around them, being related to as mere psychic extensions of their caregivers, and as a way of satisfying their own numerous and unmet needs. Where their unique gifts called out for reverence and respect, they have instead been rejected and devalued, and where love should have been shown them, they have known instead the searing pain of shame. They subsequently suffer from a profound inability to reach out to others and attain union with them, because, as Merton notes in 'The Inner Experience,'

> We are not capable of union with one another on the deepest level until the inner self in each one of us is *sufficiently awakened* to confront the inmost spirit of the other.[10] (italics added).

When children are exposed to an interpersonal environment incapable of recognizing and responding to the manner in which they manifest the Divine, they become objectified, devalued, and shamed. Their soul increasingly 'covers itself with layers of insulation. As the years pass, this protective shell may harden to the point where eventually the soul seems dormant, so out of touch with the day-to-day self it becomes so even to the tormented individual himself.'[11]

These children in essence 'become' a false self. Our task is to recognize and respond to the still-glowing embers of the true self before these extinguish altogether, and to coax this elusive 'inmost spirit' back into the world of genuine human relatedness.

In spite of the numerous traumas and repeated failures of care-taking adults to respond sensitively to their needs, the tenacity with which the Indwelling Divinity perseveres in the midst of nearly constant attack announces itself clearly in each of these children. The courage that they display is humbling. As we appreciate how such damaged children cautiously approach life, alert to the ever-present dangers inherent in revealing themselves to others, we develop an abiding appreciation and respect for the 'logic' and wisdom that their behaviors demonstrate.

We discern the soul's resolute, though often muted, quest for connection and recognition, the way in which it seeks to become visible once more in the world of interpersonal relationships. Deep within the 'layers of insulation' that slowly come to cover the souls of these children, there lies, in Merton's words from *Hagia Sophia*, 'the Child who is prisoner in all the people, and who says nothing. She smiles, for though they have bound her, she cannot be a prisoner... she does not understand imprisonment.'[12] It is in freeing this Child, that we come to free ourselves as well.

In truly opening ourselves to these children's experiences, we come to understand that their pain is our pain, their brokenness ours, and that it is not in spite of these qualities that they and we are ultimately worthy of love and care, but *because* of them. And this is a difficult yet tremendously liberating lesson for each of us. In loving another person, we achieve an intimate knowledge of that person as a unique Echo of the Divine, and thereby come not only to understand but also to facilitate the other's attaining 'his own spiritual reality, his own personal identity.'[13]

Love, if it is genuine, loves not in spite of the other person's shortcomings, faults, and failures, nor does it demand that the other somehow become worthy of our love. Rather, we are called to emulate the example of Christ, who loved all those he encountered regardless of considerations of worth.

> There is no way under the sun to make a man worthy of love except by loving him. As soon as he realizes himself loved – if he is not so weak that he can no longer bear to be loved – he will feel himself

instantly worthy of love. He will respond by drawing a mysterious spiritual value out of his own depth, a new identity called into being by the love that is addressed to him.[14]

Merton's words are particularly poignant in clinical work with traumatized children, who frequently do not feel themselves worthy of love and care, and who strenuously resist those who would suggest otherwise. And yet, their recovery and healing require that they experience love, so that they may come to love themselves and ultimately, other persons.

To close, the children whose stories have informed these thoughts teach us that what is ultimately healing and transformative in the therapeutic process is the power of love. Merton captures this truth simply yet powerfully when he writes in *New Seeds of Contemplation*:

> One of the paradoxes of the mystical life is this: that a man cannot enter into the deepest center of himself and pass through that center into God, unless he is able to pass entirely out of himself and empty himself and give himself to other people in the purity of a selfless love.[15]

To be truly able to 'pass entirely out of' the external self, and 'empty' the self of life's many distractions requires an intimacy, courage, and faith that seems exceedingly rare. Rather than being characterized by an excessive concern with one's own independence and self-sufficiency, the self that is capable of genuine love has as its hallmark a true interdependence, allowing the self to simultaneously delight in shared experiencing, while appreciating the distinctiveness of the other.

Notes and References

1. Thomas Merton, *Honorable Reader: Reflections on my work*. New York, Crossroad Publishing Company, 1991, p.116

2. Thomas Merton, 'The Inner Experience: Society and the Inner Self (II).' *Cistercian Studies*, XVII (1), 1983, p.124

3. James Garbarino, *Lost Boys: Why Our Sons Turn Violent And How We Can Save Them*. New York, The Free Press, 1999, p.38

4. Working Notebook: Holographic Journal #9. Unpublished Manuscript. 1955, p.16. The Thomas Merton Center, Bellarmine University, Louisville, KY.

5. Thomas Merton, *No Man Is An Island*. New York, Harcourt, Brace & Jovanovich, 1955 p.xxii

6. Carl R. Rogers, *A Way of Being*. New York, Houghton Mifflin Company, 1980, p.142

7. Thomas Merton, *New Seeds of Contemplation*. New York, New Directions, 1961, p.47

8. *ibid.* p.48

9. James Garbarino, *op.cit.* p.34

10. Thomas Merton, 'The Inner Experience,' *op.cit.* p.124

11. James Garbarino, *op.cit.* pp.34-35

12. Thomas Merton, 'Hagia Sophia' in *Thomas Merton: Spiritual Master* (ed. Lawrence Cunningham). New York, Paulist Press, 1992, p.260).

13. Thomas Merton, *Disputed Questions*. New York, Harcourt Brace & Co., 1953, p.103

14. *ibid.* p.125

15. Thomas Merton, *New Seeds of Contemplation*. *op.cit.* p.64

Thomas Merton and the Beat Generation:
A Subterranean Monastic Community

DAVID BELCASTRO

B Y FEBRUARY OF 1967 Merton's concerns regarding monasticism in the modern world had come to the point where he believed significant change was necessary. A journal entry dated the sixth of that month reads:

> Monasticism. I see more and more the danger of identifying the monastic vocation and spirit with a particular kind of monastic consciousness—a particular tradition, however *authentic*. A monasticism limited to the medieval western – or worse still Byzantine – tradition *cannot* survive. It is utterly finished. I very much wonder how much the Rule of St Benedict can survive in practice. This is a very serious question. Maybe monasticism needs to be stated all over again in a new way. I have no knowing how to tackle this idea. It is just beginning to dawn on me.[1]

After reading Lewis Hyde's *Trickster Makes This World: Mischief, Myth, and Art*,[2] I began to explore the possibility of understanding Merton's efforts to redefine monasticism in light of the trickster tradition. In 'An Inquiry into Merton as Trickster,'[3] I demonstrated that the primary characteristics of the trickster are present in Merton, not as marginal but as essential qualities of his person, in particular, the inclination to redefine established institutions. At the end of that paper, I suggested several lines of inquiry for further study, one of which was his place within the American tradition of tricksters, specifically, his relation to Beat writers, a connection that has long been recognized but not as yet fully explored.[4]

A study of Merton's relationship to the Beat generation provides insight into his effort to find ways to redefine monasticism in and for the modern world. This paper will focus on what I believe to have been at the core of this relationship and how it eventually became an essential aspect of his monastic identity.

The Relationship

While less celebrated than his visit with the Dalai Lama, Merton's stay with Lawrence Ferlinghetti at the City Lights apartment in San Francisco during May of 1968 was nonetheless a pilgrimage in its own right.[5] City Lights bookstore had become a Mecca for Beat writers and artists; an open place where normally apolitical persons could speak uncensored upon any subject regarding the subordination of human life and freedom to political ideologies, structures, and programs. For this reason, Merton's work caught the attention of Beat writers; in particular, the logic of such statements as:

> We equate sanity with a sense of justice, with humaneness, with prudence, with the capacity to love and understand other people. We rely on the sane people of the world to preserve it from barbarism, madness, destruction. And now it begins to dawn on us that it is precisely the sane ones who are the most dangerous.[6]

In 1961, Ferlinghetti[7] published Merton's 'Chant to Be Used in Processions Around A Site With Furnaces' in the first edition of *Journal for the Protection of All Beings*.[8] Merton's poem was printed first in a series of writings by Gary Snyder, Gregory Corso, Michael McClure, Allen Ginsberg, William Burroughs, and others. By the time of Merton's visit, he was well established within the Beat community. With regard to the visit, a line from Merton's letter to Ping Ferry may be all that is needed: 'Saw Ferlinghetti in S.F. and drank some espresso with visionaries.'[9]

This gathering of visionaries originated on the East coast at Columbia University. Jack Kerouac, Allen Ginsberg, and Lucien Carr entered Columbia shortly after Merton left in 1940. Ferlinghetti would arrive in 1946. All studied with Raymond Weaver, Lionel Trilling, and Mark Van Doren.[10] The lives of these young writers were shaped by the Columbia experience in similar ways as reflected in *Love and Living* where Merton wrote, 'Be anything you like, be madmen, drunks, and bastards of every shape and form, but at all costs avoid one thing: success.' This, he declared, was his message for his contemporaries. It was a message he attributed to his education at Columbia. There, he tells us, he learned the value of 'unsuccess.' There he was 'saved . . .

from one of those Madison Avenue jobs.' There he was 'lobbed . . . half conscious into the Village, where he came to his senses and continued to learn to imitate not Rockefeller but Thoreau.'[11] Such a statement could just as easily have been written by Ginsberg. It was at Columbia that Ginsberg's aspirations to become a labour lawyer were waylaid. It was there that he began to write wild and bewildering poetry about the best minds of his generation who studied Plotinus, Poe, St John of the Cross, and bop kabbalah, 'because the cosmos instinctively vibrated at their feet.'[12] As one person would later testify, Ginsberg's personal view of life was colored by his exposure to jazz and Columbia University where he received a liberal and bohemian education.[13]

While Merton never met Kerouac or Ginsberg, publishers Giroux, Laughlin and Ferlinghetti, as well as friends Robert Lax and Ron Seitz, would provide the necessary connections for what would perhaps be best described as solitary ships passing in the night. There were others, however, who came to Gethsemani. From 1958 to 1968, Merton's journals and correspondence reveal the development of his relationship to the Beat generation, to include Gary Snyder, Denise Levertov, Diana DePrima, Brother Antonius, Cid Corman, and Joan Baez. Merton's letter to Laughlin in February of 1958 explains how all this came about:

> Larry Ferlinghetti's stuff sounds interesting. I now have permission to read anything so there are no problems about the nature of the material... Am interested in everything that is alive, and anything that strikes you as something I ought to know about, please send.[14]

Laughlin would send Beat books. And, by March of 1960, Merton was encouraging Laughlin to bring Kerouac, Lax, and a few others down to Gethsemani to solve the problems of the world.[15]

How Merton Understood the Relationship

Definitions of Beat vary and include a variety of alternatives: beatnik, neo-beat, contemporaries of beats, each suggesting something different with regard to the nature of the relationship. Merton identified himself as a 'friend of the beats.' In a letter to William Carlos Williams dated 11th July 1961, Merton wrote:

> It has taken me a long time to get to be able to follow your advice and read *Kaddish [and Other Poems]*, because nobody sent me one. But

finally Laughlin is out in SF and the City Lights Books sent me a copy. I agree with you about it. I think it is great and living poetry and certainly religious in its concern. In fact, who are more concerned with ultimates than the beats? Why do you think that just because I am a monk I should be likely to shrink from beats? Who am I to shrink from anyone, I am a monk, therefore by definition, as I understand it, the chief friend of the beats and one who has no business reproving them. And why should I?[16]

But it was a precarious friendship. For example, by October of 1966, Merton could write:

I found some good things in the library—old articles on Camus from the immediate post-war years (1946–). And some [Gregory] Corso, R[obert] Creely and others not so good (I still can't read Charles Olson). I very much doubt whether I can or should get involved in this kind of poetry—or at least not with the people who want it. I've had enough with the pontifical Cid Corman. Maybe they all want to be gurus as well as poets.[17]

While Merton and Ginsberg had been reading each other's books, there was a tension between these two men. In an article printed in *Harpers*, November of 1965, Merton wrote:

The South American poets who had a meeting in Concepcion, Chile, last winter, considered the two Americans present to be "innocents"—should one say fools? Especially one—who was continually making a huge fuss about how poets needed lots of drugs and sex and was always the first one to go home.

The two poets were Ferlinghetti and Ginsberg, Ginsberg being the one making the fuss about drugs and sex. This difference of opinion on sex and drugs marked the relationship from the beginning as indicated by Ginsberg's journal entry of August 1955 of a dream he had of Merton after reading *Tears of the Blind Lion*:

Saw Fr Thomas Merton in the halls, come on a visit to the house, dressed in swinging robes - we talked, he brought a friend, I looked in the bathroom to see friend - a redhead (hipster looking) with small rat red mouth & pale skin, and another cat - He says, "I need to be told how I look," laughing, he's English-like, I say - "Still pimply adolescence not grown old - rather like Hamlet" (he looks awful but I don't want to insult him too much) with his long cassock & I notice big ungainly legs & wide effeminate ass under-neath, and like Auden probably tits on flabby chest and like Hol-lander long arms, then this head of his which is young English schoolboy big-eared - I say "Tell me once & for all about this divine

ecstasy - does it come once or often? How long does it last? Is it
long or short? How many times etc.?" This after I said he was like
Hamlet. My feeling a mixture of affection envy & contempt for his
body - I thought, with an ass like that no wonder he's a mystic, O
well he's no worse than anyone trying to escape not getting laid.[18]

The dream reveals radically different attitudes regarding the body;
attitudes that initially separated the celibate monk and the gay poet.
With time, however, the body would become common ground.
Compare, for example, the following two poems. The first is an excerpt
from Ginsberg's "Song."

The weight of the world
    is love.
Under the burden
    of solitude.
under the burden
    of dissatisfaction

    the weight
the weight we carry
    is love

The warm bodies
    shine together
in the darkness,
    the hand moves
to the center
    of the flesh,
the skin trembles
    in the happiness
and the soul comes
    joyful to the eye -

yes, yes,
    that's what
I wanted,
    I always wanted,
I always wanted,
    to return
to the body
    where I was born.

The second is from Merton's "May Song."

It is May
We weep for love
In the imperfect wood
In the land of bodies

O lonely little boat
Carry me away
Across the sea of wine

O small strong boat
Bring me
My child.

What Merton Found of Value in the Relationship

There are two phrases that provide some insight into what Merton valued in this relationship: 'Christians turned inside out' and 'monks in reverse.' Both refer, in different ways, to the body as an essential aspect of the contemplative life.

The first phrase, 'Christians turned inside out,' occurs in reference to non-Christian writers who are, none-the-less, of value to the person living the contemplative life. On 24th October 1958, Merton's 'Poetry and Contemplation: A Reappraisal' appeared in *Commonweal*.[19] In this article, Merton wrote:

> A sincere and efficacious desire to enter more deeply into the beauty of the Christian mystery implies a willingness to sacrifice the things which are called "beautiful" by the decadent standards of a materialistic world. Yet the Christian contemplative need not confine himself to religious, still less to professionally "pious" models... One might add that a fully integrated vision of our time and of its spirit presupposes some contact with the genius of Baudelaire and Rimbaud, who are Christians turned inside out.

Baudelaire and, in particular, Rimbaud were predecessors to the Beats. The line 'fully integrated vision of our time and of its spirit' sheds some light on the phrase 'Christians turned inside out.' There are two kinds of Christians. There are right-side-out Christians and inside-out ones. It is only by recognizing both sides that one can have a 'fully integrated vision.' So, what makes someone like Rimbaud an inside-out Christian? They approach the Gospel from the inside out, from the body, from the desires of the body, or as E. M. Forster says, 'the holiness of direct desire.'

In a letter to Bruno Paul Schlesinger dated 13th December 1961, Merton stresses the importance of this human dimension:

> That we have come to a certain kind of "end" of the development of Western Christianity is no accident...the survival of religion as an abstract formality without a humanist matrix, religion apart from man and almost in some sense apart from God Himself... is killing religion in our midst today, not the atheists. So that one who seeks God without culture and without humanism tends inevitably to promote a religion that is irreligious and even unconsciously atheistic... Sorry if I sound like a beatnik, but this is what is driving intelligent people as far from Christianity as they can travel. Hence, in one word, a pretended Christianity, without the human dimensions which *nature* herself has provided, our religion becomes a lunar landscape of meaningless gestures and observances.[20]

The second phrase, 'monks in reverse,' occurs in the following manner. On 18th September 1966, Merton wrote to *The New Yorker* in response to an article that they had printed at the time of Lenny Bruce's death.

> In *The New Yorker* for August 20 – which I have just now happened to see – there is a paragraph in "Talk of the Town" about Lenny Bruce and Bud Powell. I was very moved by it. Having been for quite some time in a monastery I had never had any occasion to hear – or even to hear of – either Lenny Bruce... What I would like to know is this: how can I now hear what Lenny Bruce was saying, and learn more about the struggle he had to face—doubtless much of it against my Church, or representatives of it. Would it be possible for the writer of that paragraph to get in touch with me and fill me in a little on this situation, and perhaps send me references that I could consult? I would be very grateful. Need I add that my interest is entirely sympathetic to Lenny Bruce and what he was evidently trying to achieve?[21]

Eighteen months later, March of 1968, Merton received a copy of *The Essential Lenny Bruce*[22] as a gift from Lionel Landry.[23] Merton wrote to Landry:

> I looked straight at the back and found that actually what he did was a marvelous adaptation of a much longer and more intricate poem of mine. This was the same poem, but cut down to a series of left hooks for the night club or wherever he did it, and much funnier. My own is very dour and quiet, this is rambunctious and wild.

Lawrence Schiller, in his book, *Ladies and Gentlemen: Lenny Bruce*,[24] tells about the routine that was based on 'A Devout Meditation in Memory of Adolf Eichmann,' with overtones from 'Chant to Be Used in Processions Around A Site With Furnaces.'

> Some nights he would end his act with a bit that had no precedent in the history of American night club humor. It was inspired by a poem by Thomas Merton that Lenny had read and treasured for a couple of years... It was much too strong for a nightclub audience. Lenny had been holding back with it, waiting till the time was right. Now was the time. Every night he would enact that chilling poem. He would call for a single pin spot. Then he would put on a very straight German accent. Staring sternly at the audience, he was Adolf Eichmann standing in the dock: *My name is Adolf Eichmann. The Jews came every day to vat they thought vould be fun in the showers.*

Merton's response? 'People like Lenny Bruce are really monks in reverse and hence I feel much closer to them than I do to say the President of General Motors.' This curious phrase, 'monks in reverse' is perhaps best understood in light of the *New York Times* article that he had read.[25]

> Lenny Bruce ...had a huge appetite for life, in all its transience, absurdity, and potentiality. What he wanted was to make it all more real, to startle his listeners into realizing how much they were missing as a result of their evasions. He kept asking them, as they laughed, why certain words were "obscene." Who had made them "obscene," and why? Similarly, he insisted on exploring – with a bizarre accuracy of perception – the chasm between Christianity and churches, between love and marriage, between law and lawyers, between the urgency of fantasies and the insubstantial safety of "normality." He had no programmatic answers. His delight was in questioning those who had given up trying to find answers. But the questioning was never malicious; it was affecting – as well as risibly – hopeful.

With this in mind, Merton may have been suggesting that there are two kinds of monks; one that moves in forward direction and another in reverse. If the above description is of a monk in reverse, we may conclude that this kind of monk engages the world in playful antics of a backward sort with the hope of opening a larger vision of life in all its grandeur that includes rather than excludes the body and all of the experiences of the body.

These two references indicate that Merton had come to recognize that there were individuals who were fulfilling the roles of monks in the modern world, even though in reverse and from the inside out. As Merton explains in a letter to Parra: 'today the poets and other artists tend to fulfill many of the functions that were once the monopoly of monks—and which of course the monks have made haste to abandon, in order to center themselves firmly in the midst of a square society.' So, forward moving monks, the ones who wear their habits right side out, fit the square world. The Beat generation, on the other hand, are monks who are moving in reverse with their habits on inside out; they neither fit nor care to fit in square society. They live outside the square establishment, beyond social conventions. They situate themselves between society's restrictions and the individual's freedom to explore and discover his or her true humanity at the deepest possible level.

This notion of a different order of monk had been developing since the late 1950s and is more fully understood in light of Merton's correspondence with Milosz, and his work on Camus. It is a notion, however, that finds its theological roots in Clement of Alexandria. In his correspondence with Milosz, Merton works out an understanding of solidarity with those who risk everything for the third position that refuses to allow life to be subordinated to political agenda. In his essays on Camus, Merton works at developing mutual understanding with a non-Christian with whom he has found common ground as reflected in his reference to Camus as 'that Algerian cenobite.' In Clement of Alexandria, Merton found a model for his approach to the world, one that affirmed, rather than negated the world whereby those outside the institutional Church may nonetheless participate in the Gospel.

Merton found in the Beat generation monks in the modern world who stand outside the structures of their day, risking everything for the third position that rebels against the subordination of human life to power and authority invested in social institutions. He saw their work as compatible with the Gospel. Living outside monastic walls, these monks howled through the dark hours of the night in the streets of America. Merton was their friend: a friend who recognized and valued what they had to offer.

It was that howling or hullabaloo that caught Merton's attention. He recognized in them what was of value to him as he was trying to redefine his monastic vocation. Merton's poem, 'Five Virgins,' written during a time of intense interest in the Beats, reveals what it was.

> There were five howling virgins
> Who came

To the Wedding of the Lamb
With their disabled motorcycles
And their oil tanks
Empty

But since they knew how
To dance
A person says to them
To stay anyhow.

And there you have it:
There were five noisy virgins
Without gas
But looking good
In the traffic of the dance

Consequently
There were ten virgins
At the Wedding of the Lamb.

Howling or hullabaloo (craziness that makes a lot of noise accompanied by disorder) described Merton's state of mind at this time. The journal entries around this date indicate his ongoing struggle to move more deeply into silence and solitude while, at the same time, very much engaged and frustrated by numerous issues ranging from political activism to theological wrangling, as well as, his relationship with M that he referred to as 'hullabaloo.' As difficult as these contradictions were, he accepted them, understanding them as essential aspects of his monastic identity. Hullabaloo had found a permanent place in his life. Faith could no longer be understood as an evasion of the absurd via endless explanations but rather a particular way of encountering the absurd as suggested in this poem.

How is one to face the absurd? With the reference to dancing virgins, we see the converging of two ideas that Merton had been entertaining for some time: the metaphor of the dance for the contemplative life and the idea of *le point vierge*[26] or what he would sometimes refer to as the 'still point' or the 'third position.' It seems reasonable to suggest that behind the images of this poem is an emerging insight that the howling virgins who know how to dance at *le point vierge* participate in the wedding of the Lamb. *Le point vierge* is a metaphysical reality and the inclusion of the howling virgins in the wedding of the Lamb is transforming his monastic community in such a way that it included persons who we could easily imagine arriving at Gethsemani on motorcycles. His understanding of the contemplative life as the obedience and vigilance of wise virgins was shifting to include the talents of those confused virgins who arrive late but get in anyway because they are good looking and know how to dance.

Who might Merton have had in mind? Around this time, Merton received a letter from James Laughlin regarding Bob Dylan's motorcycle accident. Four months earlier, Merton told Laughlin that he had been listening to Dylan's latest album, *Bringing It All Back Home*. Merton had developed an interest in Dylan as a poet and social phenomenon, as had many of the Beats. Merton referred to Dylan's music as the new liturgy.[27] Intending to write an essay on Dylan, he asked Laughlin to send him articles regarding the young rock singer. Strange as this may sound, it had become more characteristic than uncharacteristic of Merton during these years. It reveals something of the nature of Merton's growing circle of friends outside the walls of Gethsemani. He had known for some time that he needed contact with a broader community.[28] During these years, Merton's monastic community – that is to say his idea of that community or, specifically, his monastic identity – was going through a transformation. He found solidarity with another kind of monk, one as essential to the wedding of the Lamb as those he had found within the monastic walls of Gethsemani.

> Solidarity—yes. I can see it is going to be a strange kind of underground solidarity perhaps, with people who know they cannot belong to the world of the establishment, organized insanity. Who perhaps have some other, slightly better, insanity—that may make sense if anyone survives.[29]

Conclusion

Merton recognized that these wayward virgins who desired to be saints as he did had something of value to offer those who remain vigilant in solemn processions. 'Five Virgins' reveals what he had found of importance in this relationship, as well as, how it was unfolding into his efforts to understand monasticism in a new way. The Beats represented the hullabaloo, the absurd, the *mysterium tremendum*. This strange and unpredictable movement of God, Merton believed, had been walled out by the old monastic system. So he redefined his monastic identity to include body and soul, the sacred and the profane, order and chaos, tradition and improvisation. He did this by integrating back into his life that which he had left outside when he entered the monastery, that which had taken shape in him at Columbia and now presented itself to him in the Beats. For Merton, this was the only way in which monasticism could be redefined. Having embodied this new understanding of what it means to be a monk within himself, he had in effect brought a new monastic order into the world. Constructing a monastic identity that consisted of these two dimensions, one constructed above ground, one subterranean, he became the new monk wherein the subterranean world of the body would be allowed to enrich and inform a new way of being a monk.

Notes and References

1. Thomas Merton, *Learning to Love:The Journals of Thomas Merton* Vol. 6 1966-1967 (ed. Christine M. Bochen). San Francisco, HarperSanFrancisco, 1997 p.193

2. Lewis Hyde, *Trickster Makes This World: Mischief, Myth, and Art*. New York, Farrar, Straus and Giroux, 1998

3. Paper presented at the ITMS Conference in 1999

4. Brother John Albert, O.C.S.O., 'Ace of Songs - Ace of Freedom:Thomas Merton and Bob Dylan,' *The American Benedictine Review* (March 1986) pp.67-95; Ron Seitz, *A Song for Nobody*, Missouri, Liguori Publications, 1993; Robert Ginn, 'The Paradox of Solitude: Jack Kerouac and Thomas Merton,' *The Merton Seasonal* Vol. 24 (1), 1999, pp.18-26; Angus Stuart, 'Visions of Tom: Jack Kerouac's Monastic Elder Brother,' *The Merton Journal* Vol. 8 (1), 2001, pp.40-46; Peter C. King, 'Roots & Wings:Thomas Merton & Alan Watts as Twentieth Century Archetypes,' *The Merton Journal* Vol. 8 (2), 2001, pp.36-44

5. For Merton's account of this visit, see *Learning to Love, op. cit.* pp.101-102; 120. For Ferlinghetti's, see: *Merton By Those Who Knew Him Best* (ed. Paul Wilkes), San Francisco, Harper & Row, 1984, pp.29-31

6. Michael Schumacher, *Dharma Lion:A Biography of Allen Ginsberg*. New York, St. Martin's Press, 1992, p.101

7. Thomas Merton, *The Courage for Truth: Letters to Writers* (ed. Christine M. Bochen). New York, Farrar, Straus & Giroux, 1993, pp.267-272

8. *Journal for the Protection of All Beings*, (ed. Michael McClure, Lawrence Ferlinghetti, David Meltzer). San Francisco, City Lights Books, 1961

9. Thomas Merton, *The Hidden Ground of Love*, (ed. William H. Shannon). New York, Farrar, Straus & Giroux, 1985, p.239

10. For two accounts of these years at Columbia, see: Michael Schumacher, *Dharma Lion;A Critical Biography of Allen Ginsberg*, New York, St. Martin's Press, 1992, pp.23-48; Barry Miles, *Ginsberg:A Biography*, New York, Simon and Schuster, 1989, pp.36-42

11. Thomas Merton, *Love and Living*, (ed. Naomi Burton Stone and Brother Patrick Hart). New York, Farrar, Straus, Giroux, 1979, pp. 11-12

12. Allen Ginsberg, 'Howl' in Howl and Other Poems. San Francisco, City Lights Books, 1956

13. Barry Silesky, Ferlinghetti:The Artist in HisTime. NewYork,Warner Books, 1990, p.76

14. Thomas Merton and James Laughlin:Selected Letters, (ed. David D. Cooper). NewYork,W. W. Norton, 1997, p.136

15. Ibid. p.156

16.Thomas Merton, The Courage forTruth, op.cit. pp.289-290

17.Thomas Merton, Learning to Love, op.cit. p.148

18. Allen Ginsberg,Journals Mid-Fifties 1954-1958 (ed. Gordon Ball). NewYork, Harper Collins, 1995, p.154

19.Thomas Merton, The Literary Essays ofThomas Merton (ed. Patrick Hart). NewYork, New Directions, 1981, p.346

20.Thomas Merton, The Hidden Ground of Love, op.cit. p.542

21.Thomas Merton, The Road to Joy:Letters to New and Old Friends (ed. Robert E. Daggy). NewYork, Farrar, Straus, Giroux, 1989, p.342

22. Lenny Bruce, The Essential Lenny Bruce (ed. John Cohen). NewYork, Ballantine, 1967

23. John Howard Griffin, Follow the Ecstasy. FortWorth,Texas, Latitudes Press Books, 1983, p.191

24. Albert Goldman, from the journalism of Lawrence Schiller, Ladies and Gentlemen: Lenny Bruce, NewYork, Penguin Books, 1991, pp.454-457

25. NewYorkTimes, 8/20/66

26.Thomas Merton, TurningToward theWorld:The Journals ofThomas MertonVol. 4 1960-1963 (ed.VictorA. Kramer). San Francisco, HarperSanFrancisco, 1996, pp.235-236

27.Thomas Merton, Learning to Love,op.cit.p.309

28. Ibid. p.208

29. Ibid. p.245

Grace beats Karma:
Thomas Merton
and the Dharma Bums

Angus Stuart

Prologue

FINALLY AFTER PORING OVER MAPS of the United States for months, Jack Kerouac set out on the road for his great trip across the country west from New York—by heading north. It was July 17th 1947. On the map he'd traced the 'long red line called Route 6 that led from the tip of Cape Cod clear to Ely, Nevada, and there dipped down to Los Angeles' and he planned to pick this up at Bear Mountain, forty miles north of New York. Problem was, having taken the Seventh Avenue subway to the end of the line at 242nd Street then the trolley to Yonkers, transferring there to an outgoing trolley to the city limits on the east bank of the Hudson River and hitching five scattered rides to Bear Mountain Bridge, he found himself stranded on a deserted minor road with virtually no cross country traffic. On top of this, the rain was beating down, hair all wet, flimsy Mexican *huaraches* on his feet sopping. Eventually sheltering in a gas station he got a ride going the wrong way and then took a dejected bus ride back into New York.[1]

Several hundred miles south at the Abbey of Gethsemani in Kentucky it had been raining for days. Thomas Merton notes in his journal for July 16th 1947, the day before Kerouac heads out on the road for the first time:

> On top of all this year's rain we just had a tremendous storm during Vespers. The mill bottom was turned into a lake and the creek is trying to make a noise like Niagara. A moment ago every path was a torrent and were a hundred rivers coming down all the hillsides. The ducks were very happy.[2]

Introduction

I find myself drawn more and more to these two writers, the so-called father of the 'Beat Generation' and the Trappist Monk—or as his friend Ed Rice dubbed him 'a beatnik, peacenik Trappist Buddhist monk.' Robert Inchausti refers to Thomas Merton as 'Jack Kerouac's monastic elder brother,'[3] a phrase I borrowed elsewhere as I began to explore the links and parallels between these two characters.[4] What I want to do in this paper specifically, is explore further their mutual interest in, and involvement with, Buddhism and eastern traditions. This feeds into wider discussions about the Beat writers and their impact on mid-twentieth century culture in America and 'The West,' and about Thomas Merton and his increasing relationship to (or involvement in) Buddhism and 'The East.' Wider still, it feeds into questions about how Christianity and Buddhism relate to one another—about the 'grace' that is central to Christian understanding and the 'karma' (the cycle of actions and consequences) of Eastern thought. I do not conceive this in terms of opposition but rather in terms of what Christianity and Buddhism have to offer one another—conscious of Merton's caution about the birds of appetite circling the carcass for what they may gain.[5] It is my intuition that the experiences of the Beats and of Merton are not dissimilar and that they hold key insights for these discussions. Both Merton and the Beats were searching and struggling for a spiritual breakthrough, perhaps even a sloughing off of an old skin, and maybe they even achieved it or came to the brink of it before dying or going mad. And this is where it connects with my own spiritual journey – where it gets up close and personal – and where each of us is invited to engage, to ask the questions and see what will become of us.

Western Beats and Eastern Rhythms

In February 1954 Jack Kerouac walked into the public library in San Jose, California, and became engrossed with Dwight Goddard's *A Buddhist Bible* (1932), an anthology of Buddhist and Taoist writings from various traditions and periods. Soon Kerouac was devouring everything he could lay his hands on about Eastern religions. The immediate trigger for this sudden interest had been his reading of Thoreau's *Walden* and its discussion of Indian philosophy, earlier that winter. Earlier still Kerouac and Allen Ginsberg had encountered Buddhism through Oswald Spengler's *Decline of the West*; and whilst at

Columbia University in the early 1940s Professor Raymond Weaver suggested they look into the writings of Egyptian Gnostics and Zen Buddhists. The third member of the original Beat trinity, William Burroughs, also claimed in a number of letters that he had studied Zen Buddhism and practised some sort of yoga long before meeting Kerouac and Ginsberg.[6]

Kerouac's awakening to Buddhism stirred interest amongst other Beat writers, most notably Allen Ginsberg who came to pursue Buddhism much further, or perhaps more formally, than Kerouac who ultimately returned to the Catholicism which, in truth, he never really left. Kerouac's own novel The Dharma Bums (1958) inspired many young people of the 1960s disenchanted with Cold War America and the atomic age to turn to the East as well as hit the road in the 'rucksack revolution' of wandering 'Zen lunatics' prophesied by the book. The book itself fictionalises the San Francisco scene of the mid-1950s featuring depictions of other important figures of the West Coast poetry renaissance who became part of the Beat movement and were involved in Buddhism, most notably Gary Snyder and Philip Whalen who had come down from the Pacific North West.

Dharma means variously 'the way,' 'the law,' 'righteousness,' 'reality' or more fully, 'the path which a man should follow in accordance with his nature and station in life.'[7] And 'bum' refers to a bum, a tramp, a traveller, someone habitually on the road. The Dharma Bums were both the protagonists of the novel, Japhy Ryder (Gary Snyder) and Ray Smith (Jack Kerouac) and others, and the ancient Chinese poets such as Han Shan who like the Beats were chastised for their laziness and apparent purposelessness. On the penultimate page of The Dharma Bums we read:

> And suddenly it seemed I saw that unimaginable little Chinese bum standing there, in the fog, with that expressionless humor on his steamed face. It wasn't the real-life Japhy of rucksacks and Buddhism studies and big mad parties at Corte Madera, it was the realer-than-life Japhy of my dreams, and he stood there saying nothing.

The origin of the Beat movement is sometimes traced to the famous poetry reading held on October 13th 1955 at the Six Gallery in San Francisco – and described in The Dharma Bums – at which Allen Ginsberg gave his first public reading of the controversial but prophetic poem 'Howl.' But this was more of a coming-out party; the true origin goes back to 1944 when Jack Kerouac, Allen Ginsberg, and William Burroughs first met in New York City. The phrase 'Beat Generation' was coined in 1948 by Kerouac in a conversation with fellow writer, John Clellon Holmes as they struggled to describe the times in which they lived and their developing outlook.[8]

It's a state-of-being epitomized by their associate and Times Square hustler Herbert Huncke, possibly the first person they heard use the word 'beat' in this sense, who according to Ginsberg '

> was to be found in 1945 passing on subways from Harlem to Broadway scoring for drugs, music, incense, lovers, Benzedrine inhalers ... encountering curious & beautiful solitaries of New York dawn.' Huncke symbolized Spengler's 'fellaheen' with 'a deep piety that fills the waking-consciousness... the naïve belief... that there is some sort of mystic constitution of actuality.' No doubt there is some romanticizing here, but Huncke stands as one of the two archetypes of 'beat-ness.'

The other is Neal Cassady who hit New York in 1947 and is immortalized as Dean Moriarty in Kerouac's *On The Road*. He embodied energy, insatiable zest for words, ideas, kicks, cars and life. Whereas Huncke was 'beat-up' and 'beat-down,' Cassady was *upbeat*, he ran with the beat, moved with the beat and kept the beat drumming on the dashboard of whatever car he happened to be driving at full-speed, in time to the downbeat bop blaring full blast from the radio. *Joie de vie*, everyday life as a *sacrament*. Already in both these aspects of the word 'beat' we can see religious or spiritual overtones. This is made more explicit in Kerouac's development of the idea, linking the word 'beat' with 'beatific' and 'beatitude.' Blessed are the poor in spirit . . . and so on.[9]

Despite considerable misunderstanding at the time, the 'Beat Generation' was essentially a religious movement rather than a literary movement, though granted one that was rebelling against religious orthodoxy and conventional practice. Their rejection of the mid-twentieth century versions of Protestant-Catholic-Jewish traditions was taken as a wholesale rejection of religion. Furthermore they were accused of not only rejecting religion but meaning itself. In standing out against the prevailing culture and society and questioning conventional values they were caricatured as anti-social deviants bent on the pursuit of crime, violence and hedonism. Responding to a critic who described his poem 'Howl' as a nihilistic 'howl against civilization,' Allen Ginsberg defended the poem as a prophetic utterance. Speaking of *Howl and Other poems* (1956) he said, 'The poems are religious and I meant them to be.' Similarly, Kerouac responded to the charge that the Beats were 'nay sayers': 'I want to speak for things,' he explained, '

> For the crucifix I speak out, for the Star of Israel I speak out, for the divinest man who ever lived who was German (Bach) I speak out, for sweet Mohammed I speak out, for Buddha I speak out, for Lao-tse and Chuang-tse I speak out.'[10]

When Allen Ginsberg was asked whether the Beats were first and foremost artists or spiritual seekers, he responded that the two were inseparable citing the Milarepa school of Tibetan Buddhism where to be a lama one must also be an archer, a calligrapher, or a poet. 'The life of poetry,' he said, 'is a sacramental life on earth.'

The three Beat writers most involved in Buddhism were Jack Kerouac, Gary Snyder and Allen Ginsberg. Of these, Snyder spent much of the late-1950s in Japan and Ginsberg's more rigorous involvement in Buddhism developed later. So it was Kerouac who for that crucial time in the 1950s was the most prolific of the 'Beat Buddhists' leading the way in the communication of ideas and sparking new interest.

Kerouac's interest in Buddhism went beyond the study of Eastern religious texts. In the mid-1950s he chanted *The Diamond Sutra* (his favourite Buddhist scripture), meditated daily, and attempted for months at a time to live the ascetic and celibate life of a Buddhist monk. He translated Buddhist texts from French into English and took notes on his Buddhist studies that swelled to become *Some of the Dharma* (unpublished until 1997). Although both this and his account of the life of Shakyamuni Buddha, *Wake Up*, remained unpublished during his lifetime, a book of Buddhist poems, *Mexico City Blues* (1959), and a sutra called *The Scripture of the Golden Eternity* (1960) provided early published evidence of his Buddhist concerns, as did novels such as *The Dharma Bums* (1958), *Tristessa* (1960), *Visions of Gerard* (1963) and *Desolation Angels* (1965).

Buddhism appealed to Kerouac, in part at least, because of his sense of compassion and acute awareness of human suffering and the possibility he found in Buddhism to transcend such suffering and death. He was also drawn to the idea that the phenomenal world is in some sense illusory and dream-like. Although the popular press associated the Beats with Zen Buddhism, Kerouac was not drawn so much to Zen as to Mahayana Buddhism, he was less concerned with attaining mystical insight than cultivating compassion—in Mahayana the enlightened one is both a *Tathagata* and a *Bodhisattva*. The *Tathagata* passes through the world without any attachments, whilst the *Bodhisattva* is one who refuses personal salvation as longs as other beings remain unsaved. In this respect his Buddhism remained deeply Christian. Burroughs referred to him disparagingly as 'a *Catholic-Buddhist*.'

The one aspect of Zen which did connect with Kerouac however is the *haiku*, formally a three-line, seventeen syllable poem which so conveys a moment or image that one is almost able to experience it oneself. The spontaneity of the *haiku* and its time collapse and transcendence of subject and object powerfully connects with Kerouac's own developments in his writing technique—the spontaneous composition in stream of consciousness in which he sought to use the movements and patterns of his own mind as his subject matter. The first and most famous example of this technique was the composition of *On The Road* written on a continuous scroll over three weeks in April 1951 fuelled, according to legend, by Benzedrine and caffeine. After assimilating the haikus of masters such as Basho, Issa and Shiki, Kerouac produced a large number of haiku that contemporary Zen poets regard as among the best in English.

So when Jack Kerouac began seriously reading Eastern texts in the San Jose public library in February 1954, his affinity with the teachings was immediate. Both Kerouac's sense of compassion for the down-and-out, the 'beat,' who populated his novels, and his revolutionary new method of 'spontaneous bop prosody' found striking resonance with Eastern thought.

Yet in the introduction to *Lonesome Traveller*, Kerouac made the claim that he was 'actually not "beat" but a strange solitary crazy Catholic mystic,' whose final plans were, 'hermitage in the woods, quiet writing of old-age, mellow hopes of paradise (which comes to everybody anyway)...'

As early as 1952 he was planning, 'Someday I am going to be a hermit in the woods ... very soon now I'll visit my site.'[11] In *Some of the Dharma*, he again articulated his decision to become a hermit, patterning himself after Thoreau in his hut at Walden Pond. Sounds familiar.

Merton and the East

Meanwhile by 1954, down in the Kentucky backwoods, Merton was just beginning his own deeper exploration of Eastern thought and Zen in particular. By July 1956, when Merton attended a gathering in Chicago to meet the psychologist Gregory Zilboorg, we begin to hear about dinner table conversations about Zen, and that back at the monastery Merton has been going on and on about Zen.[12] His interest in Eastern thought goes back much further, though it had lain dormant during his early years of monkish enthusiasm during the 1940s. At Columbia University he had met a Hindu monk, Bramachari, who advised Merton not to read Hindu scriptures, but first to explore the mystical writings of Christianity—especially Augustine's *Confessions* and *The Imitation of Christ* by Thomas à Kempis. In studying Blake for his Masters dissertation in 1938 we find 'Suzuki—Zen Buddhism' on the reading list in Merton's Columbia Blake notebooks—though it is not ticked so it is unlikely that Merton read it at this point, but already there is perhaps a note for future reference; and we do find a couple of quotations from Chuang Tzu even at this early stage.[13] Whilst at Columbia also, Robert Lax recommended Aldous Huxley's book on mysticism, *Ends and Means*, which introduced him to apophatic mysticism – a knowledge of God gained by negation – that would later enable him to relate to Buddhist teachings about the Void and Emptiness. Going back further still in 1930, whilst still at Oakham, Merton defended Gandhi and his claims for home rule for India in a debate with the captain of the school's rugby team and head prefect.

But it was during the 1950s, at the same time that Kerouac and the Beats were discovering Buddhism, that Merton's interest in the East was re-kindled and became a major focus of his attention. In 1959 he wrote to D.T. Suzuki for the first time:

> ... when I read your books – and I have read many of them – and above all when I read English versions of the little verses in which the Zen masters point their finger to something which flashed out at the time, I feel a profound and intimate agreement. Time after time, as I read your pages, something in me says, 'That's it!' Don't ask me what. I have no desire to explain it to anybody, or to justify it to anybody, or to analyze it for myself. I have my own way to walk, and for some reason or other Zen is right in the middle of it wherever I go. So there it is, with all its beautiful purposelessness...[14]

In the letter, Merton asks Suzuki to write a preface for a collection he was preparing of the writings of the fourth and fifth century Desert

Fathers, because of 'a kind of Zen quality they have about them.' Suzuki agreed to do this, but the plan was blocked by Merton's superiors who felt that a preface by a Zen Buddhist scholar to a book of sayings by Christian Desert Fathers would be 'inappropriate.' The piece together with a response by Merton was published in the journal New Directions in 1961, and is included in the collection of essays Zen and the Birds of Appetite (1968). Eventually Merton was given special permission to meet Suzuki in New York in June 1964.

Merton also co-operated with John Wu in the production of The Way of Chuang Tzu (1965), a 'translation' of the sayings of the ancient Chinese philosopher; he also put together a collection of essays Mystics and Zen Masters (1967). His 1963 collection of poems, Emblems of a Season of Fury, also illustrates the depth to which Buddhism and Zen were influencing his thinking.[15] This also applies to much of his writing from the late 1950s onwards—even where it is not explicitly noted.

Merton as Dharma Bum

I have sketched out something of the place of Buddhism amongst the Beats, and how it connected with Jack Kerouac in particular; and I have briefly outlined Merton's growing involvement with Buddhism and the East and his particular interest in Zen. I now want to look at the ways in which Merton's connection with the East coincides with that of the Beats.

The two primary aspects of Eastern thought and experience that connected with the Beats were the sense of compassion and affirmation of life in the face of suffering and death, and the direct unmediated experience or insight into reality. These two aspects are illustrated for Merton in his famous defining and transforming experience in downtown Louisville on March 18th 1958, by which time he was well into his Buddhist studies:

> In Louisville, at the corner of Fourth and Walnut, in the center of the shopping district, I was suddenly overwhelmed with the realization that I loved all those people, that they were mine and I theirs, that we could not be alien to one another even though we were total strangers. It was like waking from a dream of separateness, of spurious self-isolation in a special world, the world of renunciation and supposed holiness... But it cannot be explained. There is no way of telling people that they are all walking around shining like the sun.[16]

This is a *satori*, in the sense of a sudden, instantaneous, unmediated revelation of reality—an awakening as if from a dream. And the content of this *satori* is clearly that of compassion—Merton realizes that he is at one with suffering humanity. There is a new level of consciousness here not simply of recognizing his own humanity but of somehow becoming aware of his identification with all humanity—the world flowing in his bloodstream.

Part of the reason for choosing this well known passage is that I came across a remarkably similar experience recounted by Kerouac in a letter to Allen Ginsberg in January 1955:

> Now let me give you this: on the subway yesterday [Jan 17, 1955], as I read the Diamond Sutra, not that, the Surangama Sutra, I realized that everybody in the subway and all their thoughts and interests and the subway itself and their poor shoes and gloves etc. and the cellophane paper on the floor and the poor dust in the corners was all of one suchness and essence. I thought, "Mind essence loves everything, because it knows why everything is." And I saw that these people, and myself to a lesser extent, are all buried in selfhood which we took to be real...but the only real is the One, the One Essence that all's made of, and so we also took our limited and perturbed and contaminated minds (hankering after appointments, worries, sorrows, love) to be our own True Mind, but I saw True Mind itself, Universal and One, entertains no arbitrary ideas about these different seeming self-hangs on form, mind is IT itself, the IT [...] If I sit with True Mind and like Chinese sit with Tao and not with self but by no-self submission with arms hanging to let the karma work itself out, I will gain enlightenment by seeing the world as a poor dream.[17]

The parallels are quite remarkable—'seeing the world as a poor dream' and the sense of waking up to reality (and the literal meaning of 'Buddha' is 'an awakened being') and the sense of compassion through his identification with not just the people on the subway but with all-that-is as being of one essence. The thrust of the insight is very similar to Merton's though expressed in more 'Buddhist' terms and being more radical in encompassing not simply all humanity but all reality. And we may blush when Kerouac disingenuously regards himself as buried in selfhood 'to a lesser extent' than those around him, but perhaps we blush knowing that is how we are too—because such an attitude seems to be inherent when we come to realize this oneness and the illusoriness of the isolated self. It's there in Merton as well: 'There is no way of telling people that they are all walking around shining like the sun.' It cannot be explained—but this, too, connects with the Buddhist awareness that enlightenment cannot be communicated, it has to be experienced. I can look you in the eye and tell you that you are walking around shining like the sun, but it won't mean anything to you unless you experience that too. You might feel a warm glow in your heart, but that is perhaps the warmth of my light falling upon you—which may in turn of course draw forth the light in you. There is a paradox, one that thwarts us in all our many attempts to communicate, all our words: I can perhaps shake you whilst you slumber, but I cannot wake up for you.

As the Pali canon says, 'When all conditions are removed, all ways of telling are also removed.'[18] Experience is untranslatable, it cannot be captured accurately in words, language can only hint at it, point toward it. So Kerouac says in The Scripture of the Golden Eternity:

> When you've understood this scripture, throw it
> away. If you can't understand this scripture,
> throw it away. I insist on your freedom.[19]

This talk of things that cannot be communicated but only hinted at or pointed towards has immediate resonance both with what Merton had to say about contemplation and what D.T. Suzuki said about Zen, providing further clues as to why Merton was drawn to Eastern thought. In the first chapter of New Seeds of Contemplation he writes:

> Contemplation is the highest expression of…intellectual and spir-
> itual life. It is that life itself, fully awake, fully active, fully aware
> that it is alive. It is spiritual wonder. It is spontaneous awe at the
> sacredness of life, of being.

Such could be also read as a description of the Beats and their outlook on life—you can almost see Neal Cassady standing there before you! Merton continues:

> It can be suggested by words, by symbols, but in the very moment
> of trying to indicate what it knows the contemplative mind takes
> back what it has said, and denies what it has affirmed.[20]

This compares with what D.T. Suzuki says in his Introduction to Zen Buddhism, 'Zen teaches nothing; it merely enables us to wake up and become aware. It does not teach, it points.'[21] And when Merton goes on to say, 'contemplation is a sudden gift of awareness, an awakening to the Real within all that is real. A vivid awareness of infinite Being at the roots of our own limited being,'[22] it is almost an exact description of his experience at Fourth and Walnut, and of Kerouac's experience on the New York subway.

Merton's words come from *New Seeds of Contemplation* published in 1961 after he had been studying Buddhism and Zen for sometime; it is highly likely therefore that his view here on contemplation is influenced by this study. However it is not too difficult to see how this also flows out of his earlier study of the Christian mystics, particularly figures such as St John of the Cross and Meister Eckhart.[23]

In Conclusion

Merton and the Beats came to find themselves coinciding in a whole area of thought and spirituality and outlook at roughly the same time. I am not aware of particularly strong links between them, though they both spent formative periods of their lives at Columbia University (the Beats arriving just after Merton had left) and it is true that Merton's close friend at Columbia, Bob Lax, also became a good friend of Jack Kerouac during the 1950s, and published some of his work. Merton also published a couple of Kerouac's poems in *Monk's Pond* in 1968. But I would not argue that either had any significant influence on the other at this point. Rather they had come from different directions to the ground on which they found themselves together : the Beats via Times Square and their visions that all life is holy; and Merton via the Kentucky backwoods and his encounters with the ancient Christian mystics. Both were struggling for a breakthrough of some sort—a sloughing off of an old skin, to be discarded inside out, with an emergence into a new state of being, a new consciousness, a new creation.

I feel I have only just begun to scratch the surface of this whole topic. The questions that still remain for me concern how in detail the 'Beat perspective' worked itself out through Buddhist ideas and practice; and how Merton's contemplative Zen spirituality was born of, and gave expression to, his own inner 'Beatness.' I find myself therefore, once again, with more questions than answers but conscious too that as I read Merton and as I read the Beats (Kerouac especially) the connections they are making with me are remarkably similar. Both Kerouac and Merton speak to me at a deep level—if I was to try and make a distinction, I would say that Kerouac is raw experience whereas Merton helps me make sense of this. But at the end of the day they blur into one another.

Epilogue

Kerouac aspired to Thoreau's ideal of a hermitage in the woods; Merton eventually achieved it: after spending much time in the early sixties in the hermitage within the monastery grounds he moved there full time in 1965. But in 1968 he was invited to make a trip to Asia and so he too at last hits the road bound for the East—by heading west (like Kerouac). On October 15th his plane took off from San Francisco:

> Joy. We left the ground—I with Christian mantras and a great sense of destiny, of being at last on my true way after years of waiting and wondering and fooling around... May I not come back without having settled the great affair. And found also the great compassion, *mahakaruna*... I am going home, to the home where I have never been in this body.[24]

And so he did. The culmination of his trip came on December 1st when he visited the shrine at Polonnaruwa in Ceylon with its huge Buddha statues. On December 4th he wrote in his journal:

> Looking at these figures I was suddenly, almost forcibly, jerked clean out of the habitual, half-tied vision of things, and an inner clearness, clarity, as if exploding from the rocks themselves, became evident and obvious... All problems are resolved and everything is clear. The rock, all matter, all life, is charged with dharmakaya...everything is emptiness and everything is compassion. I don't know when in my life I have ever had such a sense of beauty and spiritual validity running together in one aesthetic illumination. Surely...my Asian pilgrimage has come clear and purified itself. I mean, I know and have seen what I was obscurely looking for. I don't know what else remains but I have now seen and have pierced through the surface and have got beyond the shadow and the disguise.[25]

The very next day after Merton wrote this, on Friday December 5th, Kerouac wrote in a letter to his brother-in-law of his recent trip from Lowell, Massachusetts to his new home in St Petersburg, Florida:

> We made Lowell to St Petersburg in less than 24 hours, 1600 miles or so – We were stopped for speeding in South Carolina but when the cop saw Mémère and the cats and Stella in the back he just told us to pull over to a station and have our rear warning lights refurbished – [...] I stayed awake all the way, drinking and yelling and playing harmonica and watching that old road, as usual...[26]

Notes and References

1. Jack Kerouac, On The Road. New York, Viking, 1957; Penguin, 1972, pp.12-13. Also see Gerald Nicosia, Memory Babe: A Critical Biography of Jack Kerouac. New York, Viking, 1983, p.188

2. Thomas Merton, Entering the Silence: Becoming a Monk and Writer: The Journals of Thomas Merton, Vol. 2 1941-1952 (ed. Jonathan Montaldo). San Francisco, HarperSanFrancisco, 1996, p.91

3. Robert Inchausti, Thomas Merton's American Prophecy. New York, SUNY, 1998, p.5

4. Angus Stuart, 'Visions of Tom: Jack Kerouac's Monastic Elder Brother.' The Merton Journal Vol. 8 (1), 2001, pp.40-46 See also: http://pages.britishlibrary.net/thomasmerton/kerouac.htm

5. Thomas Merton, Zen and the Birds of Appetite. New York, New Directions, 1968, p.ix

6. Gerald Nicosia, op.cit.pp.139, 272, 457-459; Carole Tonkinson (ed.), Big Sky Mind: Buddhism and The Beat Generation. New York, Riverhead, 1995, p.2, 24

7. Nancy Wilson Ross cited in The Asian Journal of Thomas Merton. New York, New Directions, 1973 & 1975, p.372

8. Gerald Nicosia, op.cit.p.252

9. See 'Beatific: The Origins of the Beat Generation' (1959) in The Portable Jack Kerouac (ed. Ann Charters). New York, Viking Penguin, 1995, pp.565-573

10. Quoted in Stephen Prothero's introduction to Tonkinson (ed.), op.cit. p.8 cf 'Beatific: The Origins of the Beat Generation' (1959) see The Portable Jack Kerouac, op. cit p.556

11. Jack Kerouac, Selected Letters 1946-1956 (ed. Ann Charters). New York, Penguin, 1995, p.371

12. Michael Mott, The Seven Mountains of Thomas Merton. London, Sheldon Press, 1986. pp.293-294, see also note 352 on p.611

13. ibid. pp.117-118, see also note 75 on p.589

14. Letter to D.T. Suzuki March 12, 1959 in The Hidden Ground of Love: Letters on Religious Experience and Social Concerns (ed. William H. Shannon). London, Collins, 1990, p.561 (also New York, Farrar, Straus & Giroux, 1985)

15. See "Thomas Merton's Poetry: Emblems of a Sacred Season" by Alan Altany at http://140.190.128.190/merton/altany2.html

16. Thomas Merton, Conjectures of a Guilty Bystander. New York, Image, Doubleday, 1968, 1989, pp.156-157

17. Jack Kerouac, Selected Letters 1940-1956, op.cit. p.460-461 Letter to Allen Ginsberg dated January 18, 1955.

18. Cited in the introduction by Stephen Prothero in Tonkinson (ed), op.cit.p.20

19. Jack Kerouac, The Scripture of the Golden Eternity. San Francisco, City Lights, 1994, p.46 (Originally published in 1960 by Corinth Books, New York)

20. Thomas Merton, Seeds of Contemplation. Wheathamstead: Anthony Clarke, 1972, p.1 (Originally published as New Seeds of Contemplation in 1962 by Burns & Oates.)

21. D.T. Suzuki, Introduction to Zen Buddhism. Grove Press, 1991, p.38

22. Thomas Merton, Seeds of Contemplation, op.cit.p.2

23. An interesting study charting the development of his thought would be a detailed comparison of New Seeds of Contemplation with his earlier work Seeds of Contemplation (1948) that he was so anxious to have superseded – even so far as

wanting to retain the original title for the new book. Actually this has already been done, see: Donald Grayston (ed.), *Thomas Merton's Rewritings: The Five Versions of "Seeds/New Seeds of Contemplation" as a Key to the Development of His Thought (Studies in Art and Religious Interpretation)*. Lewiston, New York, Edwin Mellen Press, 1989

24. *The Asian Journal of Thomas Merton*, op. cit. pp. 4-5

25. ibid. pp. 233-236

26. Jack Kerouac, *Selected Letters 1957-1969* (ed. Ann Charters). New York, Viking Penguin, 1999, p. 525-526

Thomas Merton and Dorothy Day: the marriage of contemplation and action: a call to radical hospitality

DICK BERENDES & EARL JOSEPH MADARY

IN THIS PAPER WE CELEBRATE the relationship of Thomas Merton and Dorothy Day and their mutual infusion of radical hospitality into contemplative action. Through the letters of Dorothy and Father Louis (Merton), this paper will explore the personalism at the heart of the thinking of both of them, and how this relates to their attitudes towards non-violent resistance, social action, and pacifism. Thomas Merton was a citizen of the world. Dorothy Day a woman of the North American streets. They lived their Christian vocations a universe apart. Merton cloistered, and Day on the move. Yet through their letters we find many exciting bridges in their journeys. They both were converts, writers, activists, and citizens of the twentieth century, students of literature, western and eastern mystics, and scripture, and profoundly committed to prayer. Merton and Day, living the radical call of hospitality, challenged the members of their community and the wider social structures of their day. This call continues to challenge us to deeper contemplation and more direct action.

'Personalism' is about the human person and the person's accountability for self before God, the world, and finally most deeply and difficultly to oneself. Personalism became the lifeblood that flowed through the veins of the Catholic Worker movement and continues to pump life into that movement today. It is an outlook and way of being that unites the seemingly disparate worlds of a North American lay movement, the Catholic Worker, and a Trappist monk living in a hermitage. Both Dorothy Day and Thomas Merton demonstrate the synergies of personalism and a personal commitment to accountability in their own writings and in their specific correspondence with each other. For this discussion we will explore briefly the role of personalism in the roots of the Catholic Worker movement before considering it in relation to Dorothy Day and then Thomas Merton, and specifically the significance of personalism in the correspondence between Day and Merton. This foundation and these letters provide a paradigm of contemplative action built on prayer, conscience, obedience, and action.

Personalism and the Catholic Worker

In May of 1933 the *Catholic Worker* newspaper appeared in New York for the first time. The first edition became the tangible expression of a year-long dialogue between Dorothy Day and Peter Maurin. Peter Maurin had come to Dorothy Day in 1932 with his plan of action for 'social transformation.' His simple and radical plan was made up of three distinct parts: houses of hospitality, clarification of thought, and agrarian reform. These three tenets were fueled and defined by Peter's passionate commitment to *personalism*. Dorothy Day, already an active advocate for the poor and the worker, found a ready home in Maurin's ideas and dreams. The personalist focus on the human person and that person's radical accountability for their own response to God, the world, and self quickly became the foundational paradigm of the movement.

Many people have found in the personalism of the Catholic Worker movement a new vision and a way of life, a way to simply live the Gospels and their Catholic faith, and a model for a communitarian and personalist non-violent evolution in order to change the social order. Sometimes discouraged about the possibility of making any changes in our world, they have found in Peter Maurin and Dorothy Day' people who are examples, witnesses to a vital, lively faith and holiness which translates into hospitality for the poorest of the poor and all the works of mercy, into work for peace, not waiting for the government or other agency structures to ponderously begin to do something, but who simply try to act as Jesus did, or as He asks His followers to do in the Sermon on the Mount and Matthew 25:31ff.

Peter Maurin introduced personalism and the ideas of Emmanuel Mounier to Dorothy Day and to the Catholic Worker movement. As Dorothy said, he brought to us "great books, and great ideas, and great men, so that over the years, we have become a school for the service of God here and now." (D. Day, "Peter's Program," *Catholic Worker*, May 1955, p.2). However, when he introduced Mounier to the *Worker*, he did not present him as the very beginning of personalism in the Catholic Church. As Dorothy Day later mentioned, "Peter is always getting back to Saint Francis of Assisi, who was most truly the 'great personalist.'" (Day, CW, Sept., 1945, p.6). Peter knew that Mounier was bringing together the best of personalist ideas from the history and theology of the Church for this century.[1]

The thrust and meaning of personalism is vividly illustrated in Peter Maurin's poem, 'The Personalist':

The Personalist

> A personalist
> is a go-giver,
> not a go-getter.
> He tries to give
> what he has,
> and does not
> try to get
> what the other fellow has.
> He tries to be good
> by doing good
> to the other fellow.
> He is altro-centered,
> not self-centered.
> He has a social doctrine
> of the common good.
> He spreads the social doctrine
> of the common good
> through words and deeds.
> He speaks through deeds
> as well as words,
> for he knows that deeds
> speak louder than words.
> Through words and deeds
> he brings into existence
> a community,
> the common unity
> of a community.
> *Peter Maurin*[2]

The personalism proposed by Peter Maurin was not ever to be confused with a self-centered individualism. Nor could it ever be compared to Marxist social paradigms. Quite the contrary, this personalism was imbued with an intense movement towards community founded on ideal and action. In Peter and Dorothy's personalism faith, not the state, is the highest authority. Conscience tempered by obedience is the highest law. Action defined and informed by prayer is the rule. The only measure of conviction is the direct response of the individual.

Personalism and Dorothy Day

Her presence is in some ways a comfort, and in some ways a reproach.   *Thomas Merton*[3]

We are urging our readers to be neither collectivist nor individualist, but personalist. This consciousness of oneself as a member of the mystical Body of Christ will lead to great things.   *Dorothy Day*[4]

Dorothy Day was fond of sharing one of her favourite Dostoevsky folktales, *The Old Woman and the Onion*. Here is an updated version that will illustrate Dorothy's views on personalism. There was an old hag who was bitter and lonely and lived a life of harsh greediness toward all creation. One day, while at work in her garden, she dropped dead. She awoke standing before the gates of heaven and St Peter. He asked, 'Dear Sister, what righteousness, what kindness, what mercy do you wear as a crown to join the royal banquet feast of heaven?' Now the old hag was bitter, but honest, so she answered, 'Nothing.' 'Nothing?' Peter asked, 'Really nothing?' 'Nothing,' she replied. Peter with sorrow pulled the great lever to the gates of the abyss and she fell through. Millions of miles through countless screaming hordes of shame and anguish she fell until she landed with a great splash in the lake of fire. And all the demons of hell clapped and cheered!

The old hag and her poverty of virtue haunted Peter. He called for Michael, the great Archangel. He came swiftly hovering over Peter with his awful beauty. 'Michael, servant of God, search the universe. There must be one deed she could wear.' Michael went to look and to search the depths of the oceans, the valleys of Titan, the mountains of our moon and there, near the Sea of Tranquility he found it. One, old, rotten onion. He raced with angelic fury to Peter and showed him the prize. 'You see,' he told Peter, 'once the old hag was weeding her garden and Jesus appeared in the form of a beggar. He asked for food and she threw him this onion.' Peter smiled and offered, 'God is merciful. Give it a try!' Peter pulled the great lever and Michael swept down the millions of miles to the lake of fire. The demons hissed and booed. Michael flew out to the old hag and held out the rotten onion. He said, 'Grab on.' She did, and the onion held. Michael began to pull her from the fire. The other damned seeing her escape began to swim to her and grab on and so on and so on, until all the damned were hanging on to her, hanging on to the onion. When they could almost see the gates of heaven the old hag thought, 'That's my onion!' and at that moment the onion crumbled and they all fell back into the lake of fire. The demons cheered and the damned wept. Michael flew back down and hovered over the old hag. Michael wept as well and as his tears hit the flames bitter steam rose into the abyss. Michael said, 'You fools, don't you know? Either everyone goes home or nobody does.'

Indeed, in the personalist revolution of Dorothy Day nobody was expendable. Every human person had and has the potential to bring the saving power of Christ and his love to the world. All human beings bear the indelible image of the maker and are worthy of mercy, respect, hope, and ultimately love. The love of God and the love of their fellow human beings. This love finally is characterized by the willful and free choice to be a lover. The mark of love is freedom and the mark of slavery is always terror. Free will becomes the standard in any personalist response.

> We are working for a personalist revolution because we believe in the dignity of man, the temple of the Holy Ghost, so beloved by God that He sent His son to take upon Himself our sins and die an ignominious and disgraceful death for us. We are personalists because we believe that man, a person, a creature of body and soul, is greater than the State, of which as an individual he is a part. We are personalists because we oppose the vesting of all authority in the hands of the State instead of in the hands of Christ the King. We are personalists because we believe in free will, and not the economic determinism of the communist philosophy.   *Dorothy Day*[5]

Personalism and Thomas Merton

> *Afternoon* – the primary duty: to seek coherence, clarity, awareness, insofar as these are possible. Not only human coherence and clarity but also those that are born of silence, emptiness and grace. Which means always seeking the right balance between study, work, meditation, responsibility to others, and solitude. *Thomas Merton*[6]

The right balance between self and others. Thomas Merton like his contemporary Dorothy Day expressed clearly his conviction that the human person was a direct 'epiphany' of God. The life of a monk is filled with moments of self-reflection and self-examination. The order of the divine office names the hours of existence and in its prayer calls the monk to ordered accountability. Constantly emptying the monk of his own will and replacing it with the divine will. This 'perfection' is only possible because the monk, like any other human, bears the likeness and the potential of the creator. Thomas Merton expresses innumerable times, in his writings and journals, his conviction and commitment to the dignity of the human person. Emmanuel Mounier's *A Personalist Manifesto* was common reading for Catholic intellectuals of the mid-twentieth century. It is not so far fetched to imagine that Merton was well familiar with Mounier's benchmark work on personalism. Especially when one considers the consistent personalist themes that fill Merton's prose and poetry.

> The joy that I am a man! This fact that I am a man, is a theological truth and mystery. God became man in Christ. In becoming what I am, He united me to Himself and made me His epiphany, so that now I am meant to reveal Him. My very existence as true man depends on this: that by my freedom I obey His light, thus enabling Him to reveal Himself in me. And the first to see this revelation is my own self. I am His mission to myself and, through myself, to all men. How can I see Him or receive Him if I despise or fear what I am—man? How can I love what I am – man – if I hate man in others?[7]

It is significant to note that in 1965 when Merton made this journal entry he was in the midst of an active correspondence with Dorothy Day. This correspondence began in 1959 and continued until his untimely death in 1968.

Personalism in the Correspondence :
Prayer, Conscience, Obedience, and Action

We despise everything that Christ loves, everything marked with His compassion. We love fatness, health, bursting smiles, the radiance of satisfied bodies all properly fed and rested and sated and washed and perfumed and sexually relieved. Anything else is a horror and a scandal to us. How sad. It makes me more and more sad and ashamed, for I am part of the society which has these values and I can't help sharing its guilt, its illusions. Whether I like it or

not I help perpetuate the illusion in one way or another—by a kind
of illusion of spirituality which tends to justify the other and make
it more smug on the rebound. And I am not poor here. I wonder if I
am true to Christ, if I have obeyed His will. I have obeyed men, all
right. I have perhaps been too ready to obey them. I am not so sure
I have obeyed my Lord. The equation is sometimes temptingly
oversimplified. Do please pray above all that I may really and from
my deepest heart obey Him, it is crucially important now.

Thomas Merton to Dorothy Day, August 17, 1960[8]

Merton in this letter to Day works to clarify his understanding
of himself. He wonders aloud about his vocation and his life of
obedience. Has he been too willing to obey others and not willing
enough to obey his conscience, his own heart? Merton struggles to
find a complete and yet not overly simple understanding of his own
person. To really see himself as he is and not what he may appear to be.
This intense retrospective restlessness echoes Mounier in *Be Not Afraid*
where he writes, 'The Personalist is desolate, he is surrounded, on the
move, under summons.'[9] This reflection on his own personhood
forces Merton's thoughts to his relationship with world. For as Merton
writes 'How can I see Him or receive Him if I despise or fear what I
am—man? How can I love what I am – man – if I hate man in others?'
It is these questions that Merton asks that form the core of his life of
social action. How can he be human, made in the likeness of God, and
not be engaged in the world of humans? From the solitude of the
monk's hermitage a stream of action directed by prayer and
conscience begins to flow.

> Every night we say the rosary and compline in our little chapel over
> the barn, heavy with the smell of the cow downstairs and we have a
> bulletin board there with names of those who ask for prayer. Yours is
> there. There are half a dozen old men, several earnest ones, an old
> woman from the Bowery, a former teacher with one eye, a mother
> of an illegitimate child and so on. We all say the rosary, only six
> remain for compline. Do pray for us too. Your writing has reached
> many, many people and started them on their way. Be assured of
> that. It is the work that God wants of you, no matter how much you
> want to run away from it. Like the Curé of Ars. God bless you
> always.
>
> *Dorothy Day to Thomas Merton, October 10, 1960*[10]

Day recognizes the power of Merton's words to call into being radical
action. Radical in the true root of the word, that is to 'return to the

roots.' Day encourages Merton to continue; to accept his summons and to actively pursue it. Early in their correspondence we see a dependence on each other for prayer. Day's hands chaffed from dishes and floors, Merton's back bent from study, both hearts looking into the darkness of doubt. Their mutual concern seems to have been a great comfort and solace to them both.

> This, Dorothy, is sometimes a very great problem to me. Because I feel obligated to take very seriously what is going on, and to say whatever my conscience seems to dictate, provided of course it is not contrary to the faith and the teaching authority of the Church. Obedience is a most essential thing in any Christian and above all in a monk, but I sometimes wonder if, being in a situation where obedience would completely silence a person on some important moral issue on which others are also keeping silence – a crucial issue like nuclear war – then I would be inclined to wonder if it were not God's will to ask to change my situation.
>
> Thomas Merton to Dorothy Day, August 23, 1961[11]

As the letters continue between Day and Merton we see Merton focus more and more on his conscience as the catalyst for his action. Merton's journals confirm this. The struggle to discern the will of God in his conscience and yet to remain engaged actively in the life of the community: the monastic community, the ecclesial community, and community of all human beings. As the stakes rise in national and global issues Merton's summons to write, speak, and act becomes translucent. As Merton enters the public discourse his commitment to the person and personalism becomes very clear.

> Persons are known not by the intellect alone, not by the principles alone, but only by love. It is when we love the other, the enemy, that we obtain from God the key to an understanding of who he is, and who we are. It is only this realization that can open to us the real nature of our duty, and of right action. To shut out the person and to refuse to consider him as a person, as an other self, we resort to the impersonal "law" and to abstract "nature".
>
> Thomas Merton to Dorothy Day, December 20, 1961[12]

Merton clearly expresses personalism in this letter. This example could be put parallel to Peter Maurin and Dorothy Day's writings on person-alism and found to be an almost perfect match. We see in this example Merton's focus on love as the primary key to understanding who we might be in relationship to God, others, and finally ourselves. Again, Merton struggles to understand the role of obedience in being true to his own understanding of self and the call of all people to 'the real nature of our duty, and of right action.' Yet in the midst of his doubts concerning obedience this letter shows a deepening resolve to action. Merton is becoming a model of personalism. Merton's prayer is defining his conscience, his conscience is defining his obedience, and his obedience is creating his action.

> I am probably going to Rome April 16 with a group from *Women Strike for Peace* who are foolishly expecting to get an audience. I told them it will probably be with 500 other people but a pilgrimage is a pilgrimage and if we can call attention to all the things the Pope has been saying about peace, that in itself is good. We can send our message of thanks to him and if you have any suggestions to offer and if you by any chance get this letter at once instead of having to wait until Easter, do write and let me know what you think.
>
> Dorothy Day to Thomas Merton, March 17, 1963 [13]

It seems clear that Dorothy Day depended on the counsel of Merton as well. Their relationship was based on a mutuality of purpose and outcome if not method. Thomas Merton was summoned to pray for and write on behalf of peace. Dorothy Day was summoned to pray and then to act in concrete demonstrations of her conscience. Both Merton and Day struggled during this period in their lives to achieve peace first in themselves. Dorothy had the added struggle of her daughter and son-in-law and their children. Then in their communities, the monastery at Gethsemani and the myriads of houses and communities within the Catholic Worker movement. As if their lives were not turbulent enough, the United States was engaged in a very unpopular war, the civil rights movement was struggling to breathe, and the very social fabric and society norms taken for granted were being shred and re-made into a new quilt of American society. In the centre of all this, Day and Merton continued to stand with and for the call to restorative peace and equitable justice.

Merton and Day stand as examples of personalist luminaries in the midst of the twentieth century. Their correspondence reveals lives committed to prayer and discernment of conscience. As they continued in their spiritual journeys their ideas of obedience developed in the same fashion in the context of different lifestyles: Merton, a Trappist monk; Day, a Roman Catholic laywomen engaged deeply in the social apostolate and justice advocacy; both faithful to the Christ who has summoned them both. In the relationship between

Merton and Day we find expressed and, more significantly, practiced a realistic paradigm for contemplative action. Prayer is the starting point and to quote Brother Roger of Taizé prayer is the 'school of love.' From prayer conscience is formed and defined. From conscience grows genuine obedience. Direct action is a natural consequence of obedience to self. All this being said, in the end it is their faithfulness that draws us near. Dorothy and Thomas' faithfulness to each other, their God, their Church, their world and most profoundly their own conscience. Faithfulness in times of great joy and illumination. Faithfulness that is willing to walk into the desert and peer into the dark hole of emptiness. Faithfulness to the human person made fully and wonderfully in the image of its maker. Faithfulness indeed.

Non-Violence and Pacifism

Never again war! No, never again war, which destroys the lives of innocent people, teaches how to kill, throws into upheaval even the lives of those who do the killing and leaves behind a trail of resentment and hatred, thus making it all the more difficult to find a just solution to the very problems which provoked the war.

Pope John Paul II, 1991 [14]

Both Dorothy Day and Thomas Merton rooted their ethic of social responsibility in the gospel principles of nonviolence which are demonstrated clearly in their lives and found in their writing. It is based on the conviction that love is the deepest human power. As a student at Oakham School, Merton became acquainted with, and had written on, the person and the philosophy of Mahatma Gandhi for the school newspaper. Here Merton discovered a philosophy of nonviolence in the life and writings of Gandhi who, in turn, based his beliefs on the teachings of Jesus, especially in the Sermon on the Mount. In the spirit of Jesus, Gandhi embraced a practice of nonviolence and the unconditional dedication to the truth whereby one seeks to overcome one's enemies by loving them. Merton agreed with Gandhi that nonviolence insists on the truth that human rights, including the rights of one's oppressor, deserve the utmost respect. Nonviolence seeks the good of the oppressor as well as the oppressed.

Merton adopted Gandhi's philosophy that social responsibility requires the use of nonviolent methods to promote a reasonable standard of living for all, universal opportunities for education, decent work, and participation in the political and cultural life of society. Merton also felt it was imperative that issues such as racism, the Vietnam war and nuclear war be viewed from the perspective of the obligation of conscience grounded in the principles of nonviolence. Merton came to view his monastic life as a witness of nonviolence in a violent society. Although Merton was personally committed to nonviolence, he never condemned those who acted violently in self-defense. Merton's nonviolence was grounded in humility that engages the whole person in self-control. A nonviolent lifestyle offers positive, active and effective resistance to injustice and evil if it is faithful to truth and purity of conscience. The nonviolent lifestyle testifies to the truth that love is the only really nonviolent power of resistance against the forces of violence and deception.

Both Thomas Merton and Dorothy Day sought to embrace the gospel principles of nonviolence, taking seriously Jesus' commands to love one's enemies. Dorothy Day went on to adopt a position of absolute pacifism maintaining that passive resistance is the only way to oppose one's enemies. According to her, nonviolent revolution involves prayer and austerity, prayer and self sacrifice, prayer and fasting, prayer vigils, prayer and marches. The only ethical response to violence, in the teaching of Gandhi, Merton and Day, is peaceful non-retaliation which is an exercise of both freedom and love, and an outgrowth of prayer.

Both Dorothy Day and Thomas Merton decried the decision of the United States government to deploy the atomic bomb as an approach to ending World War II. In his poem 'Original Child Bomb,' in a starkly factual way, Thomas Merton narrates the brutal bombing of Hiroshima and Nagasaki and the consequent wholesale decimation of the people that inhabited these cities. Merton would advance that the bombing violated the just war theory since civilians were the primary victims. Like Merton, Dorothy Day raised her poetic voice in protest against the United States bombing of Hiroshima and Nagasaki, when she wrote:

> We have killed 318,000 Japanese. They died vaporized, our Japanese brothers scattered, men, women and children, to the four winds, over the seven seas. Perhaps we will breathe their dust into our nostrils, feel them in the fog in New York on our faces, feel them in the rain on the hills of Easton.[15]

For Thomas Merton, conscience obliges the human family to stop using such violent means to resolve disputes and conflicts between and among nations. For Merton it was imperative that the human family dismantle the existing supply of weapons of mass destruction and stop building new ones. It is worth remembering there are two decisive events that seem to have shaken him to the core of his being, and helped to expand his thinking and writing. The first was the bombing of Hiroshima and Nagasaki and his horror at the bombing of innocent men, women and children to bring a hasty and abrupt conclusion to World War II. The second was the young draft dodger, Roger LaPorte, who ignited and burned himself to death in New York City, at which point Merton telegraphed Dorothy Day trying to distance and disassociate himself from such activities in the name of peace. Merton insisted that:

> To allow governments to pour more and more billions into weapons that almost immediately become obsolete, thereby necessitating more billions for new and bigger weapons, is one of the most colossal injustices in the long history of man. While we are doing this, two thirds of the world are starving, or living in conditions of subhuman destitution.[16]

In the case of nuclear war, Merton wholeheartedly concurs with Dorothy Day that the conditions agreed upon for a just war do not apply, because citizens were the primary target. Regarding this, Merton wrote, 'A war of total annihilation simply cannot be considered a just war, no matter how good the cause for which it is undertaken.'[17] Merton and Day agreed that nuclear war would never in conscience be justified and he challenged Catholics to refuse any jobs that involved them in the making of nuclear weapons. Merton argued that the most conscientious response to the possibility of nuclear war would be for sane people 'everywhere in the world to lay down their weapons and their tools and starve and be shot rather than cooperate in the war effort.'[18] For Merton, nuclear war would lead to suicide of nations and cultures indeed the destruction of society itself.[19]

In a letter to Dorothy Day dated August 23, 1961, Merton expressed his frustration with the Church and its leadership, for their lack of a position on nuclear armaments, when he wrote:

> But why this awful silence and apathy on the part of Catholics, clergy, hierarchy, lay people on this terrible issue on which the very continued existence of the human race depends?[20]

Like Day, Merton considered nuclear disarmament an absolute moral obligation of the human community. In essence, Merton and Day agree that the only ethical armament against nuclear war, and for that matter any war, or conflict, is love. Love alone possesses the power to affect real change in the human family which can lead to peace. Just as Merton opposes nuclear war, he considered our participation in the Vietnam war one of the worst blunders of U. S. history. Merton noted that the United States dropped more bombs on Vietnam than it exploded during World War II in its entirety, even though he didn't live to see the war to its conclusion. He emphatically declared that he was 'on the side of all those who were burned, cut to pieces, tortured, held as hostage, gassed, ruined, destroyed in Vietnam.'[21] And Dorothy Day insisted that

> Christ was crucified in the death of each person in the Vietnam war.[22]

Conscientious objection was the ethically appropriate response to the war for both Merton and Dorothy Day. In her writings and actions, Dorothy consistently urged peacemaking. She believed that peace begins in each person's heart, family, office, neighborhood, and community. And that it is a telling sign of contemporary culture that most individuals and institutions fail to see war as a problem.

Like Merton, Dorothy Day constantly regretted the huge amounts of America's national budget allocated to developing weapons of mass destruction rather than, improving the life of its people. An absolute pacifist, she maintained that war is wrong under any and all conditions because it killed, maimed and rendered people homeless and hungry, destroying the land and separating families. She demanded that all weapons of war and destruction be eliminated.

Conclusion and Reflection Post-9/11

In the correspondence between Dorothy Day and Thomas Merton from 1959 until Merton's death in 1968 a wide variety of social issues were addressed (particularly in light of Merton's faith development) that related to personalism, nonviolence and the emerging social teaching of the Church. Although Dorothy Day and Thomas Merton developed a lasting friendship, it is questionable whether they actually ever met. They may have been introduced to each other when Dorothy Day came to speak at St Bonaventure's College in 1940, when Merton was on the faculty there. But an underdeveloped Merton would probably have made very little impact on the activist Dorothy Day. Over the years of their correspondence, their relationship strengthened. It is worth noting however that even prior to their relationship, Abbot Dunne of the Abbey of Gethsemani had been a regular contributor to the New York Catholic Worker House in the 1930s. So there was in fact a relationship between these two communities prior to their letters. We are quick to call everything friendship. The relationship is important to the intellectual, social and, in some ways, moral development particularly of Merton as he tries to articulate the responsibility of action in the life of a contemplative monk. Merton characterized Dorothy as 'an example of what it means to take Christianity seriously in the twentieth century.'[23] Her total commitment to nonviolence and pacifism was clearly a source of inspiration to Merton:

> When I consider that Dorothy Day was confined to a jail cell with nothing but a light wrap, (her clothes having been taken from her) and that she could only get to Mass and Communion in prison by dressing in clothes borrowed from prostitutes and thieves in the neighboring cells, then I lose all inclination to take seriously the self complacent nonsense of those who consider her kind of pacifism sentimental.[24]

Clearly Dorothy Day was one of Thomas Merton's heroes or mentors. This was a time when he was beginning to develop his writings around the social responsibility of the Christian from his unique perspective as a twentieth century American contemplative monk. Both were convinced that love is the force that binds together prayer, conscience, and Christian responsibility. Dorothy Day and Thomas Merton were convinced that Christians who developed mature consciences must employ their informed conscience in determining the most ethical response to major issues of the time such as violence, racism, and war.

The events of September 11th, 2001 have imbedded a new date in the psyche of the people of the United States. In addition to the dates of July 4th, 1776, when America declared its independence from Great Britain; and December 7th, 1941, the bombing of Pearl Harbor by the Japanese and the subsequent entry of the U.S. into World War II, we now can add September 11th 2001, the bombing of the World Trade Center in New York City. In response to the events surrounding September 11th, 2001, the current American President wants to free the world from the evil of terrorism. The same United States of America which already consumes the overwhelming majority of the earth's goods to the exclusion of much of the world's population. The United

States would choose to eliminate terrorism by terrorizing whole nations and regions. The United States would choose to eliminate terrorism while operating the US Army School of Americas at Fort Benning, Georgia, recently renamed the Western Hemisphere Institute for Security Cooperation (WHISC), which trains terrorists as Generals and soldiers who fight against their own people in Central and South America. The United States would choose to eliminate terrorism at the same time running covert CIA operations at will. Once again by drawing together people of like minds we have identified a coalition of countries and leaders, with the British Prime Minister in so clear agreement he may as well be a cabinet member in the government of George W. Bush. The United States would free the world of terrorism at the same time considering its own people not as a royal priesthood, a people set apart, not even as citizens, but as mere things, consumers—consumers who will consume and spend themselves into prosperity and happiness.

What would Dorothy Day have to say in light of these terrorist acts? What would she have to say in light of the overwhelming military response? What would she be writing and where would she choose to protest? Sitting on what street corner? In whose driveway? What would Thomas Merton say? What would the silence of this Trappist monk have to say to us? What would Merton write?

Currently we are experiencing a deafening silence or, worse, only the complicit voices of our fellow citizens and the Christian leadership and community. To quote Gandhi,

> What difference does it make to the dead, the orphan and the homeless, whether the destruction is wrought under the name of totalitarianism or the holy name of liberty and democracy?

We need frequently to be reminded that 'some of us are uncomfortably hungry and others uncomfortably full—and it becomes clear that in our broken world we are all starved for justice.'[25]

It is clear that in the writings and examples of both Thomas Merton and Dorothy Day, personalism demands a response from us and that response must embrace the practice of nonviolence and a commitment to Catholic social teaching.

Archbishop Oscar Romero, assassinated at his own altar, reminds us:

> Peace is not the product of terror or fear. Peace is not the silence of cemeteries. Peace is not the silent result of violent repression. Peace

is the generous, tranquil contribution of all to the good of all. Peace is dynamism. Peace is generosity. It is right and it is duty.

In conclusion, we quote Peter Maurin, co-founder of the Catholic Worker movement:

> Chesterton says,
> "The Christian ideal
> has not been tried
> and found wanting.
> It has been found difficult
> and left untried."
> Christianity has not been tried
> because people thought
> it was impractical.
> And men have tried everything
> except Christianity.
> And everything
> that men have tried
> has failed.[26]

It is our hope that some of what has been said here will spark a difficult yet fundamental response that welcomes the strangers (enemies) with warmth and generosity. Such a response to the gospel imperative, 'Love your neighbour, do good to those who hate you' would indeed be radical hospitality.

Notes and References

1. Mark and Louise Zwick, 'Roots of the Catholic Worker Movement: Emmanuel Mounier, Personalism, and the Catholic Worker movement,' *Houston Catholic Worker*, July-August, 1999. Available at: http://www.cjd.org/paper/roots/rmounier.html

2. http://www.cjd.org/paper/roots/rperson.html

3. Thomas Merton in the Foreword to Dorothy Day, *Loaves and Fishes*. San Francisco, Harper and Row, 1963

4. Dorothy Day, *Loaves and Fishes*. San Francisco, Harper and Row, 1963

5. *ibid.*

6. Thomas Merton, December 11th 1962 from *The Intimate Merton, His Life From His Journals* (ed. Patrick Hart and Jonathon Montaldo). San Francisco, HarperSanFrancisco, 1999, p.198

7. Thomas Merton, August 13th 1965, *ibid.* pp.254-255

8. Thomas Merton, *The Hidden Ground of Love*, (ed. William H. Shannon). New York, Farrar, Straus & Giroux, 1985, p.138

9. Emmanuel Mounier, *Be Not Afraid: Studies in Personalist Sociology*. New York, Harper & Bro, 1954

10. Department of Special Collections and University Archives, Marquette University Libraries, 1415 W. Wisconsin Avenue, P.O. Box 3141, Milwaukee, WI 53201-3141 http://www.marquette.edu/library/collections/archives/day.html

11. Thomas Merton, *The Hidden Ground of Love*, op. cit. p.139

12. *ibid*. p.141

13. The Marquette University Archives (see note 10 above).

14. Pope John Paul II, Encyclical Letter Centesimus Annus (May 1, 1991), 52. Available online at: http://www.vatican.va/holy_father/john_paul_ii/encyclicals/

15. Dorothy Day, 'We Go On Record,' *The Catholic Worker*, (September 1945), p.1

16. Thomas Merton, *The Nonviolent Alternative*. New York, Farrar, Straus & Giroux, 1980, p.118

17. *ibid*. pp.86-86, 90

18. Thomas Merton, *Passion for Peace* (ed. William H. Shannon). New York, Crossroad, 1995, p.46

19. Thomas Merton, *The Nonviolent Alternative*, op. cit. p.190

20. Thomas Merton, *The Hidden Ground of Love*, op. cit. p.139-140

21. Thomas Merton, *Faith and Violence*. South Bend, IN, University of Notre Dame Press, 1968, pp.109-110

22. Dorothy Day, 'On Pilgrimage,' *The Catholic Worker* (September 1965), p.6

23. Thomas Merton, *The School of Charity* (ed. Patrick Hart). New York, Farrar, Straus & Giroux, 1990, p.329: letter to Sister K. dated March 10, 1967.

24. Thomas Merton, *The Nonviolent Alternative*, op. cit. p.26

25. Kris Berggen, *National Catholic Reporter* Vol. 38, No.18, March 8, 2002

26. Peter Maurin, 'Christianity Untried' in *Easy Essays*. Quincy, IL, Franciscan Press, 1977. See also: http://www.catholicworker.com/maurin.htm

The World in My Bloodstream:
Merton on Relatedness and Community

THOMAS DEL PRETE

IN ONE OF THE WEEKLY TALKS THAT HE GAVE to the Gethsemani community after taking up full-time residence at his hermitage, Merton remarks that it is much better to become 'related' than virtuous. He insists that relatedness, not virtue, is what matters in spiritual and community life.[1]

Particularly in light of the fact that virtuous behavior, in some form, is held forth as the measure of tolerance and acceptable social policy by conservative religious voices in different places in the world today, Merton's distinction seems pressingly important.

The aims of this paper are to explain what relatedness means to Merton in contrast to virtue, to explore the roots of his thinking in his Christian humanism as well as his understanding of Eastern thought, and to show the importance of relatedness to his understanding of spiritual growth and community life from a Christian point of view.

Virtue Versus Relatedness

Merton has a keen sense of how misleading the idea of virtue can be in the spiritual life, and how inimical to the development of real community. As those self-consciously involved in their own spiritual journey know, there is an inevitable desire to see signs of progress. The signs one looks for are often falsely clothed in the guise of virtue—some external evidence of one's own goodness or advancing character. There is a similar tendency to judge one's own development in relation to others. In the worst case, what results is self-absorption, self-importance, and a stance of righteous judgment over and against others.

Merton, of course, knew full well our capacity for self-deception, the snares laid by what he, and many whose ideas informed his understandings, called the ego-self. Like his Cistercian forebears, he was quick to point out to his brother monks how easy it is to substitute a self-willed, self-centered pseudo-spirituality for something deeper and real. He cautioned them in particular not to make of themselves a 'project' or object of study, not to confuse their idealization of the spiritual life with the deeper reality.[2] He explained that the spiritual life is not something that we construct ourselves and is not measured by visible signs that we may have in mind. As he put it,

> When you start maturing in the spiritual life...gradually you find... that the purpose of everything is to make you drop your own plans and...place [your] hopes in God's Will.[3]

Clearly for Merton, a virtuous life and the spiritual life are hardly synonymous. It is not surprising, therefore, that in his teaching he steers a course away from virtuousness as an end in itself. In stressing the importance of relatedness, however, he is going beyond a concern for a false spirituality based on virtue, or an idealized or prescribed spirituality that is disconnected from inner openness to God's Will. A spirituality based on virtue is limited, if not hazardous, not only because of its focus on characteristic external behaviours, but because it is individualistic. In Merton's Christian humanism, spiritual growth is not only a matter of an intuitive awareness of and response to God's love at the inmost centre of our being, but involves at once a growing awareness of and response to our human relatedness in God. Self-discovery and other-discovery, so to speak, are intimately and mysteriously intertwined; Merton's spirituality is both personal and communal.[4] To be a person – to mature as a person – one has to become more and more related.

The Spiritual Roots of Relatedness

The spiritual roots of relatedness in Merton's thinking are embedded in his essentially Pauline mystical theology and traceable in his understanding of the relationship between self-discovery and other-discovery, between person and community. In his various formulations of it, self-discovery for Merton is the realization of our whole, naked, inmost self. On the deepest level, self-discovery is the inner realization of Christ in us, captured in the Pauline expression, 'I live, now not I, but Christ lives in me' (Galatians 2:20).[5]

Our full freedom and maturity as persons are realized in and through Christ, but this realization is unique for each of us. Thus Merton says, 'I have to become me in such a way that I am the Christ who can only be Christ in me.' Referring to his religious name, he adds, 'There is a "Louie-Christ" which has to be brought into existence and hasn't matured yet . . . Not just an abstract Christ but the Christ who can only be what he wants to be in us and he can't be in me what he is in anybody else.'[6]

Becoming is an important theme here. Paradoxically, to use Merton's words, 'I have to become me,' or, as he said in another context, we have to become what we already are.[7] The paradoxical mystery deepens when we realize, as Merton emphasizes, that 'I must look for my identity, somehow, not only in God, but in other[s];'[8] or when he writes, we cannot find ourselves in ourselves alone, but only in and through others.[9] The explanation for the paradox lies again in the deeper mystery of our identity in Christ.

Believing that self-discovery is ultimately Christ becoming what he wants to be in us, and thus in each of us becoming our 'Christ-self,' we are led to the spiritual corollary that we are related in and through Christ. We are all members one of another, as Merton reminds us. Therefore, relatedness is an aspect of our spiritual lives, part and parcel of 'other-discovery,' of discovering our mutuality in Christ and our common membership in the body of Christ. For Merton, this recognition is fundamentally important as a basis for the development of community life and for Christian social action.

Merton frequently expresses these ideas in non-theological as well as theological language from the middle of the 1960s onward. In talks that he gave to a group of clergy in Alaska, for instance, he writes, 'We are not individuals, we are persons, and a person is defined by a relationship with others' (TMA, pp.134-135).[10]

Similarly, in discussing prayer, he says,

> 'I am not just an individual when I pray...I am, in a certain sense, everybody...because this deep consciousness when I pray is a place of encounter between myself and God and between the common love of everybody...All prayer is communion' (TMA, pp.135-136).

One cannot be a person and fulfill one's unique personality in Christ without also and at the same time understanding one's relatedness.

Merton's introductions to Japanese editions of his work, in particular to *The Seven Storey Mountain* and *Thoughts in Solitude*, show him playing on the Zen concept of 'suchness,' his sense of 'withness.' Introducing *The Seven Storey Mountain* in 1963, he writes,

> I must...not retain the semblance of a self which is an object or a "thing." I too must be no-thing. And when I am no-thing, I am in the All, and Christ lives in me. But He who lives in me is in all those around me...is hidden [in them]... My monastery...is...a place in which I disappear from the world as an object of interest in order to be everywhere in it by hiddenness and compassion.[11]

These words are echoed several years later in his introduction to *Thoughts in Solitude*:

> [The] person...is one in the unity of love. He is undivided in himself because he is open to all. He is open to all because the one love that is the source of all, the form of all and the end of all, is one in him and in all... He who is truly alone truly finds in himself the heart of compassion with which to love not only this man or that, but all men. He sees them all in the One who is the Word of God, the perfect manifestation of God's love, Jesus Christ.[12]

It seems clear that the development of Merton's understanding of relatedness benefited from his in-depth study of Chuang Tzu, the ironic Taoist of the fourth and third centuries B.C.E., in the mid-1960s. Although he does not identify it as such, Merton in his introduction to *The Way of Chuang Tzu* (WCT) suggests that there is an awareness of relationship between self and other in Chuang Tzu's spiritual experience that has some parallel to the inner dynamic of self-discovery and other-discovery in the Christian spiritual life.

To draw this parallel it is important to see Chuang Tzu in context as Merton did. The Ju philosophy that prevailed during Chuang Tzu's time tended to set growth in virtuousness above a more direct, spontaneous and unselfconscious response to the Tao. This emphasis made it suspect as a spiritual philosophy in Chuang Tzu's eyes. Ends and means become confused. Concepts such as happiness and unhappiness, right and wrong, or good and evil, are sought self-consciously as ends in themselves. They frame and define the person in terms of a set of dichotomies that are either there or not there, gained or not gained, like objects.

Chuang Tzu refocused attention on the hidden Tao rather than the Tao as manifested in virtuous behavior. For Chuang Tzu, the one necessary end was to live in harmony with the Tao—albeit the Tao that is invisible, the 'nameless and unknowable source of all being' (WCT, p.20).[13] As Merton explains

> For Chuang Tzu, the truly great man is therefore not the man who has, by a lifetime of study and practice, accumulated a great fund of virtue and merit, but the man in whom "Tao acts without impediment," the "man of Tao"' (WCT, p.25).

Merton says that Chuang Tzu was not against virtue, but saw that 'mere virtuousness is without meaning and without deep effect either in the life of the individual or in society' (WCT, p.24).

For deep effect, it is much better to be non-virtuous, or, more to the point, to lose and find oneself in the Tao. Merton notes the Gospel analogy, 'For Chuang Tzu, as for the Gospel, to lose one's life is to save it, and to seek to save it for one's own sake is to lose it' (WCT, p.12). That deep effect includes and presupposes awareness of relatedness as well. One cannot be responsive to the Tao simply as an individual matter. In Merton's perception, Chuang Tzu, as a true man of Tao, 'does not set himself apart from others' and, in fact, recognizes 'his relatedness to others, his union with them' (WCT, p.30). Merton thus suggests a further implicit parallel between Chuang Tzu's experience and his own Christian humanism. In Chuang Tzu the way of the Tao was tied to identification with others in the same way that Merton says that we must find ourselves in and through others, and find others, therefore, in ourselves, that is, in the hidden ground of love in which we are one.[14]

We might cite other sources of influence in the formation of Merton's understanding of relatedness. Merton's study of Gandhi, for instance, reinforced a sense of connectedness across social and political boundaries, for at the centre of Gandhi's philosophy of nonviolence, grounded in faith in God, is an ontological argument that a universal law of truth is inherent in our very being. Gandhi offers a basis for community in the common capacity to recognize and acknowledge the truth.[15]

The idea of *sobornost*, which appears in Merton's correspondence in the sixties, had a more direct and perhaps deeper influence. Central to the theology of the Russian Orthodox Church, with its emphasis on the Holy Spirit and personal encounter with God, *sobornost* had theological roots in common with the Western Church in the Greek and Latin fathers. The term denotes community in the Spirit, an intimate form of collegiality and connectedness. For Merton *sobornost* pointed to the importance of a personalistic and spiritual basis for community as compared to the ideological or institutional basis that often substitutes for it.[16]

In elaborating the meaning of *sobornost*, Merton emphasizes that the deepest consciousness of who we are is a consciousness of closeness to other people, not of remoteness from them. As he explains,

> ...because I am a member of Christ... If I am going to pray validly and deeply it will be with a consciousness of myself as being more than just myself when I pray... I meet other people not only in outward contact with them, but in the depths of my own heart. I am in a certain sense more one with other people in that which is most secret in my heart than I am when I am in external relations with them. The two go together; you can't separate them (TMA, pp.134-135).

Relatedness and Community Life

Relatedness, in its full spiritual import, and community go hand in hand in Merton's perspective. Community in some sense is both the inner and outer realization of our relatedness, both within and across social, cultural and political boundaries. It is therefore an integral aspect of both our inner prayerful lives and daily relationships.

Merton states explicitly, 'The grace and the mystery and the sacrament of community work when there is relatedness between one another.' The grace that nourishes community life is tapped when we identify completely with and experience empathy for those with whom we live. As Merton explains in reference to the monastery, 'You not only identify with [your fellow monk], but you are able by your identification to value him. You see him as a good in himself because he is a person.' Identification in this sense is as much a matter of consciousness and spiritual insight as emotion, a felt intuitive awareness of the spiritual reality that we do not exist as isolated individuals. It means much more than virtue or even 'the moral conscience,' much more than judgment in terms of 'right' or 'wrong' (TMA, p.134). Merton elaborates,

> Relatedness means this capacity to leave oneself behind...[to think] in terms of other...not "I" ... but "we". [You] are no longer there as a mere individual; you are functioning as two related people...'[17]

Merton's characterization should not mislead. Becoming related no more means merging with another in a faceless relationship, or becoming invisible, than it means clothing oneself in virtue. In Merton's view of our spiritual maturation, the dynamic of self-emptying, or *kenosis*, means leaving behind all that stands in the way of our realization of what he calls our 'indestructible' self and the true 'ground' of our personality.[18] By leaving ourselves behind in this sense, we open up the inner space that is essential if we are to experience and express our relatedness to one another in community; for relatedness leads to an inner freedom that implies 'openness, availability, the capacity for gift.'[19]

These themes echo in talks, spurred in part by documents such as 'The Church in the Modern World' produced by Vatican II, that Merton gave to religious communities in the late 1960s, in particular those he gave to the Sisters of Loretto, neighbours to Gethsemani Abbey, and in Alaska on the eve of his trip to Asia. For them and for him 'community' was more than an abstraction. When he highlights for the Sisters of Loretto the importance of being present to others in community, he stresses in the same breath the importance of distance. It is distance that makes presence possible, and presence that ensures the capacity to give. Distance, as Merton means it, is both the inner and external space necessary for the recognition, valuing of and, finally, the response in love to each other as persons.[20]

In one of his Alaskan talks, Merton suggests further that leaving ourselves behind to be present to others, as an expression of relatedness, is ultimately letting God be present in and through us. In his words,

> [The kerygmatic aspect of community] is making present the thing that the word is about... The real education of the Christian community is something that God himself gets into. God himself teaches us. And what the human teacher has to do is to get in there just enough to be a channel and to let God work through him' (TMA, p.120).

For Merton, community is built ultimately on God's love, not our own (TMA, p.104).

For those of us whose sense of social identity is shaped by Western culture, Merton's idea of relatedness is counterintuitive. It is the spiritual counterweight to the culture of individualism and self-assertion that sets one over and against another as objects, that perpetuates an illusion of separateness. What we lose in becoming related is not ourselves in any deep sense, but the illusion of our individuality.

In Merton's spirituality, relatedness is one of the defining differences between an individual and a person, between the 'I' of our own preoccupation, and our real personality or 'Christ' self that is connected in love to others in the inmost depths of our being. In larger social terms, relatedness is the difference between an atomistic and a personalistic society, between a collectivity formed from the principle of self-interest or, worse, to borrow from Blake, from the 'mind-forged manacles' of collective control, and a community that seeks its ground in the mutuality of personhood and love. Neither an institution, be it a monastic tradition, the Church, or a government, that functions on the basis of rules and procedures, or a group or association, however well-intentioned and however just its cause, that seeks social leverage through power and control, have the basis for real community.[21]

Merton refers in this regard to Eberhard Arnold, the German Lutheran theologian who articulated the spiritual basis for community as a fellowship in the Spirit in love, even as he was confronted by, and saw as equally problematic, the political alternatives of Nazism and Communism in the 1930s (TMA, pp.108-109). The latter represent types of 'groupthink' that Merton saw as symptomatic of the unforgiving, collective will to power that co-opts our deep need to experience relatedness. More than once, Merton cautioned against the creation of these forms of pseudo-community, whether of the monolithic variety or in the guise of activist groups which zealously set cause and ideology above people.[22]

In reflecting on relatedness and community in light of Merton's insights, we must ask about the role of culture, class and ethnicity. Whether on a small or large scale, in what sense can relatedness transcend social, political and psychological boundaries? Commenting in one of his Alaskan talks on a Pauline passage that he uses to illustrate 'how community and contemplation and understanding the mystery of Christ are all linked together,' from Ephesians (Ephesians 2:11-22), Merton expresses clearly his view that historically divisive social distinctions are not inevitable. As he explains, 'In [the] creation of community ... community is based not on ethnic background, not on whether you are a Jew or go to the synagogue, but on the love of persons in Christ, personal relationships in Christ, and it isn't based on nationality or class' (TMA, p.100).

In other contexts, he makes equally clear that our development as whole persons and the development of a consciousness that transcends such divisions, go hand in hand.[23] This is not to say that relatedness is acultural for Merton, but that, insofar as the Christian community is concerned, it is transcultural. Put differently, Merton suggests that the more that we discover our inner integrity as persons, the more related we become within and across social and cultural groups.

If culture and ethnicity do not stand in the way of relatedness in a spiritual sense, neither does our capacity for relatedness make culture irrelevant or unimportant. One can readily make the case that Merton viewed the capacity for cultural understanding as important to the development of a sense of relatedness as relatedness might be for developing an understanding of different cultures.[24] The evidence is in his own effort to understand intercultural dynamics, both contemporary and historical, such as those related to the Cargo cults that he studied, and other religious traditions, and in his own capacity to establish communication with leaders in those traditions, such as the Dalai Lama. It is important to recognize, however, that his effort to understand was motivated in part by a realization that the prospect for peaceful and meaningful coexistence in the world depended on the ability to align cultural and transcultural perspectives, to inter-relate the local and the universal.

Merton strove to realize in himself what he called a universal consciousness, which, though universal, did not replace a more localized and communal consciousness, but rather helped to mold it. He felt sure that a universal consciousness could lead to the solution of communal problems in universal terms. In his words,

> There has to be one world in which we all experience our problems as common and solve them as common without repudiating national differences.[25]

Merton's hopeful conviction stemmed from his belief that the 'deepest level of communication is communion,' a belief that only a deep experience of relatedness can sustain.[26]

Finally, it should be noted that Merton's idea of relatedness is part and parcel of an ontological perspective that embraces the world of nature as well as the world of people. The intimation of God in all being, in everything that is, means that we are connected through God to nature as well as each other. Merton evokes this deep connectedness very simply in an entry in his journal in recording what might be described as a moment of being or of wholeness:

> The meadowlark, feeding and singing. Then the quiet, totally silent, dry sun-drenched mid-morning of spring, under the climbing sun... How absolutely central is the truth that we are first of all part of nature, though we are a very special part, that which is conscious of God...it is man's own technocratic and self-centered "worldliness" which is in reality a falsification and a perversion of natural perspectives, which separates him from the reality of creation...[27]

This example of contemplative perception has a surprising counterpart in an encounter Merton had with quantum physics. He was delighted when he learned of the uncertainty principle, which maintains that we cannot know precisely what is happening to matter in the sub-atomic world precisely because we influence what is happening by our very act of observation, a conclusion that can only be reached with the startling realization that we are part of what we see. He exclaims in his journal, 'This leads to a fabulous new concept in nature with ourselves in the midst of it, destroying the simple illusion of ourselves as detached and infallible observers.'[28]

Merton's declaration that the world is in his bloodstream is a metaphorical way of saying that 'we are part of nature,' and, more generally, a statement of relatedness. He has left himself behind in the world as an object so as to experience it living in him even as he lives in it. As he explained to Japanese readers, 'He is open to all because the one love that is the source of all, the form of all and the end of all, is one in him and in all.'[29]

Notes and References

1. Thomas Merton, 'Christian Hope and Relatedness' (Cassette Recording #243B, 1966). Thomas Merton Center, Bellarmine University, Louisville, Kentucky

2. Thomas Merton, 'Freedom and Spontaneity' (Cassette Recording #230B, 1965). Thomas Merton Center, Bellarmine University, Louisville, Kentucky

3. Thomas Merton, 'Christian Hope and Relatedness' (Cassette Recording #243B, 1966). Thomas Merton Center, Bellarmine University, Louisville, Kentucky

4. Thomas Merton, No Man is An Island. New York, Harcourt Brace Jovanovich, 1955, pp.xv-xxi

5. Quoted by Merton in *Love and Living* (ed. Naomi Burton and Patrick Hart). New York, Harcourt Brace & Company, 1979, p.22

6. Thomas Merton, 'The Bear' (Cassette Recording No.AA2079, 1967). Kansas City, MO, Credence Cassettes.

7. Thomas Merton, *The Asian Journal* (ed. Naomi Burton, Patrick Hart & John Laughlin). New York, New Directions, 1975, p.308

8. Thomas Merton, *New Seeds of Contemplation*. New York, New Directions, 1961, p.51

9. Thomas Merton, *No Man is an Island*, op. cit. p.xv

10. Thomas Merton, *Thomas Merton in Alaska:The Alaskan Conferences, Journals, and Letters*. New York, New Directions, 1988 (TMA)

11. Thomas Merton, *'Honorable Reader': Reflections on my work* (ed. Robert E. Daggy). New York, The Crossroad Publishing Company, 1989, pp.64-65

12. ibid. pp.112,118

13. Thomas Merton, *The Way of Chuang Tzu*. New York, New Directions, 1965 (WCT)

14. Thomas Merton, *The Hidden Ground of Love:The Letters of Thomas Merton on Religious Experience and Social Concerns* (ed. William H. Shannon). New York, Farrar, Straus & Giroux, 1985, p.115 (HGL)

15. Thomas Merton, *The Nonviolent Alternative*. New York, Farrar, Straus & Giroux, 1980, pp.182-183; TMA, p.109; Thomas Merton, *The Springs of Contemplation:A Retreat at the Abbey of Gethsemani*, New York, Farrar, Straus & Giroux, 1992, p.30

16. TMA, pp.84-85; HGL, pp.104, 360

17. Quotations of Merton in this paragraph are taken from the talk, 'Christian Hope and Relatedness,' see note 1 above.

18. Thomas Merton, *Zen and the Birds of Appetite*. New York, New Directions, 1968, 117-119; see also, Thomas Merton, *Love and Living*, op. cit. pp.5, 9

19. Thomas Merton, *Love and Living*, op. cit. p.8

20. Thomas Merton, *The Springs of Contemplation*, op. cit. p.70

21. See for example, TMA, pp.96, 109; Thomas Merton, *The Springs of Contemplation*, op. cit. p.35

22. See for example, HGL, pp.294-297; TMA, p.104

23. Thomas Merton, *Love and Living*, op. cit. p.9

24. Thomas Del Prete, 'Thomas Merton's Spirituality of Education,' *Catholic Education:A Journal of Inquiry and Practice*, 5(2), 2001, pp.157-180 (see pp.165-167)

25. Thomas Merton, *Preview of the Asian Journey* (ed. Walter Capps). New York, The Corssroad Publishing Company, 1991, p.69

26. Thomas Merton, *The Asian Journal*, op. cit. p.315

27. Thomas Merton, *A Search for Solitude:The Journals of Thomas Merton*, Vol. 3 1952-1960 (ed. Lawrence S. Cunningham). San Francisco, HarperSanFrancisco, 1996, p.294

28. Thomas Merton, *Turning Toward the World:The Journals of Thomas Merton*, Vol.4 1960-1963 (ed. Victor A. Kramer) San Francisco: HarperSanFrancisco, 1996, p.323

29. Thomas Merton, *'Honorable Reader,'* op. cit. p.112

The Mysticism of World Faiths in Merton's Inner Experience

JUDITH HARDCASTLE

THOMAS MERTON WAS FASCINATED WITH RELIGIONS, and enthusiastically explored the catholicity of the ancient Asian, Taoist, Confucian and Buddhist traditions, as well as Islam, Judaism and Hinduism, so that he could be a better Christian monk. Merton came to approach interfaith dialogue primarily from an experiential perspective, focusing on the inner experience of God beyond the doctrines that characterize the various faith traditions. He acknowledged these fundamental doctrinal differences while affirming the deeper truths that bound them together. Merton's artistic spirit, his intellect, his insatiable curiosity, and his wisdom profoundly influenced his own intimate relationship with the infinite God dwelling within him. Ironically, perhaps, it was only as he became more and more immersed in his own spiritual and monastic heritage that he found himself encountering others from widely differing traditions—encounters in what he came to call 'the hidden ground of love.'

For most of his adult life, he engaged in sustained correspondence with people committed to other religious traditions, eager to glean understanding of the truth of these traditions so as to deepen his own faith. Among his many contacts Merton corresponded with renowned Zen scholar and practitioner, Dr Daisetz T. Suzuki from 1959 until Suzuki's death in 1966; he corresponded with John C. H. Wu, the Christian Asian Studies expert who taught at Seton Hall University in New Jersey; he met and conversed with the Dalai Lama three times during his visit to Asia in 1968, and corresponded with Thich Nhat Hanh, a Buddhist monk from Vietnam, as well as other Eastern monks and religious; he explored Islam and Sufism through correspondence with Abdul Aziz who lived in Karachi, Pakistan; he expressed a long-held admiration for Mahatma Gandhi in his essay, 'Gandhi and the One-Eyed Giant'; and he worked towards rapprochement between Christians and Jews with Rabbi Abraham Heschel in the 1960s.[1]

Contributing to his enormous understanding of other faith traditions, and his ability to converse intelligently and openly with others about their faith, was his extensive, methodical and in-depth study of world religions. Merton's engagement in inter-religious dialogue was startling for his time, and something to emulate today if we are to have peace and healing in our world. How rare that a Catholic monk of the Abbey of Gethsemani – someone devoted to God in a traditional Christian monastic setting – would be receptive to exploring the faith of other traditions while remaining firmly rooted in his own! Even more startling perhaps is how this openness to other faith traditions marks such a huge leap from the newly converted and narrow-minded Thomas Merton who entered Gethsemani in 1941, whose Christian exclusivist ideas are reflected in *The Seven Storey Mountain* where he dismissed Oriental mysticism as no more than techniques for relaxation.

Merton's attraction to Asia developed gradually. The first concrete evidence of it dates back to November 1937, when he was influenced by the writings of Aldous Huxley. Since the 1930s, Huxley had been attracted to mysticism and investigated Christian as well as Hindu and Buddhist mysticism. His newly acquired mystical views found expression in *Ends and Means*, which Merton read at the suggestion of Robert Lax, a fellow student at Columbia University.

Huxley not only aroused in Merton an interest in mysticism but also drew his attention to similarities in the experiences of Eastern and Western mystics. In particular, Huxley pointed out similarities in the view of the anonymous author of the *Cloud of Unknowing* and of Meister Eckhart with those of the Buddha and India's foremost philosopher, Sankara. Merton was drawn to the mystical emphasis of Asian religions, the importance placed upon contemplation and withdrawal from the world. He was deeply impressed by Huxley's contention that the practice of mystical technique could bring about peace, toleration and charity, ideals that he consistently cherished.

However, it was the Hindu monk, M. B. Bramachari, whom Merton met during his student days at Columbia University, who encouraged him to read the classics of Catholic spirituality for answers to ultimate questions. Writing in retrospect in 1964, in tribute to Bramachari's sixtieth birthday, Merton commented that his encounter with Bramachari had occurred at a crucial point in his life and had contributed to his

eventual decision to become a monk.[2] He had taught him respect and a
true love for persons of other cultures:

> To love one's fellow man consists not in depriving him of his own
> proper truth in order to give him yours, but rather to enable him to
> understand his own truth better in the light of yours.[3]

Around the time of his meeting with Bramachari, Merton became
acquainted with the writings of another Hindu, Ananda Coomaraswamy,
whose ideas greatly affected Merton's intellectual development, in
particular his outlook on art and civilization. Merton came to regard
Coomaraswamy as a role model, combining in himself the best of East
and West.[4] Direct references to Coomaraswamy's ideas are found in
Merton's *Conjectures of a Guilty Bystander*, in *Gandhi on Non-Violence*, and in
his M.A. thesis, 'Nature and Art in William Blake.'

From his entry into Gethsemani in 1941 to his ordination as a
priest in 1949, there is a gap in our knowledge about Merton's
involvement in Asian religions. However, his friend, Ed Rice, tells us
in his book *The Man in the Sycamore Tree* that 'in the fall of 1949 Merton
had begun to correspond with a Hindu who had written him about
Patanjali's system of yoga, and this led to numerous contacts in India,
with Hindu monks and mystics on yoga.'[5] As Merton studied yoga, he
discerned similarities between Patanjali and St Gregory of Nyssa and St
John of the Cross. During the 1960s he continued his studies of
Patanjali, and took extensive notes on the eight steps of Patanjali's
yoga leading to the stilling of the mind. The ultimate goal of the yogis
appeared to Merton similar to that of the apophatic mystics of the
West.

While praising the virtues of yoga, however, Merton warned about
irresponsibly mixing Christianity and yoga. He believed by using
Hindu techniques for breath control, bodily postures and methods of
concentration one could attain a more authentic Christ-centeredness.

In his essay, 'Gandhi and the One-Eyed Giant,' Merton claims:

> [Gandhi] neither accepted Christianity or rejected it; he took all
> that he found in Christian thought that seemed relevant to him as a
> Hindu. The rest was, at least for the time being, of merely external
> interest...here was no syncretism and no indifferentism. Gandhi
> had the deepest respect for Christianity, for Christ and the Gospel.[6]

Merton ends his essay by affirming:

> Peace cannot be built on exclusivism, absolutism, and intolerance.
> But neither can it be built on vague liberal slogans and pious

programs gestated in the smoke of confabulation. There can be no peace of earth without the kind of inner change that brings man back to his "right mind."[7]

From 1961 on Merton studied Asian spirituality in a more systematic manner. Asia became his major concern to the end of his life, as is apparent from some of his significant publications: The Way of Chuang Tzu, Mystics and Zen Masters, Zen and the Birds of Appetite and finally, the posthumously published Asian Journal of Thomas Merton.

Well in advance of Vatican II, Merton recognized the need to dialogue with representatives of Asian spirituality in the conviction that Asian wisdom could enrich his own Catholic tradition and contribute to a renewal of Christianity, especially of monasticism. It was primarily the ancient monastic and contemplative tradition of the East that attracted him.

Studying the spiritual treasures of Asia, Merton discovered striking similarities with the teachings of Christianity—teachings which modern western society had discarded. Merton became increasingly convinced of the need for a return to a life balanced between contemplation and action, a life of self-transcendence rather than egocentricity. Above all, he became a fervent advocate of co-operation between East and West. Asian wisdom undoubtedly enlarged Merton's vision and deepened his insight into life's mystery.

Among all aspects of Asian wisdom, Zen made the greatest impact on Merton. In his book Zen and the Birds of Appetite, he wrote:

> I believe that Zen has much to say not only to a Christian but also to a modern man. It is non-doctrinal, concrete, direct, existential, and seeks above all to come to grips with life itself, not with ideas about life . . .[8]

In regard to how Merton viewed the relationship of Zen to Buddhism, he writes:

> To define Zen in terms of a religious system or structure is in fact to destroy it—or rather miss it completely, for what cannot be 'constructed' cannot be destroyed either... Zen is consciousness unstructured by particular form or particular system, a trans-cultural, trans-religious, transformed consciousness.[9]

Merton looked for ways to reach transformed consciousness through Sufism as well as Zen. Abdul Aziz, a young Pakistani Muslim who was interested in Christian mysticism, wrote to Merton on November 1, 1960, beginning a correspondence that lasted until

Merton's death in 1968. They enthusiastically engaged in book talk, recommending titles and authors to each other on Christian and Islamic mysticism.

Although Merton sent him copies of his own books, he refused to send *Seeds of Contemplation*. Merton said, 'The book was written when I was much younger and contains many foolish statements, but one of the most foolish reflects an altogether stupid ignorance of Sufism.' In the letter, Merton does not say what the foolish statement is, but William H. Shannon, the general editor of Merton's published letters, notes that in *Seeds of Contemplation*, Merton had spoken of 'the sensual dreams of the Sufis as poor substitute for the true contemplation that is found only in the Church.'[10] *Seeds of Contemplation* was written in 1949. More than a decade later, in the same letter dated November 17th, 1960, Merton wrote to Abdul Aziz:

> As one spiritual man to another (if I may so speak in all humility), I speak to you from my heart of our obligation to study the truth in deep prayer and meditation, and bear witness to the light that comes from the All-Holy God into the world of darkness where He is not known and not remembered. May your work on the Sufi mystics make his name known and remembered, and open the eyes of men to the light of His truth.[11]

In his essay, 'As One Spiritual Man to Another—The Merton-Abdul Aziz Correspondence,' Sidney Griffith points out:

> These letters are rare in that they contain a correspondence between a notable Christian and practicing Muslim in religious dialogue in modern times. Of course, Merton had long been writing letters to other scholars of Islam, some of them Muslims. But the letters to Abdul Aziz are uniquely personal and religious. Indeed one has the impression that Abdul Aziz pushed Merton, sometimes quite persistently, to express himself on themes that he would not other-wise willingly have addressed. The result is that Merton was compelled to state his position on matters of inter-religious dialogue, and other topics, in ways that other Catholic writers and scholars have adopted in print only in recent years.[12]

A similar kind of correspondence began in 1960 between Rabbi Abraham Heschel, a gifted writer and professor at the Jewish Theo-logical Seminary in NewYork City, and Merton in which they explored Jewish and Christian relations. (This correspondence is also published in the first volume of Merton's letters—*The Hidden Ground of Love: Letters on Religious Experience and Social Concerns*.) Heschel sent Merton a

mimeographed statement about the declaration at the Vatican Council
on Jewish-Christian relations on September 3rd, 1964, pointing out
that the declaration had been rewritten in a way that made it ineffective
and even offensive to Jews. In response, Merton wrote:

> This much I will say: my latent ambitions to be a true Jew under my
> Catholic skin will surely be realized if I continue to go through
> experiences like this, being spiritually slapped in the face by these
> blind and complacent people of whom I am nevertheless a
> "collaborator." If I were not "working with" the Catholic
> movement for ecumenical understanding, it would surely not be
> such a shock to take the three steps backward after each timid step
> forward.[13]

In the recently published Merton: Essential Writings, Christine M. Bochen
has gathered quotations by Merton from his journals and letters, some
previously unpublished, that are thematic to the last chapter's title—
A Call to Unity. These quotations demonstrate Merton's ability to
articulate principles of genuine ecumenism – and inter-religious
dialogue – with simplicity and clarity. Here are just three such
examples:

> One must cling to one tradition and to its orthodoxy, at the risk of
> not understanding any tradition. One cannot supplement his own
> tradition with little borrowings here and there from other tradi-
> tions. On the other hand, if one is genuinely living his own tradi-
> tion, he is capable of seeing where other traditions say and attain
> the same thing, and where they are different. The differences must
> be respected, not brushed aside, even and especially where they are
> irreconcilable with one's own views. Letter to Marco Pallis, Easter
> 1965, HGL, p.469[14]

Here Merton expresses the importance of being rooted in one's own
tradition whilst respecting the integrity of other traditions. As Ed Rice
affirms, he is not interested in 'baptizing' Buddhism for example,
or taking bits and pieces of other religions and adapting them for
Christianity. Rice continues, 'Buddhism had its own very valid and
true existence, and he was trying to shed the restriction of the Western
mind in reaching out for it.'[15] There is a paradox here, and not a little
tension—shedding restrictions of the Western mind whilst clinging to
one's own tradition and its orthodoxy. This tension is perhaps
transcended, if not resolved, by seeking to communicate and share at a
deeper level:

Genuine ecumenism requires the communication and sharing, not only of information about doctrines which are totally and irrevocably divergent, but also of religious intuitions and truths which may turn out to have something in common, beneath surface differences. Ecumenism seeks the inner and ultimate spiritual "ground" which underlies all articulated differences. A genuinely fruitful dialogue cannot be content with a polite diplomatic interest in other religions and their beliefs. It seeks a deeper level, on which religious traditions have always claimed to bear witness to a higher and personal knowledge of God than that which is contained simply in exterior worship and formulated doctrine.

'Contemplation and Dialogue' in *Mystics and Zen Masters*, p.204[16]

More controversial and illustrating Merton's profound understanding of 'Christ' and his incarnation in humanity—he had come to embrace a transforming cosmic vision of Christ paradigmatic of Christ everywhere, a vision that transcended boundaries and bridged cultures:

It was certainly right that Christian Europe should bring Christ to the Indians of Mexico and the Andes, as well as to the Hindus and the Chinese: but where they failed was in their inability to *encounter Christ* already potentially present in the Indians, the Hindus and the Chinese. . .

It is my belief that we should not be too sure of having found Christ in ourselves until we have found him also in the part of humanity that is most remote from our own.

Christ is found not in loud and pompous declarations but in humble and fraternal dialogue. He is found less in a truth that is imposed than in a truth that is shared.

'A Letter to Pablo Antonio Cuadra Concerning Giants', *The Collected Poems of Thomas Merton*, pp.380-388[17]

Commenting on this in a letter to Dona Luisa Coomaraswamy (Ananda's widow), Merton says that the missionaries thereby both did and did not preach the Gospel and were and were not true to Christ and that this 'awful ambiguity has been the tragedy of Christianity since the Middle Ages.'[18]

In the introduction to *Thomas Merton: Spiritual Master*, Lawrence Cunningham reminds us that when Merton made his fateful trip to the Far East in 1968, 'he had behind him nearly two decades of intense study of Buddhism, the Sufi tradition of Islam, and, to a lesser degree, Hinduism.'[19] Merton was reaching for a deeper communion of mysticism that made him radically open to the presence of the Spirit in the world. This was Merton's approach to inter-religious dialogue—to engage in conversation and enquiry that would allow an experience of the deepest level of communication that is communion.[20] Neither Christian exclusivism nor Christian inclusivism was acceptable to the mature Merton; neither were relativism and syncretism. Rather a genuinely appreciative and respectful desire to understand other faith traditions underscored Merton's approach to inter-religious dialogue, while staying deeply committed to Christian monasticism.

In one of his last recorded conferences at Gethsemani, Merton encouraged his brothers to be less concerned about finding the correct 'keys' to unlock their hearts to God and more concerned with 'breaking' the lock. After all, he insisted, 'We made a vow to open our hearts to love, not to be "correct."'[21] In so saying, Merton expresses his embrace of a universalist and pluralist Christianity, rejects a purely Western one, and acknowledges that our pilgrimage is inward, beyond geography, even beyond rational thought. In his practice of this highly integrative approach to interfaith dialogue, Thomas Merton remains for us an icon of our own religious future, the union of all in 'the hidden ground of love.'

Notes and References

1. Thomas Merton, *The Hidden Ground of Love: Letters on Religious Experience and Social Concerns* (ed. William H. Shannon). New York, Harcourt Brace Jovanovich, 1985 (HGL). For correspondence with Suzuki see pp. 560-571; Wu, pp. 611-635; Hanh, pp. 381-382; Aziz, 43-67; Heschel, pp. 430-436. Merton's essay 'Gandhi and the One Eyed Giant,' published originally in the January 1965 issue of *Jubilee*, became the introduction to Thomas Merton, *Gandhi on Non-Violence: A Selection from the Writings of Mahatma Gandhi.* New York, New Directions, 1965

2. Thomas Merton, 'Dr. M. B. Bramachari: A Personal tribute.' Collected Essays. Volume 9, pages 27-29. Unpublished Manuscript on file at The Thomas Merton Center, Bellarmine University, Louisville, Ky.

3. Ibid. p. 29

4. HGL, p. 126

5. Edward Rice, *The Man in the Sycamore Tree (The Good Times and Hard Life of Thomas Merton): An Entertainment.* New York, Doubleday, 1970, p. 76 (Paperback, 1972, p. 101)

6. Thomas Merton (ed. & intro), *Gandhi on Non-Violence.* New York, New Directions, 1965. p4

7. Ibid. p. 20

8. Thomas Merton, *Zen and the Birds of Appetite.* New York, New Directions, 1968, p. 32

9. ibid. pp. 3, 4

10. HGL, p.44

11. HGL, p.45

12. see Bob Baker and Gray Henry (eds), Merton & Sufism:The Untold Story (A Complete Compendium). Louisville, Kentucky, Fons Vitae, 1999, p.103

13. HGL, pp.434-435

14. Cited in Christine M. Bochen, Thomas Merton: Essential Writings. Maryknoll, New York, Orbis Books, 2000, p.167

15. Ed Rice, op.cit. p.92 (paperback, p.131)

16. Cited in Christine M. Bochen, op.cit. pp.167-168; see also, Thomas Merton, Mystics and Zen Masters (New York, The Noonday Press, 1961) p.204

17. Cited in Christine M. Bochen, op.cit. p.153; see also The Collected Poems of Thomas Merton (New York, New Directions, 1980) pp.381, 382-383

18. Letter of September 24th, 1961, HGL, p.132

19. Lawrence S. Cunningham, Thomas Merton: Spiritual Master (The Essential Writings). New Jersey, Paulist Press, 1992, p.46

20. Thomas Merton, The Asian Journal of Thomas Merton. New York, New Directions, 1968, p.308

21. Thomas Merton, 'Solitude: Breaking the Heart,' (Cassette Recording, Merton Tape No.A2165). Kansas City, MO, Credence Communications

Redeeming the Rhinoceros:
The Healing Power of the Night Spirit
and the Dawn Air

Paul M. Pearson

For devoted readers of Thomas Merton the sixties were a traumatic and challenging time. The quiet voice of monasticism had seemingly disappeared into the Gethsemani woods and the new Merton was disturbing and could grate on his readers' sensibilities. The reaction of some readers was noted by Merton writing in a letter of 1968 'Conservative Catholics in Louisville are burning my books because I am opposed to the Viet Nam war. The whole thing is ridiculous.'[1]

It is not necessary even to open his books from the sixties to encounter this change, it is evident in the titles alone. The titles of his early books – *The Seven Storey Mountain*, *The Sign of Jonas*, *The Ascent to Truth*, *Seeds of Contemplation*, *Bread in theWilderness*, *The Living Bread*, *Thoughts in Solitude* and *Life and Holiness* – titles which conjure up images from the scriptures and literature, images of the monk's fervent spiritual journey, these titles have gone. As Merton himself says, he is no longer 'roaring in the old tunnel.'[2] In contrast, the reader encounters titles such as *Emblems of a Season of Fury*, *Raids on the Unspeakable*, *Seeds of Destruction* and *Conjectures of a Guilty Bystander* ending with, for many people, Merton's two most incomprehensible works, his epic poems *Cables to the Ace*, subtitled *Familiar Liturgies of Misunderstanding*, and *The Geography of Lograire*.

In this paper I want to look in more detail at *Conjectures of a Guilty Bystander* as I think it not only sets out the issues Merton is concerned with in this period but also he suggests a way of living with these issues and, of possibly resolving them, a way based on his own experience.

The title of this book, *Conjectures Of A Guilty Bystander*,[3] points to some of the changes and developments taking place in Merton's life at this time. In an essay Merton published in 1958 entitled 'Letter to an Innocent Bystander' the changes in his attitude to the world can be seen as he reflects on his position as 'an innocent bystander.'[4] He suggests that if he, or another person, were 'bystanding' from a sense of inertia this could be a 'source of our guilt.'[5] He questions whether non-participation is possible and whether complicity can be avoided. Merton then looks at the role of intellectuals as bystanders, pondering how they could stand between those in power and authority and the majority who find themselves subject to such people. From this position Merton suggests that the vocation of the innocent bystander is to speak the truth at all costs.

The position of the innocent bystander, among whom Merton includes himself, is vastly different from the position he held in his early years at Gethsemani. The beginnings of this change can be seen in The Sign of Jonas as Merton discovers through his work as Master of Scholastics that his new desert was compassion, and the change continued from there, developing rapidly in the final years of the fifties. By 1959 Merton is beginning to question the term 'innocent' bystander moving towards the term 'guilty' bystander instead. This can be seen most clearly in letters Merton wrote to Czeslaw Milosz where he questions his use of the term innocent suggesting that the only answer he knows is 'to be responsible to everybody, to take upon oneself all the guilt.'[6] This essay was written in the year of Merton's Louisville epiphany[7] and at a time when his correspondence was burgeoning, particularly with his contacts in Latin America. It was a year marking a distinctive change in Merton and, by the time he was preparing Conjectures for publication, the enormous broadening of his horizons in the fifties and early sixties resulted in Merton changing his view of himself from that of an 'innocent bystander' to a 'guilty bystander.'

Conjectures is 'a confrontation of twentieth-century questions in the light of a monastic commitment, which' Merton says, 'inevitably makes one something of a "bystander"' (CGB, p.vi). But during the challenging events of this period, innocent bystanding was no longer possible; just to bystand made a person guilty because they were a part of the human race and therefore deeply implicated. In his introduction to a Japanese edition of The Seven Storey Mountain in 1963 Merton expressed this succinctly writing

...the monastery is not an "escape from the world." On the contrary, by being in the monastery I take my true part in all the struggles and sufferings of the world...by my monastic life and vows I am saying No to all the concentration camps, the aerial bombardments, the staged political trials, the judicial murders, the racial injustices, the economic tyrannies, and the whole socio-economic apparatus which seems geared for nothing but global destruction in spite of all its fair words in favor of peace.[8]

And again, in his 1966 essay 'Is the World a Problem?' in *Contemplation in a World of Action*, he spoke in more personal terms of his involvement with the world:

> That I should have been born in 1915, that I should be the contemporary of Auschwitz, Hiroshima, Viet Nam and the Watts riots, are things about which I was not first consulted. Yet they are also events in which, whether I like it or not, I am deeply and personally involved.[9]

Merton comes to the conclusion in *Conjectures* that instead of bystanding 'you must be willing, if necessary, to become a disturbing and therefore an undesired person, one who is not wanted because he upsets the general dream'(CGB, p.83). Merton's awareness of events in the world prompted him to become for some, including his own order,[10] a disturbing and undesired person as he felt 'the time had come to move from the role of bystander (guilty by association and silence) to that of declared witness.'[11] The position he was taking in relation to the events of his day from within the monastery is reflected in one of the epigrams Merton used on the title page of *Conjectures* (a quote from Po Chu-i):

> My life is like the crane who cries a few times
> under the pine tree
> And like the silent light from the lamp
> in the bamboo grove.

Similarly the other epigram taken from Deuteronomy – 'Remember that you were a slave in the land of Egypt, and the Lord your God brought you out of there' – reflects Merton's own experience of God's mercy, an experience which consequently enabled him to reach out to others with compassion and mercy.

Conjectures is divided into five parts each of which has a sub-title and epigrams indicative of the essence of that chapter. Before looking at some of the major themes of *Conjectures* it is worth looking at the structure of the book. In the first part, entitled 'Barth's Dream,' Merton begins by recounting a dream experienced by Karl Barth the theologian. In the dream the composer Mozart implies Barth would be saved more by 'the Mozart in himself than by his theology.' Merton suggests that Barth's attraction to the music of Mozart was an attempt to awaken the 'hidden sophianic Mozart in himself,' to awaken the '"divine" child' and concludes his account by telling Barth to 'trust in the divine mercy' as 'Christ remains a child in you' and 'your books (and mine) matter less than we might think! There is in us a Mozart who will be our salvation' (CGB, pp.3-4). In the first part of Conjectures, Merton presents a myriad of issues to his reader: questions about the monastery, the church, his relationship to the world, peace, Gandhi, race issues and the exploration of space. The title given to this chapter, 'Barth's Dream,' serves to present a contrast between the issues and questions Merton raises, and the presence of a higher wisdom, the wisdom of the monk and the solitary on the margins.[12]

In the second part of Conjectures, 'Truth and Violence: An Interesting Era,' Merton paints a picture of the early part of the sixties as 'an interesting era,' a phrase taken from a story told by Camus. In Camus' story a wise man prayed regularly to be spared 'from living in an interesting era' and Camus suggests that since we are not wise 'the Divinity has not spared us, and we are living in an interesting era' (CGB, p.51). In this chapter Merton discusses many issues he was developing an interest in relating to truth and violence, suggesting that humanity has perverted its understanding of truth, and what is desired is 'not the truth, but rather that our lie should be proved "right," and our iniquity be vindicated as "just."' Everyone is convinced they 'desire the truth above all' but what 'we desire is not "the truth" so much as "to be in the right"' (CGB, p.65) and violence comes from this perversion of truth, as 'a truthful man cannot long remain violent' (CGB, p.71). For Merton there is a confrontation with a choice: 'either to live by the truth or be destroyed' (CGB, p.79)—a choice he himself had come to terms with. To live by the truth, for Merton, is to do all things in the name of the logos, the word who is truth, Christ. Following the truth will then be a way of love and compassion. The period in which Merton was writing this was the height of the cold war when truth was being perverted in many areas of life. Merton concludes this chapter by suggesting that calling this era, 'the era of disaster and fulfillment,' interesting could be to underestimate it (CGB, p.113).

Part three, 'The Night Spirit and the Dawn Air' is a pivotal chapter, drawing on the wisdom images of part one and laying key foundations for the remainder of the book. Earlier in the fifties Merton had read Pound's translations of the Ox Mountain parable by Meng Tzu, in which the 'night spirit' and the 'dawn breath' are important 'in restoring life to the forest that has been cut down.' Through rest and recuperation 'in the night and the dawn' the trees will return. Similarly 'with human nature. Without the night spirit, the dawn breath, silence, passivity, rest, man's nature cannot be itself' (CGB, pp.122-123). Meng Tzu's approach is one that would obviously appeal to Merton with his longing for solitude and in this chapter he presents it as a solution both for himself[13] and for the world. The Ox Mountain parable could also be seen as a metaphor for Merton's experience at this stage of his life and I will return to the pivotal effect of the night spirit and the dawn air upon Merton when I examine some of the themes of Conjectures, its effect is also evident in the change of direction in the remaining two sections of the book.

In a brief entry in the fourth section of Conjectures Merton points to Thoreau as someone who experienced the night spirit and the dawn air. Set against the industrial and affluent image of America, 'Thoreau's idleness (as "inspector of snowstorms") was an incomparable gift and its fruits were blessings that America has never really learned to appreciate.' After offering his gift to America, Thoreau, in Merton's words, 'went his way, without following the advice of his neighbors. He took the fork in the road' (CGB, p.227). Merton takes that phrase, 'The Fork in the Road,' as his title for this chapter reflecting a movement in his life as presented in Conjectures. After Merton's awakening to the importance of the night spirit and the dawn air (a gradual discovery over many years but which, in Conjectures, he actually names for the first time) he can approach the questions and problems he was facing earlier in the book with a new sense of freedom and a lightness of touch. The effect upon him of the night spirit and the dawn air is summed up in one of his epigrams for this chapter where Lieh Tzu says 'life comes without warning.'

The final chapter of Conjectures, 'The Madman Runs to the East,' takes its title from one of Merton's epigrams for the chapter, a Zen Proverb:

> The madman runs to the East
> and his keeper runs to the East:
> Both are running to the East,
> Their purposes differ.

In writing *Conjectures* Merton has, like many people of his day, been asking questions about the problems facing society. Having turned his back on the world by his entry into the monastery Merton is now, through his questions, returning to the world but from a different perspective, the difference between the madman and his keeper. Both are going in the same direction, but their reasons for doing so are vastly different. His final section of *Conjectures* focuses much more on the immediate, placing an emphasis on the beauty of life that is present at all times, the beauty he originally pointed to in Mozart at the beginning of the book. This beauty is continually renewed by the night spirit and the dawn air and signifies God's presence in the world. Worldliness, Merton can now say, is acceptable providing it is of the 'right kind,' the worldliness 'which sees the world redeemed in Christ' (CGB, p.289).

Having looked briefly at the structure of *Conjectures* I want to look more closely at some of the themes Merton develops in this book. The themes I want to deal with here will be the more personal themes rather than Merton's conjectures about war, race, and other such areas—namely his growing appreciation in his life of place, of nature, and his changing relationship to the world.

The Place of Nature and the Nature of Place in *Conjectures*

In *The Sign of Jonas*, one theme that grew in prominence over the course of the book was the importance to Merton of physical place. The effect of place and environment on Merton becomes increasingly important throughout the course of *Conjectures*. Every section of the book contains frequent references to place and to the nature surrounding Merton at Gethsemane.

The increasing importance of place and nature to Merton can be seen to stem from his vow of stability. In *The Sign of Jonas* stability seems to be a problem Merton has to come to terms with; by contrast, in *Conjectures* it is his salvation. This vow serves the purpose of stopping the monk from running and forces him to start an inner journey into God.[14] In Merton's case his vow of stability forced him to stop running, especially the wandering of his youth, and to delve into his own inner self and to journey towards God. Paradoxically, for much of his monastic life, Merton appears fairly unstable, moving from one crisis to the next searching for more and more solitude or for permission to travel or to do other things which many did not consider particularly monastic. Through being forced to stop running and to face his inner self Merton came to terms with himself and discovered an inner stability.

The stability of place Merton found at Gethsemani, especially compared to the sense of homelessness and exile of his youth, were essential to his development as a person. The Cistercian writer Charles Cummings has pointed out the importance of stability to human development saying that 'reaching one's full human and spiritual potential seems to be facilitated by some degree of stability in a peaceful place where one can be at ease, sort things out, and develop a feeling of being a fully existing, unique individual.'[15] Over the course of *Conjectures* it is possible to see Merton's growing sense of having discovered that 'stability in a peaceful place' and the effect this has on him making him increasingly aware of both his surroundings and the natural life he shared with those surroundings.

The Place of Nature

In *The Sign of Jonas* Merton notes the natural world around him more frequently as the journal develops, especially after his appointment as forester. This trend continues in *Conjectures* especially from the third section onwards. Part three begins with a description of the valley awakening in the early morning—an apposite beginning to the section titled 'The Night Spirit and the Dawn Air.' Having spent the previous section looking at the challenges and questions raised by the modern world Merton, in his description of dawn and the gradual awakening of nature, points to a different kind of wisdom than that of the human world, the wisdom he had earlier pointed to in his references to Mozart. He describes the early morning as 'the most wonderful moment of the day . . . when creation in its innocence asks permission to "be" once again, as it did on the first morning that ever was' and at that moment of dawn 'all wisdom seeks to collect and manifest itself at that blind sweet point.'

In the Ox Mountain parable Merton found an expression of his experience of the effect nature had upon him, especially the effect of the woods and of nature in the very early hours of the morning a time when he, as a Cistercian monk, was awake as nature itself began to awaken. The understanding of nature Merton found in Meng Tzu's parable fits into his own expression of 'paradise consciousness' so, in the early morning, Merton discovers 'an unspeakable secret: paradise is all around us and we do not understand,' the 'dawn deacon' cries out 'wisdom' but 'we don't attend' (CGB, pp. 117-118).[16]

Merton's own arrangement of *The Ox Mountain Parable* was published in 1960 in a limited edition of one hundred copies by Victor Hammer. In his introduction to the parable, Merton draws a parallel between the violence, war and chaos of Meng Tzu's age and our own age. He wrote:

> One of his [Meng Tzu's] central intuitions was that human nature was basically good, but that this basic goodness was destroyed by evil acts, and had tactfully to be brought out by right education, education in "humaneness." The great man, said Mencius, is the man who has not lost the heart of a child. This statement was not meant to be sentimental. It implied the serious duty to preserve the spontaneous and deep natural instinct to love, that instinct which is protected by the mysterious action of life itself and of providence, but which is destroyed by the wilfulness, the passionate arbitrariness of man's greed... This is a parable of mercy. Note especially the emphasis of Meng Tzu on the "night wind" which is here rendered "night spiriit", the merciful, pervasive and mysterious influence of unconscious nature which, according to him, as long as it is not tampered with, heals and revives man's good tendencies, his "right mind."[17]

It is interesting to note here Merton's stress upon the need to keep 'the heart of a child,' once more echoing his words to Karl Barth, as well as his description of the parable as a 'parable of mercy.'

The Nature of Place

In *Conjectures* a theme intimately connected to that of nature is the continuing growth in the importance of place to Merton. In *The Seven Storey Mountain* there is a strong contrast between the instability of Merton's life before joining Gethsemani and his early years in the monastery. The early part of his autobiography contained descriptions of the many journeys Merton undertook and alongside his lack of a stable family background, his sense of homelessness and exile were prominent. Over the course of *The Sign of Jonas*, place gradually took on an important role in Merton's life and writing. This trend continues in *Conjectures* and besides being noticeable in his careful and detailed references to nature Merton also makes some very specific references to the importance place has for him.

Merton's attitude to place changes markedly from section three of *Conjectures* onwards. In one entry contained in the section 'The Night Spirit and the Dawn Air,' probably dating from the early sixties, Merton begins by describing 'the "way" up through the woods' and how he 'appreciate[s] the beauty and the solemnity' of it, going on to describe the sunrise before stating: 'it is essential to experience all the times and moods of one good place. No one will ever be able to say how essential, how truly part of a genuine life this is— to experience all the times and moods of one good place.' (CGB, p.161)

Merton's statement about 'one good place' seems to be brought about by the effect upon him of his natural surroundings and by being allowed to spend a limited amount of time in solitude at the hermitage. The influence of these two factors on Merton can be seen in an entry in his personal journal from December 1960, in which Merton records one of the first evenings he spent at the hermitage:

> Lit candles in the dusk. *Haec requies mea in saeculum saeculi* [This is my resting place forever] - the sense of a journey ended, of wandering at an end. *The first time in my life* I ever really felt I had come home and that my waiting and looking were ended.
> A burst of sun through the window. Wind in the pines. Fire in the grate. Silence over the whole valley.[18]

In this quote Merton combines the natural surroundings and the solitude of the hermitage creating a sense of having, at last, found a home. Merton's vow of stability enables him to notice the physical space around him, space that, as he states elsewhere, he never noticed when he was in the world and more mobile. Dwelling 'for long periods in one place among familiar, congenial surroundings'[19] was essential for Merton to come to know God and to know himself.

Sacramental Visions of the World

Among Merton's wide and varied interests referred to in *Conjectures*, two groups in particular attracted him because, I would suggest, of their emphasis on nature and place. In the entries immediately following on from Merton's reflection on the awakening valley at the beginning of 'The Night Spirit and the Dawn Air' he refers to the Shakers and the Celts.

There is no time to explore Merton's interest in these two groups now, but I would just like to draw a parallel between Merton's essay 'Rain and the Rhinoceros'[20] in which he describes some of the times he had spent in the woods, in solitude, living a life very different from that of an average Cistercian monk in his day, and the stories of some of the Celtic monks. Merton describes very simply an evening spent at the building where he would eventually become a hermit in 1965:

> I came up here from the monastery last night...and put some oatmeal on the Coleman stove for supper. It boiled over while I was listening to the rain... The night became very dark. The rain surrounded the whole cabin with its enormous virginal myth, a whole world of meaning, of secrecy, of silence, of rumor. Think of it: all that speech pouring down, selling nothing, judging nobody, drenching the thick mulch of dead leaves, soaking the trees, filling the gullies and crannies of the wood with water, washing out the places where men have stripped the hillside![21]

In the same manner as some of Merton's descriptions of nature and place in *Conjectures* this passage celebrates a wisdom and a way of life reminiscent of some of the Celtic hermits in solitude on their islands surrounded by the ocean and the elements. For Merton, the wind and the rain and the darkness and the solitude of the night in his cabin had a restoring effect similar to 'The Night Spirit and the Dawn Air' in *The Ox Mountain Parable*. The rain helped to heal the damage done to the woods by men who had 'stripped the hillside' and it also had a similar effect on Merton as he continues:

> ...in this wilderness I have learned how to sleep again. Here I am not alien. The trees I know, the night I know, the rain I know. I close my eyes and instantly sink into the whole rainy world of which I am a part, and the world goes on with me in it, for I am not alien to it.

In his essay 'Rain and the Rhinoceros' Merton brings together his own experience of life in the hermitage, where he experienced in 'one good place' the effect of 'the night spirit and the dawn air' with some reflections on the writings of a sixth century hermit, Philoxenos, suggesting that in the modern world similar insights are not found in the writings of theologians but in the meditations of the existentialists and the Theater of the Absurd. In Ionesco's play *Rhinoceros*, as all Berenger's friends and fellow citizens gradually become rhinoceroses, he is faced with the crises that he no longer resembles anyone and 'solitude and dissent become more and more impossible, more and more absurd.' For Ionesco rhinoceritis is the sickness that lies in wait 'for those who have lost the sense and the taste for solitude'—for those who are no longer open to the experience of the night spirit and the dawn air.

A New Perspective on the World and His Life

In *Conjectures* a dominant question for Merton is the Christian's relationship to the modern world. Over the course of *Conjectures* Merton is struggling with his response to the world. From the very beginning of the book his approach is more open than previously. Early on in *Conjectures* he suggests the *Rule of St Benedict* contains 'nothing whatever of the Ghetto spirit' (CGB, p.6) in its attitude to the world and Merton adopts Benedict's attitude to the world and not that of the Cistercian Order which at the time he was writing was still very closed. Throughout *Conjectures* the list of topics Merton writes about and the various people with whom he is in contact reflects a universal vision of the world from within the confines of the monastery, a vision he expressed in his introduction to an Argentine edition of his work:

> In the silence of the countryside and the forest, in the cloistered solitude of my monastery, I have discovered the whole Western Hemisphere. Here I have been able, through the grace of God, to explore the New World.[22]

Merton approaches the question of his attitude to the world directly a number of times in *Conjectures*, an attitude now based on his belief that 'God became man, because every man is potentially Christ' (CGB, p.69). This stress on the importance of the incarnation continues throughout *Conjectures*. When Merton is passing through the novitiate on his fire watch, he feels Christ 'was as truly present here, in a certain way, as upstairs in the Chapel' (CGB, p.193) and this feeling is not confined to the monastery as attested to by the revelatory experience Merton had on a visit to Louisville in March 1958. Although the account was elaborated by Merton in his preparation of this material for publication, the essence was there in his original text. On the corner of a busy street in Louisville, Merton was 'overwhelmed with the realization that I love all these people, that they were mine and I theirs, that we could not be alien to one another even though we were total strangers' (CGB, p.140). Significantly this incident is placed by Merton in the pivotal chapter of *Conjectures*, 'The Night Spirit and the Dawn Air.'

Merton's horizons had begun to broaden rapidly in 1958. The mercy he felt so strongly in *The Sign of Jonas* led gradually to an overflowing of mercy and compassion from himself towards others: beginning with those with whom he was in contact in the monastery, the scholastics and then novices, through his expanding correspondence, the stream of visitors who came to Gethsemani to see him and in his writings. Merton's 1963 collection of poetry poetically mirrors *Conjectures* and was aptly entitled *Emblems of a Season of Fury*.[23] The range of subjects covered reflects Merton's realisation of his need for other people, a need expressed in a letter of the same year to James Baldwin saying,

> I am therefore not completely human until I have found myself in my African and Asian and Indonesian brother because he has the part of humanity which I lack.[24]

The Merton writing in *Emblems of a Season of Fury* is no longer turning his back on the world and its problems but, as in *Conjectures*, is looking at them from his place on the margins and asking the important questions. His sense of being an exile and a pilgrim with 'no proper place in this world' made him feel 'the friend and brother of people everywhere,' especially exiles and pilgrims.[25]

By the end of *Conjectures*, Merton conveys a very strong sense of being at home with himself, of having found a 'stability in a peaceful place' which allowed him to 'be at ease, sort things out, and develop a feeling of being a fully existing, unique individual, ready to deal with life and with God on their terms.'[26] Merton's sense of homelessness and exile are now expressed in a new, creative way seeing the monk as a solitary and marginal person, and in understanding his own need for solitude. He came to realise 'The Night Spirit and the Dawn Air,' discovered through some 'stability in a peaceful place,' gave him life and enhanced his prophetic and poetic voice so he could declare that life to others:

> There is the hope, there is the world that remakes itself at God's command without consulting us. So the poet . . . sees only the world remaking itself in the live seed (CGB, pp.319-320).

As the figure of the prophet Jonas expressed Merton's understanding of the paradox of his life in the early fifties so the metaphor of the 'guilty bystander' encapsulated it a decade later. The compassion Merton discovered in *the Sign of Jonas* expands in *Conjectures* to embrace the world outside the cloister. Merton's sights are no longer set on a paradise reached by disowning the world. In *Conjectures* Merton sees God's presence in the world and in people outside the cloister and the 'deep and mute sense of compassion'[27] he had discovered in *The Sign of Jonas* finds a growing voice as seen in his title for this book which expresses his interrelationship and unity with other people and with the world.

In Merton's later works his message, expressed most clearly in his introduction to *Raids on the Unspeakable*, is that Christian hope can stand in the void where every other hope stands frozen stiff before the face of the unspeakable. His message is be human in this most inhuman of ages and guard the image of man, for it is the image of God. And how are we to do this? In *Conjectures* Merton suggests a number of ways we can redeem the rhinoceros:

> Through rediscovering solitude and experiencing some sense of stability in a peaceful place.
>
> Through paying attention to 'the night spirit and the dawn air.'
>
> Through awareness of a deeper wisdom and finding the divine child in each one of us.
>
> And, finally, through our experience of God's mercy which will ultimately bring each one of us out of slavery into the Promised Land.

Notes and References

1. Thomas Merton, *Striving Towards Being: The Letters of Thomas Merton and Czeslaw Milosz* (ed. Robert Faggen). New York, Farrar, Straus and Giroux, 1997, p.175
2. Thomas Merton, *The Collected Poems of Thomas Merton*. London, Sheldon Press, 1978, p.395
3. Merton suggested a number of different titles for this book to his publisher including 'A Temperature of My Own,' (Thomas Merton. *Witness to Freedom*. (ed. William H. Shannon). New York, Farrar, Straus, Giroux, 1994, p.144) an interesting title reflecting the personal nature of his thought in it.
4. Thomas Merton, *Raids on the Unspeakable*. London, Burns & Oates, 1977, p.34
5. *Ibid*. p.37
6. Thomas Merton, *The Courage for Truth* (ed. Christine M. Bochen). New York, Farrar, Straus, Giroux, 1993, pp.62, 64
7. Thomas Merton, *Conjectures of a Guilty Bystander*. London, Burns & Oates, 1968, pp.140-142. (Abbreviated to *Conjectures* or CGB.) Referred to in more detail later in this paper.
8. Thomas Merton, *Honorable Reader: Reflections on My Work* (ed. Robert E. Daggy). London, Fount Paperbacks, 1989, p.74
9. Thomas Merton, *Contemplation in a World of Action*. London, George Allen & Unwin, 1971, p.145
10. For a period in the early sixties Merton was prevented by his order from publishing on issues of war and the arms race.
11. Mott, Michael, *The Seven Mountains of Thomas Merton*. London, Sheldon Press, 1986, p.368
12. His epigrams for this chapter reflect this contrast. The first from Kabir is a few lines from a song to Sadhu advising him to stop his 'buying and selling' and to

'have done with your good and your bad' as 'there are no markets and shops in the land to which you go.' The other quote from Thomas Traherne suggests that, though an infant does not often realise it, when compared to the world and all its treasures the child is 'the cream and crown of all that round about did lie,' (CGB, p.1) pointing the reader in the direction of the important themes in part one, the wisdom figure of the child and the Mozart figure.

13. In a letter to Abdul Aziz Merton spoke of 'the hour of dawn when the world is silent and the new light is most pure,' as 'symbolizing the dawning of divine light in the stillness of our hearts.' Thomas Merton, *The Hidden Ground of Love* (ed. William H. Shannon). New York, Farrar, Straus, Giroux, 1985, p.46

14. Philip Sheldrake has suggested 'an engagement with "place" (as, for example, in desert monasticism's mystique of "the cell" or St Benedict's teaching on stability) may enable a spiritual, inner journey.' Philip Sheldrake, *Living Between Worlds: Place and Journey in Celtic Spirituality*. London, Darton, Longman & Todd, 1995, p.8

15. Charles Cummings, *Monastic Practices*, Cistercian Studies Series: no. 75. Kalamazoo, Michigan, Cistercian Publications, 1986, p.177; for a more detailed exploration of the relationship between journey and stability in Merton's life see:
Paul M. Pearson, 'The Whale and the Ivy: Journey and Stability in the Life and Writing of Thomas Merton,' *Hallel* 21 (1996), pp.87-103

16. References to nature, to the birds, the sky, sun, moon and stars, the country-side, the weather and to other aspects of nature continue throughout the remainder of *Conjectures* and some have a Zen-like quality in their stark simplicity. Describing a vase of red and white carnations in the novitiate chapel Merton rapidly moves from describing the flowers into Zen-like reflections: 'Eternity. He passes. He remains. We pass. In and out. He passes. We remain. We are nothing. We are everything. He is in us. He is gone from us' and the 'flower is itself. The light is itself. The silence is itself. I am myself' (CGB, p.131). Later in *Conjectures* Merton reflects in a similar way on the dawn: 'Dark dawn. Streaks of pale red, under a few high clouds. A pattern of clothes lines, clothes pins, shadowy saplings. Abstraction. There is no way to capture it. Let it be' (CGB, p. 227). Similar references to nature occur in Merton's letters in the early sixties, especially his more personal letters. Merton tells Thérèse Lentfoehr of an occasion when a 'meadowlark was singing outside the window, in the sun . . . and I thought I would go through the roof, it was so beautiful.' Thomas Merton, *The Road to Joy* (ed. Robert E. Daggy). New York, Farrar, Straus, Giroux, 1989, p.244

17. The Ox Mountain parable. [With notes and text arrangement (after the translation of I. A. Richards) by Thomas Merton] Lexington, KY, Stamperia del Santuccio, 1960

18. Thomas Merton, *Turning Toward the World: The Journals of Thomas Merton* Vol. 4, 1960-1963 (ed Victor A. Kramer). San Francisco, Harper Collins, 1996, pp.79-80

19. James McMurry, 'On Being "At Home": Reflections of Monastic Stability in the Light of the Philosophy of Gabriel Marcel,' *Monastic Studies* 4 (1966), p.82

20. This essay, included in *Raids on the Unspeakable*, was completed by Merton in December 1964, although written during the period covered by *A Vow of Conversation* the substance of it is relevant to this discussion.

21. Thomas Merton, *Raids on the Unspeakable*, op. cit. pp. 7-8

22. Thomas Merton, *Honorable Reader, op. cit.* p.48

23. Besides poems which continued to reflect his reading of the Desert and the Church Fathers, the range of subjects covered in this volume is as wide and as varied as the subjects covered in *Conjectures*.

24. Thomas Merton, *The Courage for Truth, op. cit.* p. 245; see also *Contemplation in a World of Action, op. cit.* pp. 155-156

25. Thomas Merton, *The Hidden Ground of Love, op. cit.* p.52

26. Charles Cummings, *op. cit.* p.177

27. Thomas Merton, *The Sign of Jonas.* London, Hollis & Carter, 1953, p.87

Thomas Merton's World Discourse: Economic Globalization versus Religious Universality

FERNANDO BELTRÁN LLAVADOR

& SONIA PETISCO MARTÍNEZ

> I rescue all who cling to me,
> I protect whoever knows my name,
> I answer everyone who invokes me,
> I am with them when they are in trouble;
> I bring them safety and honour.
> I give them life, long and full,
> and show them how I can save
> (*Psalm* 91:14-16)

ONE OF THE MAIN MERITS OF MERTON'S literary impact is that it can greatly contribute to untying the knots and dilemmas of personal and social conflicts by providing ever new symbolic 'pray-grounds' for voicing, and therefore building, personal, communal, and value-bound, value-able modes of being, seeing and acting in our times. It is in this Trinitarian dynamics, at the root of the Christian notion of 'person,' where both criticism of selfishness and hope for true relatedness lie.

Many contemporary representatives of our civilization have unanimously advocated a spiritual revolution to stop warfare and the disintegration of our world. Merton's transformative metaphors may help us honour the best and most universal of our human civilization by bringing forth the most regenerative radiance from deep inside the heart of contemplation.

The following reflection attempts to address the contrasting discourses of Merton's universality – as conveyed in both his prose and poetry – and of economic globalization, 'a world without direction' which Ignacio Ramonet, director of *Le Monde Diplomatique*, has graphically described as the PPII system, i.e., 'that which is planetary, permanent, immediate and immaterial' thus claiming the right to act in a god-like manner demanding submission, faith and new rituals.[1]

I

In his Millennium Lecture (*Time and Again: Poetry and the Millennium*), delivered at the University of Liverpool (22nd March 2000), Seamus Heaney concluded by highlighting the risk of our being blinded, rather than enlightened, by the glitter of the new information technologies. For him, poetry may act as a pin-card which, while letting us approach the dazzling mass of World Wide Web news and views, also prevents us from being merely bewildered by eclipsing novelties. 'Hold it up to reality and an image comes through,' he says, 'time and again, that allows us to see ourselves and the world we inhabit in a contemplatable light.'[2]

Merton devoted his monastic life to tracing back the radiance of yet another sun, an inner light which streams out from deep within the springs of contemplation and allows the human family access to the divine loving gaze which is the very foundation of the world and indeed, the stamp and breath of our human condition. Were we to love as we are loved, to see as we are seen, to create as we are created and to shine as we are being shone upon, as he discovered in Louisville, at the corner of Fourth and Walnut, there would be no more wars, no more self-deceptions, no more feelings of abandonment or scarcity.[3]

It is in the difference between these two lights that we may find Thomas Merton's crucial choice and the impulse for his radical leap of faith. Merton saw both his personal dilemmas as a young man and the painful contradictions of his own time articulated in Huxley's seminal work *Ends and Means* which, by his own appraisal, played a 'very great part' in his conversion.[4]

In the first chapter of his work, Huxley expressed his arguments in unambiguous terms:

> Technological advance is rapid. But without progress in charity, technological advance is useless. Indeed, it is worse than useless.'[5]
> How can this be possible? Perhaps we have been simply blinded by the brilliance of our technological might, a complex of means which have escalated to reach Promethean dimensions.[6]

Huxley continues:

> 'Good ends. . . can be achieved only by the employment of appropriate means. The end cannot justify the means, for the simple and obvious reason that the means employed determine the nature of the ends produced.'[7]

Obvious as it may look, it is in the forgetting of this basic axiological truth that we may largely find the dividing line between an idolatrous, insular, self-bound consciousness and the mind of the living, life-giving, loving and love-given Christ. In the same essay Aldous Huxley quotes Professor Whitehead who, in his *Religion in the Making*, suggests that 'religion is world loyalty' and sees a deep connection 'between universality and solitariness.'[8]

A person like Merton, who plunged into the depths of the world at large as well as into the abyss of his own heart, in solitude and in communion, can greatly contribute to facing global problems from a universal perspective which results from a life devoted to living 'in the company of the Trinity.'[9] Trinitarian relatedness is the very foundation of the Christian approach to self and other as 'person.' And it is this unique, specifically Christian trait, which paradoxically became for Merton the meeting point of saintly people from other religious traditions in their shared search for peace of mind and peace on earth. Thus, for instance, at a stage of monastic maturity Merton discovered 'in the "void" of Hui Neng [the Sixth Patriarch of Chinese Ch'an or Zen] a surprising Trinitarian structure' which for him meant 'inevitably a fulfilment in love.'[10]

This is indeed an unprecedented spiritual finding with enormous universal consequences at a time when economic globalization needs to be regulated by policies congenial with moral behaviour and planetary ethics.[11] Our contention is that these are to be nurtured by the sustained practice, and will develop as the natural outcome, of *contemplata tradere*, that is, they may become the ripe fruits of religious wisdom and contemplative awareness on a universal scale.

Acknowledging a Trinitarian foundation at the centre of another religion should give us enough reason for hope in the universality of the Gospel's promises.[12] In his seminal work, *Der dreiene Gott, Eine trinitarische Theologie*, theologian Gisbert Greshake defines God as relational and the Three Persons as three distinct yet inseparable relationships. Rather than an isolated, individual and objectified entity, a person is defined by his or her love and openness to the radical Other as much as to the neighbouring others in a bond of communion. Similarly, better than the modern or postmodern 'I' defined by its power to think autonomously and instrumentally, from a Christian perspective, the 'I' can only be true to himself or herself by breaking its boundaries in an attempt to reach out towards 'you' and 'him/her,' thus becoming a 'we' whose way of thinking is de-centred and altruistic. The basic assumption is, therefore, not that 'I think' but that 'I believe in love,' which has a threefold meaning: 1) God loves me; 2) you are for me as important as I am to myself because I find the Lord in you; and 3) we want to love each other as He loved us. In short, we are one, and He is always in our midst. What is more, according to Greshake, this does not merely apply to the individual person but it also provides hermeneutical keys for other 'formations of unity' in the created world, such as cultures, religions and societies. This realization opens up new avenues of understanding, collaboration and dialogue within the great human family, a plural yet singular unity of love.[13]

In a similar vein, Raimon Panikkar defines the Trinity as a primordial human experience and as indeed the core of the whole of reality.

> There are not three realities: God, Man and the World. There is not one reality either: God, or Man or the World. Reality is cosmotheandric.[14]

In other words, Reality is intrinsically Trinitarian.

This preamble may perhaps better situate Merton's contemplative critique and the universality and poignancy of his writings against the background of today's 'millennial capitalism,' which the Comaroffs define as 'a capitalism that presents itself as a gospel of salvation,' a kind of 'Second Coming of Capitalism—of capitalism in its neoliberal, global manifestation,'[15]

Merton's articulation of his monastic experience, and his specific unmasking of idolatry throughout his work, can throw much light upon the belief-system which sustains today's economic globalization and its rationality. The term *globalization*, which was included for the first time in an American dictionary in 1961, has been recently defined by Joaquín Estefanía, former director of the Spanish national newspaper *El País*, as a process whereby national policies are becoming less important while international decisions, made far away from the citizens, are gaining predominance. This description deliberately seeks to reflect both the positive and the negative sides of it. However, despite its benefits, there is growing concern about the fact that more and more things occur without the intervention of the people affected by them and important issues are decided without the say of those for whom they are designed.[16] Freedom to decide courses of action is being gradually replaced by a surrogate, fake freedom to choose material commodities. The praxis of citizenship is subtly but effectively replaced by the compulsive exercise of consumption.

It is thus not *globalization* as such which is seriously objected to but the evidence that so far its development has been predominantly financial. For it is this ambition, both virtual and material, freed from any political control or human regulation, which precisely imposes severe limits on a parallel and much needed spread of global justice, human rights and sustainable development. Only this complementary globalization can put a halt to the perverse consequences of irrational greed.[17]

At the heart of this 'structural' evil, Merton saw the artful machination of 'the father of lies' eroding the core of our spiritual consciousness and distorting our image and likeness of God. In an essay which served as an introduction to the letters of the twelfth century Cistercian Adam of Perseigne, Merton explains how St Bernard saw pride as leading us away from God to bring us, in return, 'to the feet of a false god, which is our own inordinate self-love.' For Merton, this falsity can only be given up when we see that it is false. 'No man will cling to something that he manifestly believes to be unreal,' he writes. After offering what we deem a most accurate diagnosis of the illness of our times, Merton provides us with this equally fair prognosis:

> Hence the constant need to be honest with ourselves, and to grapple with the "spirit of fiction" that is in our very blood itself, always ready to deceive us in the disguise of an angel of light.[18]

Globalization is today being overtly and covertly advocated by representatives of neoliberalism as an eschatological movement towards the definite unity and universality of the human race.[19] And who could resist such noble ends? Neither the possibility of being universally linked nor the virtual access to financial information available from anywhere in the world in real time can be denied. But this is precisely the disguise adopted by the *spiritus fictionis* in our days. Can technological connections or media communication, in all honesty, satisfy our thirst for genuine communion? Does instant access to any kind of information grant real wisdom? Could it be that we are being seduced by the media and are becoming their prey instead of their masters?

The words of Aldous Huxley in his 1946 introduction to *Brave New World* bear overtones which are terribly familiar for us today: 'A really efficient totalitarian state would be one in which the all-powerful executive of political bosses and their army of managers control a population of slaves who do not have to be coerced, because they love their servitude.' And the strategies devised to this end partially mirror the numbing and dumbing climate of our own society: 'In conjunction with the freedom to daydream under the influence of dope and movies and the radio, [sexual freedom] will help to reconcile his subjects to the servitude which is their fate.'[20]

Similarly, in one of his best known essays Merton bluntly asked, 'Is love a package or a message?'[21] Isaiah's curse should shake us out of our all too-easy complacency: 'Woe to those who call evil good, and good evil, who substitute darkness for light, and light for darkness' (Isaiah 5:20).

Felix Wilfred and Jon Sobrino caution us against the feigned universality of capital and the centripetal unity of possessive individualism. Appealing as it may seem, financial globalization is a poor and dangerous substitute for the centrifugal unity of religions and their communal and relational universality, which, on the other hand, from a genuine Trinitarian perspective, could never allow for uniformity or syncretistic fusions and confusions.[22] The antidote of falsity is reality itself.[23] Merton viewed monastic life as either a school of charity or a school of reality since, for him, the terms love and reality are interchangeable. In the words of the Carmelite contemplative Father William McNamara:

> This is what it means to become the image and likeness of God: to develop the graced capacity we have for altruistic love relationships. God does not have a social life, a community, a trinity of persons. No one of the persons of the Trinity has or is anything in and by himself. Each one is entirely for the other and is constituted in being by eternal relatedness to the other. The Trinity is the altruistic love-life of God. We are truly human to the extent that we do in fact become, existentially and not just theoretically, the living image and likeness of God.[24]

Merton himself explains the delusory dynamics of self-aggrandizement as a failed approach to gain a status of reality, which cannot and indeed does not need to be conquered because it is pure gift.

Dr Robert Imperato, in his essay on Merton and Walsh concerning the person, aptly introduces a lengthy quotation of Merton to explain the crucial difference between an individual and a person:

> Psychologically, the individual is what is constructed by discrimination from all other individuals; the unique person is constituted by divine love.[25]

The quote in question is from *New Seeds of Contemplation*:

> People who know nothing of God and whose lives are centered on themselves, imagine that they can only find themselves by asserting their own desires and ambitions and appetites in a struggle with the rest of the world. They try to become real by imposing themselves on other people, by appropriating for themselves some share of the limited supply of created goods and thus emphasizing the difference between themselves and the other men who have less than they, or nothing at all.
>
> They can only conceive one way of becoming real: cutting themselves off from other people and building a barrier of contrast and distinction between themselves and other men. They do not know that reality is to be sought not in division but in unity, for we are members of one another.
>
> The man who lives in division is not a person but only an individual.

Former UNESCO general secretary Federico Mayor Zaragoza has recently written that we need to first acknowledge the fact that it is the spiritual poverty of a few which has been the cause of the material poverty of far too many.[26] Similarly, President of the Czech Republic Vaclav Havel has declared that the time has come to lift the Iron Curtain of the spirit:

> It is not enough to invent new machines, new regulations, new institutions. We must develop a new understanding of the true purpose of our existence on this earth ... Perhaps the way out of our current bleak situation could be found by searching for what unites the various religions...[27]

For his part, in response to the tragic events of September 11th and thereafter, Buddhist monk and Zen teacher Thich Nhat Hanh, whom Merton came to know and considered his 'brother,' wrote a circular letter inviting all readers to cultivate compassion as the way out of violence. His seems a spiritually intelligent commentary:

> We are all co-responsible for the making of violence and despair in the world by our way of living, of consuming and of handling the

problems of the world. Understanding why this violence has been created, we will then know what to do and what not to do in order to decrease the level of violence in ourselves and in the world, to create and foster understanding, reconciliation and forgiveness.

Equally sensitive, and also universally applicable are Nobel Peace Prize Aung San Suu Kyi's commentaries, even if the context in which they were made was different:

> Truth is a very powerful weapon. People may not think so but it is very powerful. And truth – like anything that is powerful – can be frightening or reassuring, depending on which side you are on. If you are on the side of truth, it's very reassuring—you have its protection. But if you are on the side of untruth—then it's very frightening.[28]

And in reading about the fear which comes from 'unreality,' 'untruth' or 'the spirit of fiction,' we cannot but share Merton's alarm against the possibility of 'global suicide' in one of his incendiary essays whose plea is even more urgent today than when it was first published in 1962. At the end of The Root of War is Fear readers find the following statement and subsequent exhortation:

> Many men...have asked God for what they thought was "peace" and wondered why their prayer was not answered. They could not understand that it actually was answered. God left them with what they desired, for their idea of peace was only another form of war. The "cold war" is simply the normal consequence of our corruption of peace based on a policy of "every man for himself" in ethics, economics and political life. It is absurd to hope for a solid peace based on fictions and illusions! So instead of loving what you think is peace, love other men and love God above all. And instead of hating the people you think are warmongers, hate the appetites and the disorder in your own soul, which are the causes of war. If you love peace, then hate injustice, hate tyranny, hate greed—but hate these things in yourself, not in another.[29]

Not only the above mentioned people but many others are unanimously claiming the need for a global spiritual revolution, that is, a universal, yet at the same time absolutely personal, therefore relational, metanoia to prevent the destruction of our world. From the point of view of consciousness, this revolution would consist in the reversal and radical conversion of instrumental reason into a Trinitarian 'structure of thinking and feeling.' Here we are deliberately attempting to stretch Raymond Williams' appropriate categorization beyond its material confines from within the core of materiality, as it were.[30]

Consciousness cannot be abstracted from language. And Merton saw the crisis of language as both a symptom and an expression, the cause and the effect of a mindset ever prone to war. Interestingly for us, a few years after Merton's death, linguists George Lakoff and Mark Johnson wrote a most revealing study on the metaphors we live by in which they profusely disclosed how metaphors pervade our lives to the extent that our ordinary conceptual system is basically metaphorical. So much so that it governs our normal functioning to the most mundane details. 'The essence of metaphor,' they explained, 'is understanding and experiencing one thing in terms of another.'[31] And then, they added, acting according to the way we conceive things. They showed this systematically through examples taken from everyday speech, which still strike us for their very simplicity.

Even more shocking and provocative was a later paper by George Lakoff which was publicly presented at the University of Berkeley, California, on January 30, 1991 on 'the metaphor system used to justify war in the gulf' which began by directly claiming that 'metaphors can kill,' a provocative statement which he qualified in his conclusion as 'metaphors backed up by bombs can kill.' In this paper, Lakoff took as a case study the thought system evinced by the metaphors used in the discourse over whether to go to war in the Gulf. Let us take just one example of a loaded set of metaphors, for today they still serve as the main conceptual justification for the so-called economic globalization. These metaphors fall under the following umbrella heading: 'Rationality is the maximization of self-interest.' Lakoff explains some of the Protean corollaries of this implicit injunction in the context of the gulf situation: 'Since it is in the interest of every person to be as strong and healthy as possible, a rational state seeks to maximize wealth and military might.' Under this frame of thought, Lakoff discovers three very logical deductions: 1) 'violence can further self-interest,' 2) 'morality is a matter of accounting' and 3) 'a just war is thus a form of combat for the purpose of settling moral accounts.'

Lakoff adds nuances to these assumptions with further metaphorical scaffolding in case there could be any possible mind-gaps, as if even ellipsis itself has a role to play in the very working of the metaphor system which rules our way of thinking. For our purpose, we would like to simply call your attention now to the way the term 'person' has been used. The concept, as seen in this context, would clearly correspond to what Merton called 'an individual,' that is, a measurable entity, a separate material body, a numbered subject, or an objectified human. However, it would never apply to a 'person' as regarded from a Trinitarian standpoint, that is, the uniquely interrelated play of freedoms which constitutes the reality, relationality, and indeed the charitable rationality and the ineffable beauty, goodness and truth of each and every loved-lovable-and-loving human being. The very fact that a person, in the real Christian sense, cannot but conceive self-interest as inclusive of the interest of the others, explains the miraculous and paradoxical condition of universality and uniqueness, the unity and differentiation of the human condition.

Christian humanism is built upon and depends on personal and communal dignity. Their very intertwining within a Trinitarian alliance shapes the extraordinary conviviality of humane life. Conversely, a real 'person' could never interpret 'interest' as just 'material wealth' for oneself, as if 'interest' were synonymous with mere individual possession or the accumulation of goods. On the other hand, a faithful Christian could not and should not interpret collective, or rather communal, strength as 'military might.' In the Gospel narratives, the kingdom of God was never compared to the Roman Empire. The blessing goes for the meek because, sadly enough, the powerful are too reluctant to accept whatever may be freely given. Certainly, the rationale of the metaphor system which governs the beatitudes runs counter-power-wise. Lakoff finished his case study by affirming that 'it is in the service of reality that we must pay more attention to the mechanisms of metaphorical thought.'[32]

This is what Merton himself had already tried to do in his 1968 prophetic piece of writing 'War and the Crisis of Language' in which he viewed 'the gap between words and actions' as a 'worldwide illness' and 'a universal malaise' affecting both the particular domains of war and politics in general, even religion. The same logic of power which justifies madness is made manifest, says Merton, in 'the language of escalation,' characterized by 'circularity,' oversimplification, ambiguity, 'self-enclosed tautological clichés,' 'double-talk,' 'banality and apocalypse,' 'self-righteous and doctrinaire pomposity' which, unfortunately, still plague the rhetoric of today's global power politics, only to hide, as Merton discovered, 'a massive death wish,' 'a total callousness and moral insensitivity, indeed a basic contempt for man.' And all of this to 'mask the ultimate unreason' of technological strategy becoming an end in itself and leading the fascinated players into a maze which seems to call for self-destruction as its only desperate way out.[33]

We are coming full circle. What Robert Inchausti very appropriately termed Merton's 'American prophecy'[34] has largely outgrown the scope of the American dream. And what Merton announced as much as what he denounced about America for his fellow citizens is of universal import today. Thanks to him, nowadays the 'spirit of fiction' can be better seen everywhere for what it is, 'a father of lies,' a process of unreason, the mirror of death and, in the words of Indian writer Arundhati Roy, 'the end of imagination.'[35]

Indeed, we can see the worldwide spread of this falsity adopting the inflated guise of globalization every time the means (instruments, technologies, goods, commodities, devices and media of all sorts) become the ends; whenever war is madly advocated as the only way of achieving peace; when people are emptied of their freedom and their kinship and end up instead functioning as replaceable units in a production-consumption chain; every time busi-ness is ruled by self-ish-ness; whenever man is thought an 'island, entire of himself;' whenever financial benefit acts as the only driving force for personal or social change; when, caught by the birds of appetite and lost in the fog of unreality, we mock the living God and distort His image and likeness.

In contrast, Merton suggests:

> The Christian life is a return to the Father, the Source, the Ground of all existence, through the Son, the Splendor and the Image of the Father, in the Holy Spirit, the Love of the Father and the Son. And this return is only possible by detachment and "death" in the exterior self, so that the inner self, purified and renewed, can fulfil its function as image of the Divine Trinity [...] Christianity...is a return to the infinite abyss of pure reality...a recognition of ourselves as other Christs.[36]

A Trinitarian look at the world will doubtlessly make us share Merton's clear realization that 'the stranger we meet is no other than ourselves, which is the same as saying we find Christ in him.'[37]

The following story may perhaps illustrate, better than any further elaboration, the tiny but insurmountable distance which separates today's spurious economic globalization from religious universalism:

> A Zen master in deep samadhi visited heaven and hell after death. First he went to hell, where everyone was having dinner. They were

all seated at long tables, facing one another. The tables were loaded with delicious food, but the chopsticks were over a meter in length, and try as they would, the people were unable to get the food into their mouths. There was a great commotion.

Next, the master went to one of the heavens and he found the people also seated around tables loaded with delicious food, just as in hell. Here, too, the chopsticks were exceedingly long, but everyone was using them very naturally, putting the food into the mouths of the people across the table! They were all enjoying dinner, and the atmosphere was quiet and happy.[38]

II

The title of this conference, *The World In My Blood Stream: Thomas Merton's Universal Embrace*, is taken from one of Merton's love poems which seems appropriate to illustrate our reflection. This fine composition was written by a mature monk and poet who by the end of his life had somehow managed to solve his inner conflict between solitude and solidarity, contemplation and action, silence and writing. By the time he wrote the poem Merton seemed to have reached or to be on the verge of reaching a global and transcendental vision of reality beyond false divisions. Let us coin a neologism and call his compassionate look a 'contemplactive' gaze which mirrored and was conducive to the experience of universal love.

This sacred and unifying perception of life is in fact the underlying theme not only of this poem but of his whole poetic production. Needless to say that the unity alluded by Merton differs greatly from any of the notions fostered by the advocates of 'economic globalization' viewed as the current process of marketization of the world and the set of pseudo-theological arguments which seek to legitimate it.

In many of his writings, instead, Merton stoutly criticized this western 'unmitigated arrogance towards the rest of the human race.'[39] He fiercely denounced the apparently inherent drive of human beings to subject the 'other.' Strongly opposing this xenophobic inclination to wipe out all that is unfamiliar or interferes with our clear rationalizations, Merton saw the urge to re-create a political and poetical space wherein humanity could imagine new forms of consciousness and communal experience.

He envisioned the transformation of a world metaphorically built upon 'empires' into one thought of and felt as a 'dwelling' place and he charted a sacred geography where there would be no need to artfully justify any sort of personal or structural violence for the sake of power or gain over others. He invited us to recover our original unity in Christ's light, underlining the need to overcome division and warfare within ourselves and between people of different faiths. For, as he wrote,

> the deepest level of communication is not communication, but communion…we are already one. But we imagine that we are not. And what we have to recover is our original unity. What we have to be is what we are.'[40]

Merton's main concern throughout his life was to become what he really was and to listen to the Word incarnated within himself and his brother, a living presence between himself and the other.[41] He considered life as a process from birth to new birth through 'unbirth' and resurrection. In this most personal and universal agenda, the command of the Delphic oracle, 'know thyself,' plays a relevant role. Indeed, Merton encouraged us to transform our life into a journey towards the core of our 'true self,' the ground where one can hear one's true name pronounced and gain access to the mystery of creation, as given, and creativity, as giving.

Near the end of Merton's life, metaphorically experienced as a journey into the wisdom of love, on the 23rd March 1966, Father Louis met a nurse from St Joseph's Hospital (Louisville) who acted for him as a transparent mirror of his own authentic identity: 'You have come/bringing the truth I need,' he wrote then.[42] Merton dedicated *Eighteen Poems* to her. 'With the World in my Blood Stream' was written in April 1966, after surgery to his spine, and it is, in fact, the first poem he composed for her, inspired by the loneliness he felt when the student nurse left the hospital for the Easter holiday and flew to Chicago in order to see her fiancé.[43] According to Jim Forest's biography,[44] she received the lines during a meeting they had at a restaurant in Louisville on 26th April, where the monk confessed his love for her.

The poem shows some of the characteristics of Merton's latest poetry, rich with imagery, allusions and synaesthesias. The stanzas stand as a profound and solitary meditation on the authentic meaning of life by a poet who, after an unceasing search for unity and purity of heart, had transcended his own solitude and was capable of embracing all cultural and religious differences in God's 'palace of nowhere.'[45]

The poem begins with a stream of musical metaphors,[46] which voice the poet's desolate situation after a surgical operation:

> I lie on my hospital bed
> Water runs inside the walls
> And the musical machinery
> All around overhead
> Plays upon my metal system
> My invented back bone
> Lends to the universal tone
> A flat impersonal song
> All the planes in my mind
> Sing to my worried blood
> To my jet streams

In these very first lines we already find a continuum between the physical condition of the individual narrator and a cosmic perspective. Thus, from the very beginning we encounter a monk who has gone beyond his individual consciousness and dwells in the realm of a greater, global awareness. This is reinforced in the last verses of this strophe, when Merton adds that he swims 'in the world's genius.'

And it is here when, as readers, we may attune to Merton's feelings as he confronts the central question of his entire life: 'Who the hell am I ?' Having reached a stage of spiritual maturity, after years of solitude, prayer, and silence, this monk is still trying to grasp the mystery of his true self, which is not constituted by images, ideas, or symbols but goes beyond them and lives in the pure 'isness' or what the Buddhists call 'suchness.'[47] In short, he longs for the elusive realization of a self who is no-self.

The second stanza persists in Merton's inquiry as to his true nature and origin. Here is a monk who no longer feels isolated from the rest of the world. Life is medically preserved, as it should be, and the world goes on, and yet the quest for identity remains; for now Merton's religious dialectics provide him with a kind of double citizenship, both as a member or a cell of 'this' particular city, Louisville,[48] which keeps him 'functioning,' and as the inhabitant of an eschatological Kingdom and a member of a Mystical Body:

> The world's machinery
> Expands in the walls
> Of the hot musical building

Made in maybe twenty-four
And my lost childhood remains
One of the city's living cells
Thanks to this city
I am still living
But whose life lies here
And whose invented music sings?

In these lines, the poet has a strong intuition that the rhythmic life which breathes within himself is not his own, that he belongs to a much wider scheme for which he is just an instrument, a channel, an expression, even an invention. Again, there is evidence of a double binding or belonging. As part of the world's musical machinery, the poet's life follows its tune, whereas as part of God's self-gift, his life celebrates the song of Creation and has a share in it through his own creativity as conveyed in a life devoted to art and prayer. This is Life so abundant and yet so simple that it can really live in us and through us, as we also freely move in it on condition that it is not interfered with by the noises of the ego. According to Merton, very much influenced by the Benedictine Rule exhorting monks to listen ('obsculta oh, filii,' RB, Pról 1), this life is a subtle music which can be heard everywhere if we only develop our capacity to listen intently, as the Lord would have us do: "Incline your ear, and come unto me: hear, and your soul shall live" (Isaiah 55:3).

The next stanza ties this life in with the figure of Christ: '. . . all my veins run/ With Christ and with the star's plasm.' This is the Christ he discovered in Rome, looking at the frescos in the old run-down chapels beside the Palatine, the One Person he decided to serve as 'My God and my King.'[49] It is also the Christ depicted in the recondite Byzantine chapels of the Italian city: St Cosmas, St Damian, St Mary Major to whom he dedicated such moving poems as 'The Biography' or 'The Communion.'

Here we can still distinguish a dichotomy between an earthly plane, full of suffering and doubt, and a heavenly sphere, which he associates with the reign of Christ. Without neglecting their difference, Merton came to transcend this duality, as inspired by St Augustine, when he realized that God's flame of love pervades the whole created world.

His search for the origin and his longing for home continues throughout the whole poem. In the fourth stanza, the healing presence of masters and saints from different times and traditions is made manifest. Thus, 'recovery' and 'home' hold the same metaphorical rank in one of these lines to the extent that they are interchangeable. This particular lexical choice is most meaningful as it broadly suggests redemptive policies for our society, lost and wounded. The Buddhist narrative of the world has people become sick because they are blind and thus ignore their true nature. Consequently, the prescription is awakening and seeing. In the Christian story the leading metaphors revolve around the images of loss and belonging, exile and return, separation and union.[50] Be it under the grand Buddhist cosmology or within the Christian metaphorical system of belief, the human task can be said to be a Trinitarian enterprise, one rooted in and aiming towards the Mystery of Love, its Incarnation in the world and our spiritual fulfilment by partaking, as image and likeness, in the very Self of the Living God.

As a committed contemplative, Merton was conversant with both Western and Eastern religious expressions. 'Only the Catholics who are still convinced of the importance of Christian mysticism,' he wrote, 'are also aware that much is to be learned from a study of the techniques and experiences of Oriental religions.'[51] In his dialogue with the Zen master D. T. Suzuki, he discovered that there was a great similarity between the Christian concept of innocence or purity of heart and the Buddhist vacuity or *Sunyata*; between Christian knowledge or moral and metaphysical differentiation and Buddhist ignorance, which obscures the original light of the void. He was also inspired by the Desert Fathers (like St Jerome or St Paul the Hermit) and, like them, regarded true wisdom as union with divine light,

> not considered as an "object" or "thing" but as the "divine poverty" which enriches and transforms us in its own innocence. The recovery of Paradise is the discovery of the "Kingdom of God within us" [...] It is the recovery of man's lost likeness to God, in pure, undivided simplicity.[52]

Merton held the view that man has been clothed over with confusion as with a double cloak. Influenced by the writings of St Bernard, he wrote: 'our only task is to get rid of the "double" garment, the overlying layer of duplicity that is not ourselves.'[53] However, the recovery of our initial simplicity is not so easy as it may seem. It requires a process of complete unlearning, a leaving of everything behind, even our warm and comfortable house, in order to start the journey back to our divine inner self in solitude and silence as beautifully rendered in St

John of the Cross's *Dark Night of the Soul*: 'On a dark night, restless of soul, afire with love, oh blessed fortune!, unnoticed went I forth, my house left now at peace.'[54]

Like him, Merton has abandoned his false refuge and departs in search of the divine abode:

> I have no more sweet home
> I doubt the bed here and the road there

And like Jesus himself, Merton has no place to lay his head. He has become very sceptical and can no longer bear the hectic, oppressive and superficial life of the urban society which he condemned in poems such as 'So, goodbye to cities,' or 'Hymn of not much praise for the city of Miami.' Now, lying on a hospital bed, he tries to rid himself of any false relief or self-deception, and adopts a questioning attitude:

> Here below stars and light
> And the Chicago plane
> Slides up the rainy straits of night
> While in my maze I walk and sweat
> Wandering in the low bone system
> Or searching the impossible ceiling
> For the question and the meaning
> Till the machine rolls in again

The quest for his true identity becomes more and more pressing. Merton feels expelled from paradise, because his beloved is flying on the Chicago plane, and her absence makes him feel lost in a labyrinth. She seemed to be the answer to his search,[55] his resting place, but without her he begins to hunger for 'invented air,' 'community of men,' 'Zen breathing,' 'unmarried fancy,' 'wild gift' and 'compromising answers.'

Meanwhile the prophet-poet keeps depicting the oppression of technical society, the endless want of men, and the logic which runs the world as much as his blood system.

According to Merton, it is precisely the desire, craving, appetite or thirst of our own isolated individual ego, which poses the main obstacle for the discovery of our real, non-illusory nature: 'Ego desire can never culminate in happiness, fulfilment and peace, because it is a fracture which cuts us off from the ground of reality in which truth and peace are found.'[56] Therefore, by our unrest, as creatures, we remain cut off from the loving wisdom in which we should be grounded and live in a condition of brokenness and error. In sharp contrast to this selfishness and avidity, Merton refers to Christ's behaviour, when he abandoned everything and even gave his life for us:

> Nameless, bloodless and alone
> The Cross comes and Eckhart's scandal
> The Holy Supper and the precise wrong
> And the accurate little spark
> In emptiness in the jet stream
> Only the spark can understand
> All that burns flies upward
> Where the rainy jets have gone
> A sign of needs and possible homes
> And invented back bone
> A dull song of oxygen
> A lost spark in Eckhart's Castle
> World's plasm and world's cell
> I bleed myself awake and well.

The emphasis is now on the need to die in order to live, like Jesus did. The Cross becomes an engaging symbol for the death and resurrection of men in Christ as well as the door to a new life of love 'in the Spirit.' John Howard Griffin pointed out that in the hospital 'Merton plunged into a study of Eckhart.'[57] He was impressed by his sermons and his way of penetrating the core of inner life. Michael Mott also wrote: 'Merton was making notes on Eckhart in his reading notebooks when yet another student nurse came in to announce she had just been appointed to this floor of the hospital.'[58]

Merton was fascinated by Eckhart's concept of *die eigentlichste Armut* or absolute poverty, that is, when a man is empty of 'self and all things,' and he learnt from him that a man should become so poor and dead as not to have even a place for God to act in: 'it is here, in this poverty, that man regains the eternal being that once he was, now is, and evermore shall be.'[59]

Thomas Merton borrowed Eckhart's image of the 'spark of the soul' or *scintilla animae* which the German mystic himself described as 'free of all names, bare of all forms, . . . empty and free,'[60] 'something in the soul so closely akin to God that it is already one with him and need never be united to him.'[61] This mystical spark, this divine likeness in us is the core of our being and is in God even more than it is in us. It is a basic unity within ourselves at the summit of our being where we are, in Eckhart's words, 'one with God.' Merton rephrased it as 'His

Name written in us; as our poverty, as our indigence, as our dependence, as our sonship.'[62]

As Erlinda Paguio has pointed out, when Merton calls himself 'a lost spark in Eckhart's Castle,' he is recalling Meister Eckhart's Sermon 24 which is inspired by Luke 10:38: 'Our Lord Jesus went into a castle and was received by a virgin who was a wife.' The monk's contradictions and suffering at that point in his life might have led him to identify himself with these telling lines.

Finally, at the end of the poem Merton considers the spark or living flame of love as our true identity in God, the everlasting birth of Christ within us:

> Only the spark is now true
> Dancing in the empty room
> All around overhead
> While the frail body of Christ
> Sweats in a technical bed
> I am Christ's lost cell
> His childhood and desert age
> His descent into hell

Merton's spark of the soul is 'dancing in the empty room' because, as he pointed out in his book *New Seeds of Contemplation*, 'the world and time are the dance of the Lord in emptiness.'[63] In these verses, there is an association on the part of the poet between Eckhart's divine spark, the Buddhist experience of emptiness and the Christian search for innocence or selflessness as Paradise. All seems to indicate that in that difficult situation in hospital, Merton had an experience of true void, solitude, poverty, or desert, and he lived the within and the beyond of this nothingness as a source of rich inexhaustible possibilities. He followed Christ's path into death, left everything behind and gave up all, descending into hell only to find himself infused with light and blessed by union with the divinity. By overcoming his alienation from the inmost ground of his identity, he reached a fresh awareness of his true self, as hidden in the ground of Love:

> Love without need and without name
> Bleeds in the empty problem
> And the spark without identity
> Circles the empty ceiling.

According to Sister Thérèse Lentfoehr, an earlier version of this poem had a different ending and read as follows:

> And love without need without name
> Without answer without problem

Love is the way and love is the home[64]

By the end of his life Merton achieved the wisdom of universal love, grounded in Christ, shining through everything: an 'absolute emptiness' and yet, paradoxically, the womb of 'absolute fullness.' Through his human and divine love for a woman, thus, Merton reached a deeper awareness of the Trinitarian economy of Being which is infinite Giving, Spirit and Life. According to Merton:

> This realization is...not simply the awareness of a loving subject that he has love in himself, but the awareness of the Spirit of love as the source of all that is and of all love.
> Such love is beyond desire, and beyond all restrictions of a desiring and self-centered self . . . Christian charity seeks to realize oneness with the other "in Christ." Buddhist compassion seeks to heal the brokenness of division and illusion and to find wholeness not in an abstract metaphysical "one,"... but...in the void which is Absolute Reality and Absolute Love.[65]

It is in this unlimited Love that Merton sees authentic unity to be possible rather than in an abstract, idealized 'globalization' which is but the mask of a new imperialism and implies the domination of the giants or 'spectres' and the oppression of the weakest. The poet denounced the distortion of looking at the other as enemy and considered it a 'subjective abstraction' based on particular interests. He writes:

> A society that kills real men in order to deliver itself from the phantasm of a paranoid delusion is already possessed by the demon of destructiveness because it has made itself incapable of love. It refuses, a priori, to love. It is dedicated not to concrete relations of man with man, but only to abstractions about politics, economics, psychology, and even, sometimes, religion.[66]

However, the unity that Merton advocates is neither abstraction nor mere communication or virtual connection at the level of ideas but a communion of hearts that share the same love for the living truth since, rather than rejoice in the need to conquer or possess, they rejoice in giving.

Throughout his love poems, the monk of Gethsemani teaches us that real communion is incompatible with a sort of economic globalization whose practices plainly reflect man's choice of a false master:

> For what he needs will be given him when he needs it, and in this sense, God will think and act for him. Modern man may have been tempted to look upon this as an evasion. In actual fact it is the

highest and simplest courage: the courage without which life cannot be faced as it is, and loses its real meaning. This was the central
message of the Sermon on the Mount. ...It is fashionable today to
point to the evil in the world as though it could be put forward as
evidence against this teaching on Providence. But the ironical thing
is that the greatest evils in the world today (wars, genocide, slave
labor, mass exile, poverty and degradation) are all the direct result
of man's rejection of this teaching of Christ... If we have rejected
God and chosen Mammon, and if the result is what we were told to
expect, then why do we complain?[67]

Only by becoming aware of our 'inmost center,' 'spark' or 'apex,' a
'freedom beyond freedom,'[68] which 'smashes louder than lightning in
the great night and was made by God with outlaw fire without rule
and reason,'[69] will we be able to recognize God's providence for all
and his presence among the poorest. And only then shall we act
accordingly.

In his poetry, Merton dreamt of a promised land, or, as Michael
Higgins has pointed out, a 'spiritual locus' and 'rootedness.'[70] A place
where there can be a coincidence of all in all, a final integration or
'ingathering.' In an atomic age, when western religion and philosophy
are in a state of crisis, and human consciousness is threatened by the
deepest alienation, he tried to awaken us to a new awareness of our
dignity as co-creators with God, entitled to love and name things for
the first time. Moreover, he attempted to revive the divine inscription
which is already in us since we are born, that spark of the soul which
is a source of endless creativity and the most powerful weapon against
death. In short, he showed us the path to unbounded Life. 'With the
World in my Bloodstream' is the creation of a man who at the end of his
life's journey learnt to be a lover and a giver.

Let us pray that Merton's poetic and prophetic witness help us
redeem today's sinful economies, based on fear, hatred and ignorance,
and contribute to creating in their place a new global politics
of sharing based on a Trinitarian experience of reality: one that
acknowledges that we are all loved, that consequently demands that
love be made present in our world and one that finally allows the
Source of love and the Word of life to speak to our hearts and inspire
in us a new language filled with living metaphors[71] of hope and
wordings for a world 'charged with the grandeur of God.'

ACKNOWLEDGEMENT

The authors wish to express their profound gratitude to Sr Ana Maria Schlüter Rodés, member of the Bethany Community, Zen Roshi and the heart of Zendo Betania in Spain, for her initiative to start a series of seminars to explore the consequences of the encounter of Zen and Christianity, and most particularly for exhorting Christian practitioners of Zen to deepen their understanding of the Christian notion of 'person' from a Trinitarian perspective, which can both illumine and be illumined by the Zen experience.

Notes and References

1. See Ignacio Ramonet, 'Pensamiento único y sistema PPII,' *Un mundo sin rumbo: crisis de fin de siglo*, Madrid, Debate, 1997. The same tenets are also developed in his books *La tiranía de la comunicación*, Madrid, Debate, 1998 and *La golosina visual*, Madrid, Debate, 2000. See also the following excerpt from Susan George's *The Lugano Report: On Preserving Capitalism in the Twenty-first Century*, London and Sterling, Virginia, Pluto Press, 1999, as quoted in *The New Internationalist*, January/February 2000, p. 27: 'If capitalism can be said to possess an ontology, an essence, it is surely that the market, in its full sweep and scope, is harmonious and wise. Like God, it too can create good from apparent evil. From destruction it draws the betterment and the highest possible equilibrium possible.' Susan George is vice-president of Attac (Association for the Taxation of Financial Transactions for the Aid of Citizens <www.attac.org>) and *The Lugano Report* is actually a fictional work which tried to show the horrific consequences of taking the logic of the global economic system to its conclusion.

2. Seamus Heaney, 'Time and again: poetry and the millennium,' an abbreviated version of a Millennium Lecture delivered at the University of Liverpool, 22 March 2000, *The European English Messenger*, Vol. X/2, Autumn 2001, pp. 19-23

3. Merton's actual words were: '. . . it was as if I suddenly saw the secret beauty of their hearts, the depths of their hearts where neither sin nor desire nor self-knowledge can reach, the core of their reality, the person that each one is in God's eyes. If only they could all see themselves as they really are. If only we could see each other that way all the time. There would be no more war, no more hatred, no more cruelty, no more greed . . .' (*Conjectures of a Guilty Bystander*, New York, Doubleday, 1966, p.158

4. See Chalmers MacCormick, 'Huxley's *Ends and Means* Revisited,' *The Merton Seasonal*, 19:3 (1994) pp.24-27

5. Aldous Huxley, *Ends and Means*, Chatto & Windus, London 1937, p.8. Volume 13 (200) of *The Merton Annual* includes two clarifying articles on Merton's views on technology: Phillip M. Thompson's 'The Restoration of Balance: Thomas Merton's Technological Critique,' pp.63-79 and John Wu's 'Technological Perspectives: Thomas Merton and the One-Eyed Giant,' pp.80-104. Lugano Report fictitious authors sum up their eschatological rationale to suppress to billion people by 2020 as follows: 'Our message is not merely that "the ends justify the means," though this may well be so. It is, rather, that Western culture and the liberal

market system must, in the twenty-first century, choose between the ends and The End' (Susan George, *op.cit.* p.28).

6. In his 'Prometheus: A Meditation,' (*Raids on the Unspeakable*, New York, New Directions, 1966, pp.79-88), Merton establishes a distinction between the Prometheus of Hesiod, Cain, and the Prometheus of Aeschylus, Christ on the Cross. The essay seems to us an excellent metaphor of today's neoliberal craving frame of mind. For a historical account of the many versions of the myth up to the 20th century (including Italian, Spanish, English, French pictorial and literary renderings as well as the readings of Voltaire, Goethe, Shelley, Camus, Unamuno, etc.), see Gregorio Luri Medrano, *Biografías de un mito: Prometeos*, Madrid, Trotta, 2001.

7. Aldous Huxley, *op.cit.* p.9

8. *Ibid.* p.250

9. 'To live in the company of the Trinity is our contemplative experience, our life of prayer,' concludes the Cistercian monk from St. Joseph's Abbey, Spencer, Massachusetts, Joseph Chu-Cong, OCSO, (*The Contemplative Experience: Erotic Love and Spiritual Union*, New York, Crossroad, 1999, p.122).

10. Thomas Merton, *Mystics and Zen Masters*, New York, Farrar, Straus & Giroux, 1967, p.40

11. Leonardo Boff claims that ethos and pathos should go hand in hand within any agenda seeking to address the three most urgent issues of our times: the problematic social situation, the ecological crisis and massive unemployment. See his *Ética planetaria desde el Gran Sur*, Madrid, Trotta, 2001.

12. '. . . many will come from the east and west to take their places with Abraham and Isaac at the feast in the kingdom of heaven' (Matthew 8:11)

13. These are rephrased excerpts from the Spanish edition of the book by Gisbert Greshake, *El Dios Uno y Trino: Una teología de la Trinidad*, Barcelona, Biblioteca Herder, 2001, p.312.

14. Although English, German, Italian and French versions of Raimon Pannikkar's work are available, this second Spanish version is a revised expanded edition of the former, *La Trinidad: Una experiencia humana primordial*, Madrid, Siruela, 1998, p.92. For a contextualized approach to this Trinitarian perspective see Chapter IV, 'Panikkar: The Systematic Theology of the Future,' in Ewert H. Cousins, *Christ of the 21st Century*, Rockport MA, Element, 1992.

15. Jean Comaroff and John L. Comaroff, 'Millennial Capitalism: First Thoughts on a Second Coming,' in Jean Comaroff and John L. Comaroff (eds), *Millennial Capitalism and the Culture of Neoliberalism*, Durham & London, Duke University Press, 2001, pp.2, 4.

16. Joaquín Estafanía, *¿qué es la globalización? La primera revolución del siglo XXI*, Madrid, Aguilar, 2002, p.28. In the words of Anthony Giddens, 'Globalisation can . . . be defined as the intensification of worldwide social relations which link distant localities in such a way that local happenings are shaped by events occurring many miles away and vice versa' (*The Consequences of Modernity*, Cambridge, Polity Press, 1990, p.63).

17. For a detailed description of these, see Josep F. Mària i Serrano's 'Ah, yes, globalization! A marvellous excuse for many things (R.M. Solow, Nobel Prize for Economy),' *Cuadernos Cristianisme i Justicia*, no.103, December 2000, Barcelona. (available in English at <http://www.fespinal.com>) and 'Las otras caras de la

globalización,' *Documento Social: Revista de Estudios Sociales y de Sociología Aplicada*, (ed. Cáritas Española) <http: www. Caritas-esp.org> no. 125, October-December 2001

18. Thomas Merton, 'The Feast of Freedom: Monastic Formation according to Adam of Perseigne,' *The Letters of Adam of Perseigne*, translated by Grace Perigo, Vol. I, Cistercian Fathers Series Number 21, Kalamazoo, Cistercian Publications, 1976, pp. 13-14

19. A detailed clarification of the connections between God and the goods, can be found in the following works: Jung Mo Sung, *Desejo, mercado e religiâo*, Petrópolis, RJ, Brazil, Editora Vozes, 1998; José Ma. Mardones, *Capitalismo y religión: la religión política neoconservadora*, Santander, Sal Terrae, 1991; Cristianisme i Justicia, *¿Mundialización o conquista?*, Santander, Sal Terrae, 1999; Bas de Gaay Fortman and Berma Kelin Goldewijk, *God and the Goods. Global Economy in a Civilizational Perspective*, World Council of Churches Publication 1998

20. Aldous Huxley, 'Foreword' (1946), *Brave New World* (1931)

21. Thomas Merton, *Love and Living*, London, Sheldon Press, 1979, pp. 25-37

22. Felix Wilfred, 'Las religiones ante la globalización,' in Jon Sobrino & Felix Wilfred (eds), *Concilium: La Globalización y sus Víctimas*, 293, November 2001, p. 716

23. See Xavier Melloni, SJ, 'La experiencia de Dios como experiencia de lo Real,' *Vida Nueva*, no. 2315, 2 February 2002, pp. 23-29

24. William McNamara, OCD, *The Human Adventure: The Art of Contemplative Living*, Rockport, Element, 1991, p. 55

25. Dr. Robert Imperato, *Merton and Walsh on the Person*, Wisconsin, Liturgical Pub., 1987, p. 99

26. Federico Mayor Zaragoza, 'Propuestas para cambios inaplazables,' *El País*, Wednesday, 9, January 2002, p. 12

27. Václav Havel, 'The Divine Revolution: Lifting the Iron Curtain of the Spirit,' *Civilization*, April/May 1998

28. Aung san Suu Kyi, *The Voice of Hope*, Penguin Books, England 1997, p. 29

29. Although originally written as chapter 16 of *New Seeds of Contemplation*, it is worth reading the context of its publication in *Passion for Peace: The Social Essays of Thomas Merton* (ed. William H. Shannon), New York, Crossroads, 1995, pp. 8-19

30. Williams defines 'structures of feeling' as 'affective elements of consciousness and relationships: not feeling against thought, but thought as felt and feeling as thought: practical consciousness of a present kind, in a living and interrelating continuity.' (Raymond Williams, *Marxism and Literature*, Oxford University Press, 1977, p. 132)

31. George Lakoff and Mark Johnson, *Metaphors we Live by*, The University of Chicago Press, 1980, p. 5

32. George Lakoff, *Metaphor and War: The Metaphor System Used to Justify War in the Gulf*, type-scripted copy of the paper presented on January 30, 1991 on the campus of the University of California at Berkeley. An earlier version had been distributed widely via electronic mail, starting on December 31, 1990.

33. Thomas Merton's essay seems to apply to our own global issues today and, but for a few words which refer to concrete scenarios, his message bears the same urgency as when it was originally written and deserves a very careful reread. 'War and the Crisis of Language,' *Thomas Merton on Peace*, London & Oxford, Mowbray, 1984

34. His prophetic contribution has been wonderfully summed up by Robert Inchausti in *Thomas Merton's American Prophecy*, State University of New York Press 1998, as follows: 'Merton's chief contribution to contemporary thought may just be his overt refusal to employ conventional political categories in his analysis of cultural phenomena in order to raise political issues to a higher level where spiritual themes enter into dialogue with questions of social ethics. His defense of the contemplative life subverts the grand narratives of both the right- and left-wing political theorists - and directly challenges both the conservative unilinear version of history and the Marxist materialist dialectic. In their place, he offers an eschatological view where progress in the realms of charity, compassion, and gratitude matters more than progress in material prosperity because material progress only feeds the insatiable human desire for more; whereas, an increase in charity and compassion curbs our self-centred inclinations and makes possible the beloved community' (p. 75).

35. Arundhati Roy's 'The End of Imagination' (*The Cost of Living*, New York, Modern Library, 1999) was written as a reaction of alarm and protest against nuclear tests conducted in the Thar desert, which transformed first India, and then Pakistan, into nuclear weapon states.

36. Thomas Merton, 'The Inner Experience: Christian Contemplation (III),' *Cistercian Studies*, Vol. XVIII (1983: 2), p. 202

37. Thomas Merton, *Mystics and Zen Masters, op. cit.*, p. 112

38. Kôun Yamada, translations and comments, *Gateless Gate*, Tucson, The University of Arizona Press, 1979, p. 215

39. 'A Letter to Pablo Antonio Cuadra Concerning Giants,' in *The Collected Poems of Thomas Merton*, New York, New Directions, 1977, p. 380

40. Thomas Merton, *The Asian Journal of Thomas Merton*, New York, New Directions, 1975, p. 308

41. In his article 'Theology of Creativity,' Merton tells us that the responsibility of every Christian is to restore all things, including himself, in Christ, so that the whole creation becomes an epiphany and revelation of God's love (*The Literary Essays of Thomas Merton*, New York, New Directions, 1985, pp. 369-370).

42. A line from his poem 'Six Night Letters,' included in the collection *Eighteen Poems* (unpublished).

43. Merton describes his feelings on that occasion in his journal of March 23, 1967: 'the rainy evening when M. came to say goodbye before going to Chicago and when I was so terribly lonely, and lay awake half the night, tormented by the gradual realization that we were in love and I did not know how to live without her.' (*Learning to Live: The Journals of Thomas Merton* Vol. 6, 1966-1967 (ed. Christine M. Bochen), San Francisco, Harper Collins, 1997, p. 208)

44. Jim Forest, *Living with Wisdom: A life of Thomas Merton*, Maryknoll, New York, Orbis Books, 1991, p. 174

45. After the metaphor of James Finley in his fine resumé of Merton's message, *Merton's Palace of Nowhere: A Search for God through Awareness of the True Self*, Notre Dame, Indiana, Ave Maria Press, 1978

46. Merton was very fond of melodic images. He even entitled one of the poems in his book *The Strange Islands* 'Elias-Variations on a Theme,' as if it were a musical piece divided into different variations. It should also be remembered that Merton loved listening to music, especially jazz and blues.

47. Thomas Merton, *The Literary Essays of Thomas Merton, op. cit.* p. 364

48. Merton did not completely overcome his rejection of big artificial and inhuman cities, which are portrayed in poems like 'So, goodbye to cities' or 'Hymn of not much Praise for the city of Miami' (*The Collected Poems of Thomas Merton*, NewYork, New Directions, 1975, pp. 19-20).

49. Thomas Merton, *The Seven Storey Mountain*, NewYork, Harcourt Brace & Company, 1976, p. 109

50. However, a careful reading of the two narratives and a meeting of Jesus and Buddha, love and wisdom, is being proposed by representatives of both religions as necessary to heal our common world. Suffice it to mention here two seminal books out of a growing body of literature along the same lines: Thich Nhat Hanh, *Going Home: Jesus and Buddha as Brothers*, NewYork, Riverhead Books, 1999 and Aloysius Pieris, SJ, *Love Meets Wisdom: A Christian Experience of Buddhism*, Maryknoll, NewYork, Orbis Books, 1988

51. Thomas Merton, *Zen and the Birds of Appetite*. NewYork, New Directions, 1968, p. 21

52. Ibid. p. 102

53. *Thomas Merton on St. Bernard*, Michigan, Cistercian Publications 1970, p. 119

54. San Juan de la Cruz, *Obra Completa (I)*, ed. de Luce López-Baralt y Eulogio Pacho, Madrid, Alianza, 1994, p. 66

55. Just after meeting Margie for the first time, he remembers some lines of his favourite poet, Rilke: '... Were you not always/distracted by expectation, as though all this/ were announcing someone to love? ...' (Quoted by Michael Mott, *The Seven Mountains of Thomas Merton*. Boston, MA, Houghton Mifflin Company, 1984, p. 435).

56. Thomas Merton, *Zen and the Birds of Appetite, op. cit.* pp. 85-86

57. John Howard Griffin, *Follow the Ecstasy*. Fort Worth, JHG Editions, 1983, p. 79

58. Michael Mott, *The Seven Mountains of Thomas Merton, op. cit.* p. 435

59. Quoted by Merton from Blakney's translation of Meister Eckhart in *Zen and the Birds of Appetite, op. cit.* p. 10

60. Quoted by Erlinda Paguio in 'Blazing in the spark of God: Thomas Merton's References to Meister Eckhart', *The Merton Annual*, Vol. 5, 1992, p. 256

61. Thomas Merton, *Zen and the Birds of Appetite, op. cit.* p. 11

62. Thomas Merton, *Conjectures of a Guilty Bystander*, NewYork, Doubleday Image Paperback, 1968, pp. 140-142

63. Thomas Merton, *New Seeds of Contemplation*, NewYork, New Directions, 1972, p. 297

64. Quoted by Sister Thérèse Lentfoehr, *Words and Silence: On the Poetry of Thomas Merton*, p. 69.

65. Thomas Merton, *Zen and the Birds of Appetite, op. cit.* p. 86

66. Thomas Merton, 'A Letter to Pablo Antonio Cuadra Concerning Giants,' *The Collected Poems of Thomas Merton, op. cit.* p. 375

67. Thomas Merton, 'The Inner Experience: Prospects and Conclusions (VIII),' *Cistercian Studies*, Vol. XIX (1984:3), pp. 344-345

68. Thomas Merton, *Love and Living*, NewYork, Farrar, Straus Giroux, 1979, pp. 8-9

69. Thomas Merton, *Working Notebook #21*, April-June 1966, Thomas Merton Studies Center, Bellarmine University, Louisville, KY

70. Michael Higgins, 'Merton and the Real Poets: Paradise Rebugged,' *The Merton Annual: Studies in Religion, Culture, Literature, and Social Concerns*, Vol. 3, New York, AMS Press, 1990, p.175

71. 'La metáfora es el proceso retórico por el que el discurso libera el poder que tienen ciertas ficciones de redescribir la realidad.' (Paul Ricoeur, *La MetáforaViva*, Madrid, Ed. Europa, 1985, p.15). See the work of the philosopher synthesized by Jesús Díaz Soriano, *Revelación y lenguaje: Una lectura hermenéutica de la palabra de Dios a través de la filosofía de Paul Ricoeur*, Doctoral thesis presented at the Faculty of Theology at the University of Fribourg, Switzerland. Salamanca, San Esteban, 2001

THOMAS MERTON
the world in my bloodstream

POETRY SUPPLEMENT

A selection of the poems perfomed at the Conference Poetry Reading

Valley Road, Louisville
(for Paul, Helen, and Anne Pearson)

THANKS BE to God
that sometimes we can
walk in Eden. Quiet
in the morning, I catch
the shadow and the sun,
so neither hurt.
I know there's a world
elsewhere, but am allowed this one.
Whatever the six-fold lips
of the lily say, they say it kindly.
Trees there are in plenty
arching like Blake's tall angels
over me, each a blessing, none
bearing the troublesome apple.

Ibn Abbad Woke Early

IBN ABBAD woke early, put on
his patched garment, turned to God
and said, *Peace be to us, and to all this day.*

Rabbi Schmelke of Nikolsburg,
when a rich and distinguished man
tried to make him look ridiculous,
read the forty-first psalm, and
translated verse eleven, *By this
I know that you delight in me:
my enemy will suffer no ill because of me.*

Father Louis in his American hermitage
wrote to Abdul Aziz, *Let us
have great love for truth, and open our hearts
to the spirit of God our Lord and Father,
Compassionate and Merciful.*

All three went to Paradise,
Ibn Abbad, Rabbi Schmelke of Nikolsburg,
and Father Louis, and sat to eat
at the same table. They drank the water of life
and ate the meat of friendship. Whenever
their cups ran dry or their plates were empty
a little Nazarene came by and filled them up.
Who are you? they said.
I am Jesus, son of Mary. Can I sit awhile?
Be our guest, they said.

As they sat, the ground beneath them shook,
their faces paled and their eyes were filled
with knowledge, and with grief. *Today,*
said Jesus, *they will hate more and*
love more, than on any other day since
the world began. Hold hands,
and ask our God to speak to us
in Spirit. And there they sat
in love and prayer, all day, all day,
Ibn Abbad, Rabbi Schmelke of Nikolsburg,
Father Louis, and Jesus, Mary's son.

   and their silence was more profound than words
   and their communion was most eloquent
   and they willed the world to peace

After a long time they opened their eyes,
and there were only three at the table.
Jesus, Mary's son, had gone.

   had gone to join some other hands in love
   sit by some other beds in pain
   pray with some other desperate men
   break for some other hearts the loaf
   share with some other faiths the way

and that goes on today
unceasing in his care to see beyond the robes
of different length, and hue, and cloth,
the common beating heart, and to mark again
as on the Bethlehem night, the angel's call:
Peace on earth, goodwill to all, to all.

DAVID SCOTT

Absence

YOU'RE BACK. Two years is a long time.
I should ask where you've been;
was I so dense, so unteachable?

Not that I have any right to your company.
You are free to choose your fireside.
Perhaps you think the anguish time well spent:

Stroking an empty page with my fingers,
Scanning the distant hillside for any movement
That could be the far-off footsteps of a poem.

A Postcard for Thomas Merton

AT FOURTH and Walnut today, it's just
Any old crowd milling: I guess it always was.
But you're there too among them, helping us remember.
And from these books you get under my skin,
Firing the ache for something whole and simple: the truth.

It's funny how the cheese and the conflicts
Don't matter now. There's so much cheese
We have to deal with. But you needed that, too:
It had its place in the mountain climb, one of many paths
Leading to the crossed roads of your heart.

I want to thank you for staying with them all; not going
Anywhere much: letting those roads worry you awake.
Smile on us then, reclining at you must now, at home
Among buddhas, saints and outcasts; their familiar.
And pray for blessing on our small wits,
And on our turbulent, distracted hearts.

MICHAEL WOODWARD

Ice Dance

ONCE, IN icy February,
I watched a flock of geese
land on a frozen lake,
land and glide across
in a great, silent dance.

Each bird put down
one webbed foot,
slid it forward,
hesitated for an instant
before shifting weight to it.
They all did this:
step, hesitate, slide.

Rising and falling together,
the whole flock waltzed forward,
each one testing the ice,
each one ensuring
the other's safety.

Not birds of the air
nor any creeping thing,
not beasts of the field
nor human kind in God's image
can safely dance alone.
The ice is too thin;
the dance is too dangerous.

Geese on a Foggy Day

FROM FALLOW fields,
from fog's ghostly gray,
they rose at first unrecognised,
a chevron of geese
on seasonal sojourn.

In ordered formation
and splendid profusion,
life rises up
around inattentive me,
and everything sings, "I AM."

Creation's cup overflows
with a million ordinary miracles,
like geese on a foggy day
lifting me on the world's wild wings,
making my heart soar.

Gardener's Eden

EARTH HAS begun to thaw.
One purple crocus
proclaims it.
I can smell
rich, wet rottenness
as last fall's leaves
sink into soil.
I know that dirt
is springing to life.

I was made of dust,
to dust cheerfully return,
human to humus.
I ache to go back
to the garden
to sink my hands
in the stuff of my making,
to seek high things
in low places.

Earth is not,
and has never been,
an unheavenly direction.

BONNIE THURSTON

Fragments of a Poetic Journal

Tuesday June 5, 2001

> 27,000 ft Angel flying.
> Destination Louisville
> Filled with unspeakable
> heaviness of joy
> at this homecoming.

Wednesday June 6, 2001

Sitting here on a bench near the corner of Fourth and Walnut (except now it's called Muhammed Ali) in the Center of the Shopping District in Louisville (pronounced by locals as Loo-ville) where the people are still somehow walking about 'Shining Like The Sun.' Smells of humid southern heat of the not-so-early-but-not-got-going-yet morning. It's just after 10am. I've been wandering around for ¾ an hour. People cutting along or ambling to work, now some standing outside buildings for final cigarette moment of contemplation before work in smoke-free air-conditioned shops or offices. Fed-Ex van pulls away giving me a clear view of the corner on which stands the Seelbach Hotel. Sparrow flits down before me and then back into the tree beneath whose bows I sit. Shoppers beginning to appear. Baggy shorts and baseball caps. Heart is full with just being here. Eyes brim with tears that not overflow.

> Holy community standing
>   bench sitting
> human touch of
>   nicotine fellowship.   spoken.   silent.
>   alone.   together.

Somewhere a bell tolls. A quarter after ten. A signal to move.

Monday June 11, 2001 Gethsemani

> old monk enters abbey church
>   in sneakers
> crosses himself.

14th June 2001. *Thursday. Evening. About 9.30pm*

Father Louis' Grave

THE fireflies danced
around your grave
when I came at last
to sit at your feet.

A stranger pilgrim
unknown inconceived
seeking your spirit
not amongst the dead.

But in the heart
of life-overflowing
sunshine fecundity
pulsing through Kentucky heat.

'Be what you are'
you said. You said.
wisdom draws forth
heart question:

And what am I?
Who am I?
Walking this wilderness path
open-eyed to vision behold.

Illusion beholding illusion
Disappearing trick
you are gone
and I am too.

ANGUS STUART

A Note from Gethsemane, California

During the early part of summer last year I fulfilled one of my dreams—to travel on the Pacific Rim from Vancouver in the north via Washington, Oregon and California State to Mexico. This was a journey of some 7,800 km round trip much of it spent on the Californian Coast line, Salinas, Big Sur, Monterey, San Francisco on and down to the border. The road back cut inland and out of LA into Death Valley, up the interior, over the top of the Sierra Nevada round Lake Tahoe, up west to Portland then north east following the mighty river Columbia past Mt Adams into the Northern Cascade Mountains, leaving me with a last minute dash back to Vancouver for the flight home.

I did not travel alone but with a good friend from Theological college days. We spent a good deal of time planning the trip, agreeing to meet some folks along the way. (Robert Inchausti was one of them.) We were travelling light, and camping when were unable to bum a bed. We read poetry (mostly Ginsberg's *Howl*) Kerouac's *On the Road*; listening to jazz and rock and roll—and wild preacher men giving the gospel on the radio air-waves. The trip was all that it was meant to be and much, much more.

On this particular day we were on our way to the Abbey of Our Lady of the Redwoods—our reason for going was that Thomas Merton had visited this Abbey, in fact he set off from this place to the far east, his final journey. A travelling companion of Tom's bought a painting of Christ by the artist Jamini Roy; it was a painting Merton wanted to buy but couldn't afford. It was presented to the community of Our Lady of the Redwoods by Dr Chakravarty, Merton's companion
during the autumn of 1968.

This a short extract from my own journal written on that day, 5th July 2000:

> Hurled the 4X4 down the small back road, through woods which 'towered like Cathedrals' to quote Tom Merton ~ Gt. Redwoods all around. My companion Angus unsure of the speed I maintained as I am pulled by the excitement of meeting.
>
> Beyond is something more than a frontier across which we must travel; if this journey is to be more than one long drive down the US West Coast. This is the moment ~ one that neither of us will have again. We are propelled and called towards the Abbey ~ my companion urges me to go slower ~ but I feel it! And I feel Him

beyond us calling, calling. I am familiar with these roads and this vehicle it seems in this moment that I have known them all my life, I have never been here before. It is as if I were born, destined for this moment ~ I am fully present to myself and Him ~ as if driving to the beyond ~ right through 'The Church' ~ through this ancient garden. I'm striving for God ~ I'm called ~ set apart to be here at this time. This is my time, here in this place. This is spiritual.

I muse at my impatience to be there!!! I want to express the otherness to which I am being drawn. I feel solitude and holiness, although accompanied now by a reluctant passenger. I know our welcome will be only short, we are not really welcome; interlopers, just some more disciples looking for reflections of Tom; even so the meeting will have meaning.

We arrive on time "Sanctus" Holy, Holy, Holy is God. Bread and Wine are set before us, and an invitation to come in from a sister. Bread and Wine are set before us Sanctus. God calls ~ we can do no more than respond in awe at His call to see through and go beyond.

Later Reflection:

I remember now sitting in the Chapel at Our Lady of the Redwoods. It was a hot dusty day, and late in the afternoon. We had driven hard to get there, and battled even harder to get an invitation. Two Anglican Priests.

We looked for a short while at the picture, asked our questions, then moved around the grounds shooting camera film, reading passages from An Asian Journal and then onwards to another Merton Rendezvous down on the coast line.

This encounter was one of many moments that could be defined as spiritual on the road, when Christ met with me, with us almost in secret. Maybe all God's children should carry a translucent cross!

SEAN ROBERTSHAW

Notes on Contributors

CANON A.M. ALLCHIN is Honorary President of the Thomas Merton Society and a friend and correspondent of Thomas Merton. He is   Honorary Professor of Theology at the University of Wales, Bangor.

DAVID BELCASTRO is professor of Religious Studies at Captial University in Bexley, Ohio. He is both an ordained pastor in the Disciples of Chirst Church and a lay person in the Roman Catholic Church and the Chair of the Religion and Philosphy Department of a Lutheran University.

RICHARD BERENDES is a registered nurse and is currently a health care administrator. He spent a portion of his young adult life as a religious brother, and was introduced to the work of Thomas Merton at that time.

TOM DEL PRETE is past recipient of an ITMS award for scholarship, and past-president of the ITMS. He is author of *Thomas Merton and the Education of theWhole Person* (Religious Education Press, 1990).

DONALD GRAYSTON is director of the Institute for the Humanities at Simon Fraser University in Vancouver. An Anglican priest, he is Vicar of St Oswald's Church in Port Kells, south of Vancouver. He is author of *Thomas Merton's Rewritings: The Five Versions of Seeds of Contemplation as a Key to the Development of His Thought* (Edwin Mellen, 1989) and *Thomas Merton: The Development of a Spiritual Theologian* (Edwin Mellen, 1985).

JUDITH HARDCASTLE is a founding member of the ITMS, British Columbia Chapter. Judith is the ITMS International Advisor for Canada. She received a Shannon Fellowship from the ITMS in 2001 conducting research on Merton and interfaith dialogue.

ROBERT INCHAUSTI is a Professor of English at California Polytechnic University, San Luis Obispo. He is the author of three books: *The Ignorant Perfection of Ordinary People* (SUNY, 1989), *Spitwad Sutras* (Bergin & Garvey 1993), and *Thomas Merton's American Prophecy* (SUNY, 1998) and has recently edited the Merton anthology, *Seeds* (Shambhala, 2002). He is a member of the Catholic Commission on Intellectual and Cultural Affairs.

FERNANDO BELTRÁN LLAVADOR is currently serving his third term as an ITMS International Advisor. He is author of *La contemplación en la acción:Thomas Merton* and translator of various Merton books into Spanish. He teaches at Salamanca University.

EARL MADARY teaches in the Religious Studies and Philosophy department at Viterbo University. Earl is a Catholic Worker and a founding member of the Place of Grace Catholic Worker House in La Crosse, WI. Earl has also written, along with William J. Reese, an introduction to the New Testament titled, *These Things Are Written*, and a recording of original music titled *Prodigals*.

SONIA PETISCO MARTÍNEZ is the former recipient of a Robert Daggy Youth Scholarship and has recently completed her Ph.D thesis at the Universidad Complutense in Madrid, on the poetry of Thomas Merton.

PAUL M. PEARSON is Director and Archivist of the Thomas Merton Center in Louisville, Kentucky. A founding member of the TMS - GBI, and editorial advisor to *The Merton Journal*. He has presented papers in the United Kingdom, USA and Canada.

SEAN ROBERTSHAW is Vicar of New Mill in Yorkshire and a Chaplain in the Territorial Army.

DAVID SCOTT is Rector of St Lawrence's in Winchester. He is a poet, a founding member of the Thomas Merton Society and poetry editor of *The Merton Journal*.

MICHAEL SOBOCINSKI is a staff psychologist at the Denver Children's Home. In addition, he is on the faculty of the Counselling Psychology Program at the University of Denver. He is the author of *Distracted by Difference: Thomas Merton's Vision of the Self and the Role of Love in Psychotherapy* (University Press of America).

ANGUS STUART has been Chair of TMS since 2000 and a member of the society since 1998. His particular area of interest concerns Merton and 'The Beats,' especially Jack Kerouac. He has a day job as a Chaplain at the University of Bristol.

BONNIE THURSTON is a founding member of ITMS and served as its 3rd president. After 27 years as a university professor she resigned her position as William F. Orr Professor of New Testament at Pittsburgh Theological Seminary to begin life as a solitary in West Virginia. She is the author of 10 theological books, 1 volume of poetry and over 100 articles, 20 of which are on Thomas Merton.

MICHAEL WOODWARD is a writer and a publisher. He edits *The Merton Journal* and was recently elected leader of the Lay Community of Saint Benedict.

Acknowledgements

'Ice Dance' ©2002 Theology Today. Originally published in Theology Today 59 (2002):
pp.104-05. Reprinted with the publisher's permission.
'Ice Dance' appears in Bonnie Thurston's new collection Hints and Glimpses
(Three Peaks Press 2004, ISBN 1-902093-09-7)
'A Postcard for Thomas Merton' is reprinted from Thirst
(Three Peaks Press 2001, ISBN 1-902093-04-6)

MADE AND PRINTED IN WALES BY
GWASG DINEFWR PRESS
LLANDYBIE FOR
THREE PEAKS PRESS
9 CROESONEN ROAD, ABERGAVENNY,
MONMOUTHSHIRE NP7 6AE